Peter Strawson

Philosophy Now

Series Editor: John Shand

This is a fresh and vital series of new introductions to today's most read, discussed and important philosophers. Combining rigorous analysis with authoritative exposition, each book gives a clear, comprehensive and enthralling access to the ideas of those philosophers who have made a truly fundamental and original contribution to the subject. Together the volumes comprise a remarkable gallery of the thinkers who have been at the forefront of philosophical ideas.

Published

Donald Davidson
Marc Joseph

Nelson Goodman
Daniel Cohnitz & Marcus Rossberg

Saul Kripke
G. W. Fitch

David Lewis
Daniel Nolan

John McDowell
Tim Thornton

Hilary Putnam
Maximilian de Gaynesford

Wilfrid Sellars
Willem A. deVries

Peter Strawson
Clifford Brown

Bernard Williams
Mark P. Jenkins

Forthcoming

David Armstrong
Stephen Mumford

Thomas Nagel
Alan Thomas

John Rawls
Catherine Audard

Peter Strawson

Clifford Brown

McGill-Queen's University Press
Montreal & Kingston • Ithaca

192

S 9/ z b

H

ISBN-13: 978-0-7735-3171-0   ISBN-10: 0-7735-3171-8 (bound)
ISBN-13: 978-0-7735-3172-7   ISBN-10: 0-7735-3172-6 (pbk.)

Legal deposit third quarter 2006
Bibliothèque nationale du Québec

Published simultaneously outside North America
by Acumen Publishing Limited

McGill-Queen's University Press acknowledges the financial support of
the Government of Canada through the Book Publishing Development
Program (BPIDP) for its activities.

Library and Archives Canada Cataloguing in Publication

Brown, Clifford, 1923-
    Peter Strawson / Clifford Brown.

Includes bibliographical references and index.
ISBN-13: 978-0-7735-3171-0   ISBN-10: 0-7735-3171-8 (bound)
ISBN-13: 978-0-7735-3172-7   ISBN-10: 0-7735-3172-6 (pbk.)

1. Strawson, P. F. I. Title.

B1667.S384B76 2006   192   C2006-902313-1

Typeset by Kate Williams, Swansea.
Printed and bound by Cromwell Press, Trowbridge.

Contents

Abbreviations   vi

Introduction   1

1. "On Referring" and *Introduction to Logical Theory*:   17
   The basic questions

2. *Individuals: An Essay in Descriptive Metaphysics*:   51
   Towards a basic ontology

3. *The Bounds of Sense*: Kant's first *Critique* under   93
   analysis

4. *Skepticism and Naturalism*: Hume revisited   143

5. *Analysis and Metaphysics*: Summing up   167

   Notes   199
   Bibliography   203
   Index   207

Abbreviations

AM   *Analysis and Metaphysics* (1992)
BS   *The Bounds of Sense* (1966)
IE   *Individuals: An Essay in Descriptive Metaphysics* (1959)
ILT   *Introduction to Logical Theory* (1952)
OR   "On Referring" (1950)
SN   *Skepticism and Naturalism* (1985)

Introduction

> The questions which at the time most seriously engaged my attention were questions in the philosophy of logic and the philosophy of language. While ... lecturing on these matters, I had become deeply concerned with the matter of singular reference and predication, and their objects – a topic which has remained central to my thought throughout my working life.   (Strawson 1998a: 7)[1]

That time and place were the late 1940s in Oxford, at the beginning of the diverse, productive and lengthy career of Peter Strawson, whose accomplishments clearly place him at the forefront of Anglophone philosophers in the latter half of the twentieth century. The questions that engaged him at the outset concern our common use of expressions to refer to particular persons and things as the fundamental objects of reference. That use is fundamental, but since anything whatsoever can be identifyingly referred to, the *individuals* of our discourse will include not only particular objects, but also all manner of concepts, such as those of species, qualities and relations. This linguistic use is indeed common but, on Strawson's own account, an attentive investigation of what that presupposes leads us straightaway not only to the most fundamental questions of logic, but also to those of ontology and epistemology.

It is remarkable that while the theme of singular reference and predication, and their objects, has been consistently central to his work, that one theme has at the same time given entry to a broad world of descriptive metaphysics, and to a consequent fresh and critical view of contemporary scepticism and naturalism. Thus Strawson's work is not a narrowly contained special interest; rather, it embraces an attempt to confront with rigour many of the traditional questions of Western philosophy. A sure sign of the catholicity of his thought is his acknowledgement of Aristotle and Kant as the greatest of our predecessors.

It is equally remarkable that while the questions he addresses are in the tradition of Western philosophy, he comes to them with an insider's view of all the accomplishments in the philosophies of logic and language that are the hallmarks of contemporary academic philosophy. Moreover, the list of philosophers with whom he has been engaged – many in direct correspondence and dialogue – is a roll call of the leading thinkers of our time: J. L. Austin, Hidé Ishiguro, Peter Geach, G. E. Moore, W. V. Quine, Gilbert Ryle, Hilary Putnam, D. F. Pears, J. O. Urmson and John Searle mark only a beginning. None of this is to say that his views have been accepted by all. But he has certainly done his share "to keep the conversation going", and the views that so sharply divide him from many of his peers have consistently shed new light on the major questions raised by philosophers in our time.

In this brief introduction, I intend first to give an overview of what Strawson himself calls his intellectual autobiography, marking the striking continuity between his life and his thought. Peter Strawson was born on 23 November 1919, one of his schoolteacher parents' four children. He was educated at Christ's College, Finchley, where he developed a liking for grammar and an enduring devotion to English poetry and prose. He won an open scholarship in English to St John's College, Oxford, but on arriving at Oxford he persuaded the Fellows to allow a change from the Honour School of English to that of Philosophy, Politics and Economics. He soon discovered that he had no real interest in economics, much more in the historical part of politics, and that philosophy was for him "congenial and absorbing" from the start.

He was fortunate in his tutors. His principal philosophy tutor throughout was J. D. Mabbott, whom he found a very reasonable and helpful teacher. He enjoyed one tutorial term with H. P. Grice, whom he regarded as one of the cleverest and most ingenious thinkers of our time, and from whom he learned the most about the difficulty and the possibility inherent in philosophical argument. So engaging was this programme that he knew by the end of his undergraduate years that being a Tutor and a Fellow in one of the colleges in Oxford was the occupation he most desired, but two events conjoined to prevent any immediate realization of that goal. His final examination was a disappointment to him and to his tutors, and the outbreak of the Second World War took him quickly enough into the Royal Artillery for six years. An ongoing and rigorous pursuit of academic philosophy was for the time impossible, but the years left their mark.

I was sent for basic training to a territorial searchlight battery in Sussex, where, in between learning to drill and to shoot, I had an excellent view of the aerial Battle of Britain during the day, and, at night, of the red glow of the Northern sky where London was undergoing bombardment by the Luftwaffe ... In the summer of 1946, having unhesitatingly declined the bait of further promotion, I was demobilized. I had served for six years, thinking a little, but not much, about philosophy, and devoting most of such leisure as I had to reading the greater French and English novelists. My ambitions, however, for a career as an academic philosopher had not changed. *(Ibid.*: 5–6)

An immediate return to Oxford seemed difficult at best, and his former tutor John Mabbott suggested that he apply for the post of Assistant Lecturer in Philosophy at the University College of North Wales, Bangor. Once elected, he prepared earnestly for his lectures, especially for those in the philosophy of logic and Kant's moral philosophy. But during that same academic year, he won the competitive examination for the John Locke Scholarship at Oxford, and so in 1947 he returned to Oxford as a College Lecturer. In the following year he was elected a Fellow.

Having thus achieved, at the age of 28, my prewar ambition, I set seriously to work at the two tasks of tutorial teaching and of thinking my own thoughts. They are not unconnected tasks, for the first is of immense benefit to the second, as the second is to the first. Indeed I think there is no better or more mutually profitable method of philosophical instruction than the one-to-one tutorial exchange. The pupil, who brings and reads to his tutor a weekly essay, prepared on the basis of recommended reading, gains from the attention and criticism of his more experienced listener. The tutor, striving to understand and clarify his pupil's thoughts, will frequently succeed in clarifying his own. This admirable system, like many good things, is under threat. *(Ibid.*: 6–7)

His university lectures in Oxford beginning in 1948 concentrated on a critique of Bertrand Russell's theory of descriptions. At the request of Gilbert Ryle, editor of *Mind*, the content of those lectures appeared in that journal in 1950 as "On Referring" (OR). This work, published at the outset of his career, remains probably the best known of all his writings. He takes issue there with Russell's claim that all singular or general statements are either true, false or meaningless. That trichotomy is the framework for Russell's theory of definite descriptions, according to which asserting "The king of France is wise" would be asserting (1) There is a king of France, (2) There is not more than one king of France, (3) There is nothing which is the king of France and is not wise. Consequently, under the conditions of Russell's trichotomy, the assertion "The king of France is wise" is false, and therefore meaningful.

For Strawson, Russell's theory goes wrong in its failure to distinguish among (a) a sentence, (b) the use of a sentence and (c) an utterance of a statement. The sentence "The king of France is wise" is meaningful in as much as there are varied circumstances in which its utterance would result in a true or false statement. Ordinarily, a speaker uttering that statement *presupposes* the existence of the king, and his uttering neither asserts nor entails that existence. Hence, while the statement is meaningful, its utterance at the present time is neither true nor false, since what it presupposes is false. Thus presupposition must be carefully distinguished from both assertion and entailment.

That initiating question of the relation between our ordinary language and the prescriptions of formal logic was soon, again with Ryle's urging, both explicated and developed in *Introduction to Logical Theory* (ILT) in 1952. A linguistic rule on the boundaries of applicability for the words we use in one particular language can indeed lead to logical appraisals that transcend any particular language. And now, for Strawson, it is an easy but fatal step to suppose that there are logical rules that are independent of linguistic facts. The rules of formal logic typically establish a common use for truth-functional constants, then make that use standard, and end by mandating a rigidity that is foreign to the uses of ordinary language. The logician's rule of material implication, for example, does not correspond exactly to the diverse uses of "if ... then" in ordinary language, where there are no precise rules. The range of application of referring terms is therefore the appropriate territory for the lexicographer, not the logician.

To indicate the limitations of formal logic is not to deny its power both to clarify our thoughts and to put us on the track of useful formal analogies. Strawson accordingly gives an account of the genesis of the logician's second-order vocabulary, and how this leads to both a deductive and a mechanical truth-tabular method of systematizing logic.

Introduction to Logical Theory moves then to a fuller consideration of the treatment of subjects, predicates and existence as they are found in both modern logic and in the older logic of Aristotle. The modern's assumption is that the older logic, if rightly understood, is just one small part of the modern's predicative system. That assumption turns on the issue of existential import. But if we interpret Aristotle's logic as holding that the question of whether statements are true or false does not arise unless the subject class of the categorical statement has members, then all the problems posed by the modern disappear at a stroke. At this point, the tie to the earlier article, "On Referring", is manifest. Strawson thinks that the reluctance of moderns to accept his interpretation is probably rooted in their commitment to that bogus trichotomy of "true", "false" or "meaningless" that underlies Russell's theory of definite descriptions. That error is in turn rooted in the failure to distinguish between sentence and statement.

In sum, formal logic and the ways of ordinary language are related but clearly distinct. From the formalist's viewpoint, the ideal sentence is one that has no contextual commitments. But the vast majority of statement-making sentences we ordinarily use are not of that sort. The effort of the formalist to impose his rule on ordinary language may well be termed revisionary. Strawson's counter is to offer a modestly descriptive account of the manner in which ordinary language makes its way in our world.

Recognition of the challenge posed by *Introduction to Logical Theory* came early in a lengthy review by Quine in *Mind*. Strawson's stance has consistently marked him as a member in opposition to one prevalent contemporary view of logic's role.

> My double concern in the book was to explain the nature of standard elementary logic while at the same time emphasizing the point that, perspicuous, powerful, and elegant as it is, modern formal logic is not an adequate instrument for revealing clearly all the structural features of language as we use it. Rather, it is an idealized abstraction of great power and beauty, an indispensable tool indeed for clarifying much of our thought, but not, as some are tempted to suppose, the unique and sufficient key to the functioning of language and thought in general. (*Ibid.*: 8–9)

At this stage of his career, the major influences on Strawson had in the first place been those of Russell and Moore, to whom had now been added Ryle, Austin, Frege and Wittgenstein. Those influences were of a mixed sort:

> Ryle, whose verve and brilliance might excuse, if they sometimes masked, a certain lack of rigor in thought, and Austin, consistently clear, precise, witty, and formidable; more remotely,

Wittgenstein, whose Blue and Brown books began to circulate in pirated copies at the beginning of the 1950s, at once breathtakingly impressive and profoundly enigmatic; and Frege himself, whose articles on Sense and Reference and Concept and Object were made available in English translation by Geach and Black in 1952. Nor should I fail to mention A. J. Ayer whose *Language, Truth and Logic* I had read, enthralled, in the gardens of St John's as an undergraduate – even though, by now, I no longer found satisfying his undiluted classical empiricism.　　　*(Ibid.*: 8)

With the publication of *Introduction to Logical Theory*, Strawson no longer gave his introductory lectures in logic and began to turn his attention to the application of his original concern with reference and predication to questions in ontology and metaphysics, questions that span the history of Western philosophy from Aristotle to Quine. This led naturally enough to the publication of *Individuals* (IE) in 1959 where his central concern is with the identification and reidentification of particulars. This represents both a continuation of and a move beyond the concentrations of his earlier works. The logical and linguistic issues of singular reference and predication and their objects continue in play, but their ties to the ontological commitments that are now addressed take us to a broadening philosophical perspective.

Thus, the identification of particulars is now linked to the same questions of reference to singulars and their predications that were dominant in "On Referring" and *Introduction to Logical Theory*. For Strawson, a speaker making reference to and identifying particulars such as historical occurrences, material objects, people and their shadows, is always done through the use of expressions with some demonstrative, egocentric or token-reflexive force, all done within a single public spatiotemporal framework.

The theoretical indispensability of a demonstrative element in identifying thought about particulars ... necessarily holds for any system incorporating particulars, in which the particulars are spatial or temporal or spatio-temporal entities .... It [also] seems to me necessarily true ... that no system which does not allow for spatial or temporal entities can be a system which allows for particulars at all .... This [is Kant's point] that space and time are our only forms of intuition. If we take these two points together, it follows that ... identifying thought about particulars necessarily incorporates a demonstrative element.　　　(in Hahn 1998: 119)

Thus ontologically armed, Strawson next addresses those questions of the relationship between minds and bodies that have been central since the time of Descartes: why are one's states of consciousness ascribed to anything at all, and why are they ascribed to the very same thing to which we ascribe certain corporeal characteristics? Strawson argues here against both a Cartesian view of the ego as a thinking substance distinct from the body as an extended substance, and the no-ownership view that ego is an illusion, attributable perhaps to Moritz Schlick and Wittgenstein. To free ourselves from such difficulties, we must instead recognize the primitiveness of the concept of person, that is, of an entity such that both "M-predicates" ascribing states of consciousness, and "P-predicates" ascribing corporeal characteristics, are equally applicable to a single individual of that single type. In this manner, Strawson thinks we arrive at a "descriptive metaphysics" rooted within the boundaries of our ordinary experience, and set over against the "revisionary" claims of those metaphysicians such as Leibniz whose claims to go beyond those boundaries have been permanently discredited by Kant.

Part II of *Individuals* fully considers the link between Strawson's original concerns with logic and his consequent concerns with ontology. He argues that the relation in the logical or grammatical distinction between subject (reference) and predicate (predication) and the ontological distinction between particular and universal is indeed fundamental, but not exclusive, since while particulars can never be predicated, universals can certainly be referred to and can be the subjects of predication. There is always a way in which subject expressions are complete, while predicate expressions are incomplete. Strawson finds here an additional depth to Frege's metaphor of the saturated and unsaturated constituents of a sentence.

The year of publication of *Individuals* (1959) was also the year in which Ayer was elected to the Wykeham Chair of Logic at Oxford and initiated a series of weekly meetings, which in their own way replaced the Saturday morning meetings over which Austin had presided before his untimely death.

> With Austin proceedings were informal and no standard philosophical issues were tackled head-on; instead, particular concepts or concept-groups (words or word-groups), and the conditions of their use, were examined in detail, with results that were always fascinating, and often philosophically suggestive or illuminating. With Ayer, a different member of the group each week would read a paper on a philosophical topic of his choice; then drinks would be

> served by the host for the term and discussion, usually spirited,
> never acrimonious, would begin.   (Strawson 1998a: 11)

Individuals had attempted to investigate the conditions that are
presupposed by the knowledge and experience we actually have. It
was an altogether natural consequence that in the years immediately following its publication, Strawson began to lecture regularly on
Kant's *Critique of Pure Reason*. His investigations into logic, language
and ontology had all struck the note of presupposition, and that note
is also central in all three of Kant's Critiques. *The Bounds of Sense*
(BS) (1966a) is Strawson's effort to disentangle within the *Critique of
Pure Reason* the unintelligibility of Kant's metaphysical idealism from
the specific and salutary arguments of the Transcendental Analytic
and the Transcendental Dialectic.

Kant investigates the limits of what we can conceive of as the
framework of all of our thought about the world and our experience
of the world. He argues that a certain framework is a presupposition
of all that is truly intelligible: the concepts of the understanding are
empty without the forms of the sensuous intuitions of space and time,
and it is equally true that the forms of intuition are blind without
the concepts. This framework is presupposed by all of our empirical
enquiries, but any attempt to apply that structure beyond the bounds
of sense is an illusion.

Strawson thinks that the Analytic is at the heart of the *Critique*. It
is here that we find the construction of the bounds of our experience:
that all of our experience is essentially temporal, that within that temporal series there must be what is necessary for self-consciousness,
that the outer objects of that consciousness are all spatial, and that
there is but a single spatiotemporal framework.

That is followed in the Dialectic by the claimed destruction of any
metaphysics that would attempt to transcend these bounds of sense,
hence the antinomies and the arguments against the possibility of
our knowing things-in-themselves. Kant believed nonetheless in the
existence of a noumenal world beyond the reach of our possible experience within the bounds of pure reason, and saw in this a safe haven
for the interests of morality and religion. But here Kant may appear
to be arguing both that there is a supersensible reality and that we
can have a particular kind of knowledge about it, an argument that
Strawson finds unintelligible.

Strawson thus thinks that Kant has both drawn the bounds of
sense and attempted to traverse them. Strawson's aim in *The Bounds
of Sense* is therefore twofold. He attempts to make plain, in the terms

of contemporary analytic philosophy, Kant's "brilliant and profound account" in the Analytic of that structural network of ideas and concepts that determine the limits of the world of our possible experience. Strawson also attempts to show how Kant's efforts in the Dialectic failed in his effort to provide an overarching theory that would serve to explain the possibility of the sort of account that the Analytic provides. Nonetheless, Strawson continues to think that Kant's work is the greatest single work in modern Western philosophy, but that a last word on this work is an ongoing project without any sign of a final resolution. Strawson's interest in Kant did not end with the publication of *The Bounds of Sense*. He continued to give regular graduate seminars on Kant for the following twenty years, and in a series of articles he both amended and developed the views he had established in that book. The range of his philosophical interests also continued to widen.

In 1968 he had succeeded Ryle in the Waynflete Chair of Metaphysical Philosophy at Oxford. The manner in which he continued to find thinking his own thoughts and simultaneously working with students in philosophy to be mutually supportive activities is characteristic of his academic career.

> Before taking up my duties in October of that year I worked hard at preparing a set of introductory lectures on philosophy. My aims were, first, to explain the general nature of the discipline as I conceived and tried to practice it; then to demonstrate the interdependence of ontology, epistemology, and logic; and finally to show how certain philosophical issues should, on my view, be resolved. I was incidentally concerned both to lay classical empiricism to rest and, in rejecting at least one favored conception of analysis, to resist the reductive tendency in philosophy in general. (*Ibid.*: 13)

All that served well as the framework for what followed. The general issues that had been there from the beginning remained, but the particular issues treated in greater detail varied across time. He translated and delivered a French version of those lectures at the Collège de France in 1985. An English version was given in Munich in the same year, at the Catholic University of America in 1987, and at the Sino-British Summer School in Philosophy in Beijing in 1988. The final English version of the lectures did not appear until 1992.

His next book was *Subject and Predicate in Logic and Grammar* (1974b). The primary concern here is with the philosophy of language, but the unity of his philosophical development is again manifest. He starts with his initial concern with definite singular reference and predication, and proceeds by way of *Individuals* to an account of the grammatical notions of subject and predicate.

Strawson travelled and lectured widely in the 1970s: twice to India, to Spain, and to Jerusalem for a conference commemorating the tercentenary of the death of Spinoza. Responses to his lectures reflected the temper of the times.

> In 1977 I received the honor of knighthood; immediately after the investiture in December I departed for Yugoslavia, where I gave lectures in Belgrade, Sarajevo, and Zagreb. I registered a certain difference in atmosphere in the three places …. In Sarajevo, where I was only allowed to give one of my two scheduled lectures and had minimal contact with fellow academics, one perhaps time-serving young man in my audience suggested that my lecture revealed an essentially bourgeois outlook. I replied, "But I *am* bourgeois – an elitist liberal bourgeois". My interpreter commented, *sotto voce*, "They envy you".   (*Ibid.*: 15–16)

Philosophical Subjects (Van Straaten 1980) contains critical essays along with Strawson's own replies. Notable among the contributors are John McDowell, Gareth Evans and Ishiguro. A similar collection of essays appeared in a special issue of the Israeli journal *Philosophia* in 1981. Later in the decade there were two more papers on the original question of singular reference, and travels again to Spain, the United States, Switzerland and, for the third time, India.

Lectures he gave at Columbia University formed the basis of *Skepticism and Naturalism: Some Varieties* (SN) (1985). While Strawson continues to see Kant as the greatest of the moderns, he is also prepared to see Hume as hero in his stance on some issues that continue to divide our contemporaries. *Skepticism and Naturalism* identifies two of those issues. Here Hume is for Strawson both the arch-sceptic and the arch-naturalist, under one use of those terms. Hume as sceptic does not really deny the validity of certain beliefs: they are simply our natural dispositions, which provide the framework for all of our appropriate judgements. But Hume does doubt the adequacy of any effort to justify those beliefs by criteria external to the frameworks themselves.

Strawson here distinguishes between a strict reductive "hard" naturalism, and one that is comprehensive or "soft".

> For there is an evident affinity, though by no means identity, between the scientism that pooh-poohs subjective experience,

and scientific realism which relegates phenomenal qualities to the realm of the subjective, denying them objective reality, and the reductive naturalism that represents moral and personal reactive attitudes as resting on an illusion, denying, in effect, the objective reality of moral desert, or moral good and evil. All these stances have in common ... a reductive and scientistic tendency which leads me to bring them together under the label of "reductive naturalism" ... [and] to represent them also as varieties of *skepticism:* moral skepticism, skepticism about the world as it appears, skepticism about the mental .... I have tried to set up another kind of Naturalism – a non-reductive variety – which recognizes the human inescapability and metaphysical acceptability of those various types of conception of reality which are challenged or put in doubt by reductive or traditionally skeptical arguments.

(SN: 67–8)

In a debate over the foundations of morality, the reductive naturalist will hold that any claim of objective right or wrong is either an illusion or an invention, since all that we can ever empirically observe are simply natural happenings. The opposition will argue for objective standards that transcend the empirical, and for a free will that will justify assigning moral praise and blame. Strawson's way with this dispute is not to enter the lists on either side of the argument, as he thinks Kant does. Strawson's way is not to argue, it is simply to circumvent the issue altogether. This is the way of the soft naturalist. Both the hard naturalist and the free-will defender will argue from within frameworks towards each of which we do have a natural predisposition. Within each framework, there are appropriate standards for judgements and justifications within that framework. Within neither are there grounds to support the other framework. Moreover there is no available point of view, independent of and superior to the two frameworks, that would enable us to choose between them. Thus Strawson will advocate a peaceful coexistence between the two: a truce in a war between two apparently irreconcilable points of view.

His way with the ancient quarrel between nominalists and realists is much the same.

The strong nominalist will say of his opponent, in Wittgenstein's famous phrase, that "a picture holds him captive". To the strong realist, on the other hand, it will appear that his opponent is in the grip of a reductive rage, a rage to reduce thought; and he will find it noteworthy, and ironical, that this reductive is perhaps most common today among the most scrupulous thinkers.

(SN: 94–5)

But if the conflict between nominalist and realist is irreconcilable, and if a choice has to be made, then Strawson's sympathies are with the realist. Strawson inconclusively concludes with Gibbon's epigram that philosophy's boast is that her gentle hand is able to eradicate from our minds the latent and deadly principle of fanaticism.

We have seen that in Oxford between 1968 and 1987, the year of his retirement, Strawson gave almost yearly a series of introductory lectures in philosophy. They form the major part of *Analysis and Metaphysics* (AM) (1992a). Although introductory, the lectures are certainly not elementary. He notes in the Preface that there is "no shallow end to the philosophical pool". The lectures were Strawson's attempt to explain his conception of how the issues surrounding the fields of metaphysics, epistemology and the philosophies of logic and language and their connections are to be resolved. In *Analysis and Metaphysics*, those lectures are supplemented by essays on Davidson and Spinoza. Taken altogether, the work represents not just a gathering of past considerations, but also a pointer towards issues for further consideration.

For Strawson, philosophy is an attempt to provide a systematic account of that general conceptual structure over which our daily practice shows us to have a mastery, a structure both so general and so common that all the specialized structures of all the special sciences must fit within its rule. We have in place conceptual equipment that we are well able to use long before we can say systematically what the rules are that we so effortlessly observe. But when we seek to make that general structure explicit, we run the danger of falling into the "childish habit" of looking for a single master key to everything: the methodological error of Descartes. That error is best averted if we search instead for the multiple connections among a network of concepts.

That search is the hallmark of all Strawson's work since its inception in "On Referring". He has also made common cause with Moore in identifying the trio of logic, ontology and epistemology as but three aspects of one unified enquiry. One difference is that while Moore talks about things in the universe, Strawson's concern is with the concepts we use when considering those things. The life of those concepts is in the proposition, and it is logic that studies the general forms of the proposition, and hence of all our beliefs about the world. Those general forms have what Quine calls a "canonical notation", and he thinks there is an identity of that notation with ultimate categories, and most general traits of reality, hence the tie between logic and ontology. But where Quine would render ordinary language into canonical notation in a programme of ontological reduction, Strawson's way once again is to search out connections that are not reductive. Towards the end of his career in philosophy, this approach manifests once again a continuing thread in Strawson's thinking: *Introduction to Logical Theory* (ILT) (1952) had at the outset investigated the relation between our ordinary language and the prescriptions of formal logic, and had concluded that they are related but distinct, that the rationality of ordinary language is far more varied than what formal logic captures.

Logic and ontology are joined in Strawson's account by epistemology, since the use of concepts is in making judgements, and our concepts get their sense from what is possible in our experience. Here Strawson continues to invoke Kant: a concept without the content of spacetime experience is empty. Thus Strawson supports "Kant's empiricism", while he opposes the "classical empiricism" of Hume. Typically, Hume sought the impression from which the idea of a necessary connection between two states of affairs is obtained. The consequence for Hume was that causal relationships have no objective foundation. But for Strawson, that falsely atomizes our experience: we simply see the boulder *flatten* the hut. We have no need to justify our concept of causality, properly understood, for our experience of the world presupposes it.

That stance leads naturally enough to the issues of freedom and necessity. Here Strawson opposes the position of Spinoza that freedom is an illusion, based on our ignorance of the causes of our actions. For Strawson, our sense of freedom is a natural fact, tied most closely to the very notions of self and other selves. Even if science were in theory able to identify every mental event with a physical one, such a reduction has no possibility of realization, for such an attempted reduction would *of itself* exclude the very attitudes in question.

The retirement from his Chair at Magdalen College in 1987 did not mark the end of Strawson's philosophical activity. He continued to have a room in University College and to work there, and his travels and philosophical discussions remained a constant. In 1991 he visited and lectured at the Universities of Colorado, Wyoming and Wisconsin, and at Yale. This was Strawson's first experience of undergraduate teaching in the United States, all of his previous semester-long visits having been in contacts with graduate students and faculty members. He found the differences between undergraduate and graduate levels particularly striking. In his contacts with undergraduates, he was refreshingly taken with "the informality of the proceedings and the enquiring receptiveness" of his audience (Strawson 1998a: 18). At the same time, he found a surprising difference between undergraduate and graduate students in their levels of literary and philosophical sophistication.

Strawson's academic career has indeed been diverse, productive and lengthy. His continuing passion for philosophy has taken him to all of the world's continents except Australasia. All this has been sustained by his own view on how to do philosophy. He did not set out to develop some grand metaphysical scheme in the manner of Spinoza or Kant. Instead, in the manner so well exemplified early in his career in the Saturday morning meetings with Austin, he has sought to come to a better understanding of particular concepts or concept-groups, and to draw out an awareness of parallels and connections among them that shed new light over an apparently familiar landscape. He tells us that the original moment of an apparent discovery of that sort is exhilarating, but that this is often followed by a cooler and more chastened attitude. Very early in his career he one day announced to one of his colleagues that he had a new theory of truth, only to receive the reply "Come on now, which of the old ones is it?" Nonetheless, after the initial rush of the apparent discovery has subsided, sober reflection may show a worthwhile residue, and at this point the hard work begins. This starts with getting a clear idea of the line to be pursued, organizing and detailing that line and finding good prose for its expression.

Throughout his career, Strawson has always been much engaged in public discussions and debates, from Saturday mornings with Austin to international conferences and lecture halls around the world. He has always been in earnest and open dialogue with his peers. But that activity is always rooted in an independent work that he finds native to philosophy itself.

> Agreement among experts in the special sciences and in exact scholarship may reasonably be hoped for and gradually attained. But philosophy, which takes human thought in general as its field, is not thus conveniently confined; and truth in philosophy, though not to be despaired of, is so complex and many-sided, so multi-faced, that any individual philosopher's work, if it is to have any unity and coherence, must at best emphasize some aspects

of the truth, to the neglect of others which may strike another philosopher with greater force. Hence the appearance of endemic disagreement in the subject is something to be expected rather than deplored; and it is no matter for wonder that the individual philosopher's views are more likely than those of the scientist or exact scholar to reflect in part his individual taste and temperament. (SN: vii–viii)

Strawson shares the view of the later Wittgenstein that philosophy's essential and perhaps sole concern is to get clear about concepts, and the ways in which they shape our lives. He thinks that this later Wittgenstein is the greatest among us in his effort to free our minds from those illusions that Wittgenstein's earlier work so well exemplifies. And yet Strawson does not share what he regards as Wittgenstein's distrust of general theorizing, since for Strawson Kant does indeed, in the *Critique of Pure Reason*, provide a human conceptual scheme that offers an articulated structure susceptible to a defensible description. And, again Wittgenstein notwithstanding, for Strawson even an exposed illusion way have at its source some elements of truth.

Strawson has no religious beliefs; he has trouble with the concept of God, a trouble not surprising in view of both his admiration for and his reservations about Kant. His political views are centrist; he is conservative in his tastes, liberal in his sentiments.

All in all, I count myself extremely lucky. Above all, I am fortunate in my friends and my family; friends whom I made as an undergraduate and to whom I am still close, and others, of many nationalities, whom I have come to know since; a family of wife and four children, all variously gifted and all, to my mind, invariably charming. Philosophy, friends, and family apart, my life has been enriched by the enjoyment of literature, landscape, architecture, and the company of clever and beautiful women. So far every decade has been better than the one before, though I recognize that, in the nature of things, this cannot continue indefinitely. (Strawson 1998a: 21)

The list of philosophers with whom Peter Strawson has been engaged is indeed a roll call of the leading thinkers of our time. With them he has consistently addressed the central concerns of contemporary Anglophone philosophers across a broad spectrum of issues, and he has done that in an historical context that makes Aristotle, Hume and Kant our own. His dialogues with both those in agreement and the members in opposition are always marked by mutual respect.

Peter Strawson is one of the great philosophers of our century. If I have long been an admirer of his work, it is because of the exemplary way in which, time and again, he has advanced the state of philosophical discussion and opened new ways for us to explore (while always keeping in mind the interrelatedness of philosophical issues). I particularly value the fact that he opened the way to a reception of Kant's philosophy by analytic philosophers. (Putnam 1998: 273)

His strong involvement in public debates has been matched by his commitment and skill in the very personal world of an Oxford tutorial. His way with that has left some lasting impressions:

An Oxford tutorial usually lasted an hour. It began with the student reading aloud an essay he or she had written in the course of a week .... In responding to the essay, Strawson did four things. He would, first, make a number of criticisms. In my experience he focussed on *significant* difficulties ... which were important for the case being argued in the essay .... Second, he encouraged us to develop our own ideas, by pointing out how they could have been taken in other directions, pushed through more vigorously, and linked in other ways. Third, he would reveal an approach of his own to the problem, which always seemed ... deeply considered, original and persuasive. Fourth ... he would manifestly *think* before our eyes, a thinking which issued in pellucid, ingenious, honest, and abstract responses. (Snowdon 1998: 293–4)

All in all, Strawson considered himself extremely lucky. But surely he made the most of the chances that were his, and his life was marked by an uncommon unity of purpose.

Peter Strawson died on 13 February 2006, aged 86.

The chapters that follow are an attempt to make clear the ways in which the central thoughts in logic and language with which Strawson began remained constant, while at the same time manifesting their applications across an ever broader range of philosophical topics. Each chapter is mainly concerned with one of five major books by Strawson, but together they also provide ample opportunity to consider the contents of his other books and essays, notably the debates on freedom and necessity and on the correspondence theory of truth. Each chapter includes some indication of the ways in which various philosophers have responded to Strawson's initiatives, together, in some cases, with Strawson's replies to his critics.

Chapter 1

"On Referring" and *Introduction to Logical Theory*: The basic questions

Looking back at the course of his career in philosophy, Strawson believed in 1998 that the work by which he continues to be best known remains his first, the article "On Referring". That judgement is probably correct. It is certainly true that "On Referring" is the root of the whole wide spectrum of developments in his later writings. The article is concerned with one particular aspect of the relation between our ordinary language and formal logic, and the concern with that relation is then broadened in his subsequent first book, *Introduction to Logical Theory*. The two works are therefore appropriately considered together as foundational.

"On Referring"

We commonly use expressions of a certain kind to refer to some individual person, object or event. We use singular demonstrative pronouns ("this" and "that"), proper names ("Peter Strawson"), singular pronouns ("I", "you", "it"), and we use the definite article followed by a noun in the singular ("the table", "the king of France"). The members of the last of those four classes are called definite descriptions, and they constitute the source of a number of questions that are simultaneously grammatical, logical and ontological. Those questions have a long history, going back at least to Aristotle, and contemporary efforts to deal with them are a major source and a continuing central concern among contemporary Anglophone philosophers.

Russell's theory of definite descriptions (Russell 1905) is still widely held among logicians to be a correct account. In "On Referring",[1] however, Strawson wants to show that Russell's theory contains some fundamental mistakes. In his effort to set the account straight, we find the prime source of all that was to follow in Strawson's career as a philosopher, with consequences that were to involve the most fundamental questions not only in the relation between ordinary language and logic, but ever more widely with perennial questions in epistemology and metaphysics.

We may begin by asking what question or questions Russell's theory of definite descriptions attempts to answer. Consider someone at present uttering the sentence "The king of France is wise". The sentence thus uttered certainly seems to be significant, but then the question arises of just how this can be so if there is no present king of France. One apparent answer would be this argument. Let the sentence as a whole be S, and let "the king of France" be D. Then:

(1) If S is significant, then it is either true or false.
(2) S is true if D is wise, false if D is not wise.
(3) But S and not-S are alike true only if there is D in some sense.
(4) Since S is significant, D must exist in some sense.

That is evidently a bad argument, one that Russell rejects. For him, the mistake in the argument comes from thinking that D as the *grammatical* subject of S is therefore also its *logical* subject. But D is not the logical subject of S. Indeed, S is not logically a subject–predicate sentence at all; it is instead a complex kind of existential proposition. To exhibit the true logical form of S, we should rewrite it:

(1) There is a king of France.
(2) There is not more than one king of France.
(3) There is nothing that is the king of France and is not wise.

Thus, on Russell's analysis, anyone uttering S today would be saying something significant but false. And thus for Russell we must distinguish definite descriptions such as "the king of France" from logically proper names. The latter (a) can alone be the subjects of sentences of a genuine subject–predicate form, and (b) have some single object for which they stand. Strawson thinks that Russell is wrong in this. For Strawson, sentences 1–3 above do indeed describe circumstances that are necessary conditions for making a true assertion when uttering the sentence. But that does not mean that Russell has given us an account of those sentences that is either completely or even partially correct.

In order both to show the error of Russell's way and to provide an alternative correct account, Strawson begins by drawing a distinction among

- a sentence
- a use of a sentence
- an utterance of a sentence.

The sentence "The king of France is wise" can be uttered at various times, and it has various uses. It is critically important to recognize that we cannot say that the sentence in itself is either true or false; we can only say that the sentence may be used to make a true or false assertion or to express a true or false proposition.

In line with this analysis of the sentence S, we can make an analogous although not identical analysis of a uniquely referring expression such as "the king of France". The analysis is not identical, since no use of such an expression can ever be either true or false. But there is an effective analogy, and this is at the heart of Strawson's position. Referring is not something that an expression such as "the king of France" does. Referring is instead characteristic of the *use* of an expression, just as truth-or-falsity is characteristic of the use of a sentence.

In sum, let "type" stand for "sentence" or "expression". Strawson then is not saying that there are types, and uses of types and utterances of types, in the sense in which there are ships, and shoes and sealing wax. He is instead saying that we cannot say the *same things* about types, the uses of types and the utterances of types.

> We are apt to fancy that we are talking about sentences and expressions when we are talking about the uses of sentences and expressions …. This is what Russell does. Generally, as against Russell, I shall say this. Meaning (in at least one important sense) is a function of the sentence or expression; mentioning and referring and truth or falsity, are functions of the use of the sentence or expression. (OR: 9)

Meanings do give general directions for the ways in which a type may be used, but they do not give directions for any particular use. Thus the question of whether a sentence is significant or not has nothing to do with the truth or falsity of a particular occasion of its use. Russell confuses meaning with mentioning, and that is the source of his mistake. For Strawson, the absurdity of asking whether a particular sentence is true or false is not relieved by Russell's contention that it must be one or the other on the grounds that the sentence is significant. A sentence in itself is no more true or false than it is about some particular subject. The correct question on whether a sentence is significant or not is the question of whether there are language habits, conventions or rules such that the sentence could be *used* to talk about something.

Russell's claim is that anyone now uttering the sentence "The king of France is wise" would (a) be making either a true or a false statement, and (b) be asserting that there exists at present one and only one king of France. Strawson finds Russell wrong on both counts. For Strawson, the sentence is certainly significant, because it *could* be used to say something true or false, and it *could* be used to refer to a particular person. But that does not mean that any particular use of it must be either true or false. Suppose someone were at present to utter "The king of France is wise", and were to ask me whether what he just said is true or false. I would be likely to reply that it was neither, since the question simply does not arise.

There are, of course, "secondary" uses of sentences and expressions, as in the cases of sophisticated fictions. If I at present say that the king of France is wise, and that he lives in a golden castle with one hundred wives, no one would suppose either that I was referring to an existing person, or that my utterance was false. Such secondary uses do not compromise the primary one. Someone using "the king of France" in a primary way is not asserting that there is a king of France, nor does that use entail a proposition of a uniquely existential sort. One of the ordinary functions of the definite article is to signal that some unique reference is being made, but which particular individual is being referred to is a function of the contextual features such as the time and the place of a sentence's utterance. There is thus a critical distinction between (a) using a sentence to make a unique reference, and (b) asserting that there is one and only one individual that has certain characteristics. To refer is not to assert. Russell fails to make that distinction, and is thus led to "the logically disastrous theory of names developed in the *Enquiry into Meaning and Truth* and in *Human Knowledge*" (OR: 16).

It is Strawson's claim that in the correct account we *use* expressions to make unique references, but that it is only in the rules governing those uses along with the context of those uses that we actually secure a particular use. There is thus a need to distinguish between rules for referring and rules for ascribing and attributing. Once that distinction is recognized, we are well on the way to resolving a number of ancient logical and metaphysical puzzles. We approach those puzzles with the recognition that when we state a fact about a particular, we have two tasks, the referring and the attributing. That distinction roughly and approximately corresponds to the grammatical distinction between subject and predicate. There are, of course, other methods. An example would be a game in which no expression is used in a uniquely referring way, but there are instead a series of uniquely existential sentences leading ultimately to the identification of a particular through an accumulation of relative clauses. The parlour game Twenty Questions might serve as an example. But the fact that this is a game is a sufficient indication that this is not the ordinary use we have for existential sentences.

To make a unique reference requires some device for showing both *that* a unique reference is made, and *what* unique reference it is. To do this, the context of utterance is of the greatest importance:

> The requirement for the correct application of an expression in its ascriptive use to a certain thing is simply that the thing should be of a certain kind, have certain characteristics. The requirement for the correct application of an expression in its referring use to a certain thing is something over and above any requirement derived from such ascriptive meaning as the expression may have; it is, namely, the requirement that the thing should be in a certain relation to the speaker and to the context of utterance. Let me call this the contextual requirement.   (OR: 19)

For Strawson, this irreducible distinction between ascribing use and referring use has been blurred by logicians in their neglect or misinterpretation of the conventions for referring. This is because most logicians are preoccupied with definitions, and some of them are preoccupied with formal systems. The distinctive features of referring use are ones that they seek to reduce or eliminate altogether. For Strawson, a prime instance of the folly of that attempt is made by Leibniz in his effort to establish individual identity through "complete individual concepts" done in exclusively general terms. We shall see in Strawson's subsequent *Individuals* (1959) a detailed account of just how Leibniz is judged to go wrong. Strawson thinks that Russell similarly strives desperately in his own way to make logic in a narrow sense adequate for referring to individuals.

It is important to remember that while Strawson's fundamental distinction is between referring and ascribing uses, there are expressions that can play either role, and those expressions that refer can do so in a variety of ways:

- Such expressions may differ in their degree of context-dependence, with "I" and its maximum dependence at one end of the scale and "the author of *Waverley*" at the other.
- They may also differ in their degree of descriptive meaning. "Horace" may be the name of a cat, a dog or a motorcycle. Such pure names have no descriptive meaning at all, although they may acquire such a meaning as a result of one of their uses. In contrast, a substantial phrase such as "the round table" has a maximum descriptive meaning.
- They may differ on whether or not they are governed by some *general* referring-cum-ascriptive conventions. For pronouns, having the least descriptive meaning, there are such conventions. Usually for proper names there are no such conventions, only conventions that are *ad hoc* for each particular case.

Common nouns are naturally and commonly used to refer; adjectives are not. We expect common nouns to show what unique reference is being made, *and* to mirror the salient characteristics of things. Strawson finds the difference between nouns and adjectives to be mirrored quaintly by John Locke in the claim that substances are collections of simple ideas.

> "Substance" is the troublesome tribute that Locke pays to his dim awareness of the difference in predominant linguistic function that lingered, even when the noun had been expanded into a more or less indefinite string of adjectives. Russell repeats Locke's mistake with a difference when, admitting the inference from syntax to reality to the extent of feeling that he can get rid of this metaphysical unknown only if we can purify language of the referring function altogether, he draws up his programme for "abolishing particulars", a programme, in fact, for abolishing the distinction of logical use which I am here at pains to emphasize.   (OR: 22)

It is particularly noteworthy that Strawson's fundamental distinctions between sentence and utterance, and between referring and ascribing, are in effect a challenge to the votaries of modern logic. Consider such non-uniquely referring expressions as "all", "no", "some" and "some ... are not". These are the four types of standard form categorical propositions: A (all X are Y); E (no X are Y), I (some X are Y), and O (some X are not Y). For the modern, only I and O propositions have existential import. A consequence is that the modern must deny some traditional doctrines such as the square of opposition and the validity of some forms of the syllogism. That consequence rests precisely on the modern's failure to recognize Strawson's way with the referring use of expressions.

The modern's dilemma is a bogus one. If we simply say that the question of whether or not the quantificational expressions are being used to make true or false assertions just does not arise except when the existential condition is fulfilled for the subject term, then all of the laws of traditional logic hold good. Expressions beginning with "all" or "some" are ordinarily used in a referring way. If we ask a literal-minded and childless man if all of his children are asleep, he will not answer either "Yes" or "No", because the question simply does not arise.

Strawson concludes "On Referring" with a sentence that is both a summary for this article and an augury of what was to follow in *Introduction to Logical Theory*: "Neither Aristotelian nor Russellian rules give the exact logic of any expression of ordinary language; for ordinary language has no exact logic" (*ibid.*).

Introduction to Logical Theory

This book is pivotal in the sense that it marks the way that leads from the seminal article we have been considering to all the metaphysical and epistemological accomplishments of Strawson's later works. At the outset, the book's title notwithstanding, he disclaims any attempt to add to the large number of textbooks and technical treatises on formal logic. Many of those works deal scantily or misleadingly with the relationship between formal logic and the logical features of ordinary language. For Strawson, the failure to deal adequately with that relationship also results in a failure to understand formal logic itself.

To remedy that failure, Strawson sets himself two objectives. The first is to bring out both the contacts and the contrasts of words as they occur in ordinary speech and as they occur in formal systems. The second is to provide a clear introductory account of formal logic itself as it is understood and practised at the present time. In accomplishing this second aim, Strawson establishes his credentials to stand as a partial defender of some of the claims of traditional logic and as a critic of what he regards as the ill-founded and exclusionary claims of some of the moderns.

Strawson will begin this task by noting differences among the various ways in which we make judgements about what someone says. One form of appraisal we call logical, other forms include rhetorical and moral. He then argues that within the logical form there are points of both contrast and contact between the logical vocabulary of ordinary language and that of formal logic. Once that is in place, Strawson will proceed to a thorough if introductory account of the systems of both sentential and quantificational logic. He concludes with a shorter review of the differences between deductive and inductive reasoning, and the attendant questions of probability. All things considered, I think that Strawson here provides a significantly fresh and informed view of the roles of logic, one that has shown itself on evidence to be usefully provocative. In what follows, I attempt to provide a sequential account of that view, together with some indication of how that view has been received by the critics.

Chapter 1: Logical Appraisal

What we ordinarily say or write can be judged by various criteria: by its truth, style, morality or logic. To say of a statement that it is logical is ordinarily a term of commendation; to say that it is illogical is plainly to make a criticism that differs from a disagreement on moral or literary grounds. There is a further and somewhat more complex distinction when we say of a statement that it is untrue or that it is inconsistent. To say that something is untrue is to refer to things outside the statement itself: it is to say that the statement does not square with those things. In contrast, to say that a statement is inconsistent makes no such reference: the fault lies within the statement itself.

In a deductive argument that is valid, if the premises are true, then the conclusion is necessarily true under pain of inconsistency or self-contradiction. If the purpose of speech is communication, then a man who truly contradicts himself does not really say anything. We must, however, be careful not to rush to judgement. Asked if the results of a recent election pleased me or not, I may significantly reply that they did and they did not. In appraisal, we cannot be content with words alone; we must also consider their context. For the same reason, we must exercise caution in the range of applicability of the words we use to describe things. Such words as "vehicle" and "entertainment" have only approximate boundaries for their appropriate use. The uses and hence the meanings of words are subject to both expansion and contraction, and they vary from time to time and from place to place. We must consider the context of statements that are made.

Here at the outset, Strawson thus carries over a theme already well established in "On Referring". Logical appraisal is properly applied to statements, not sentences. That appraisal is made possible by the boundaries of applicability we draw for referring expressions. To accept such a boundary for "*p*" is to establish its definition, and therefore to accept "*p* and not-*p*" as a logical contradiction. Behind logical inconsistencies between statements, there are linguistic rules for the use of expressions that are in play.

Formal logic's ultimate dependence on the workings of ordinary language is thus apparent. And, for Strawson, seeing that this is so enables us to see a further way in which we may be tempted to assign to the language of formal logic an undeserved regulatory sovereignty over ordinary language. A *linguistic* rule for one particular language can lead to *logical* appraisals that transcend any particular language. Consider "*x* is *y*'s son-in-law and *x* is unmarried". That statement is logically inconsistent on the basis of the *linguistic* rule that in English "son-in-law" means "is married to the daughter of". From a *logical* point of view, a French version of the statement is also inconsistent, but the *linguistic* rules in English and French are not identical. And now it is easy to think that logical facts are independent of linguistic facts, and hence to say that a logical statement transcends the particular language in which it is made. It is precisely here that Strawson raises a cautionary note:

> It is important also to notice that this reason for not regard-
> ing statements of logical appraisal as about particular groups of
> words (e.g., sentences) is different from, though connected with,
> that which we have discussed earlier. Earlier we pointed out
> that it is not sentences which we say are inconsistent with one
> another, follow from one another, etc., but statements; the ques-
> tion of what statement is made, and of whether a statement is
> made at all, depends upon other things than simply what words
> are used. But rules about words lie behind all statements of logi-
> cal appraisal; and it remains to be seen whether we can best do
> logic in terms directly about representative expressions, or in
> terms of logical relations between statements.   (ILT: 12)

Having thus sounded an initial caution about the relationship between ordinary language and formal logic, Strawson now addresses his second announced aim: making clear at an introductory level the nature of formal logic itself. While much of this account is in common with the orthodoxies of modern logic, Strawson also offers significantly countering views. Strawson's account is therefore valuable both for its uncommon clarity and for its establishing the foundations of his consequent metaphysical and epistemological views.

Most of the statements we make are about persons and things; they are what the logician calls first-order statements. Statements about first-order statements are second-order statements. Thus to say of two statements that they are contradictions or that they are contraries is to make a second-order statement. Appraisals made in logic are second-order statements.

A statement may be either contingently or logically true or false. For a contingent statement, we look to the world to see whether it is true or false, but for tautologies and contradictions, there is no need to look. For the logician, all the facts are in.

Two statements are contradictions if they are inconsistent with each other and there is no third statement that is inconsistent with both. Two statements are contraries if they are inconsistent with each other and some third statement may be inconsistent with both. Suppose someone says that John is over six feet tall, and someone else says that he is not over six feet tall. The two statements are contraries and not contradictions, since there is the possibility of someone saying that John is exactly six feet tall.

To say that S_1 entails S_2 is to say that it is inconsistent to affirm S_1 and deny S_2. It is also to say that it is not the case that S_1 and not S_2. With the truth-functional connectors "and", "not" and "implies" thus in place in the logician's second-order vocabulary, Strawson completes the catalogue of words used in logical appraisals. Among them:

"S_1 is logically equivalent to S_2" = "S_1 entails S_2, and S_2 entails S_1"

If S_1 entails S_2, then S_1 is a sufficient condition of S_2, and S_2 is a necessary condition of S_1

Chapter 2: Formal Logic

While a logician's work thus essentially involves entailments, it is not his task to make an exhaustive list of them; that would be an unending enterprise. He is instead concerned to develop a *general* entailment statement of this sort:

Any statement made by the use of a sentence which could be obtained by substituting a certain word or phrase for the variable

in the formula "x is a younger son" ... entails the statement made
by the use in the same context of the sentence obtained by making
the same substitution in the formula "x has a brother" ....

(ILT: 30)

And thus in abbreviation we have the general statement that "*x* is a
younger son" entails "*x* has a brother". And in turn we have the less
general but still general statement that "Tom is a younger son" entails
"Tom has a brother".

Once again, for Strawson, it is to *statements* and not to *sentences*
that the words of logical appraisal are correctly applied, and there
is no reason why "entails" should not also be applied to the relation
one formula has to another. A formula is an expression such that by
substituting words or phrases for the variables we can obtain sentences that could be used to make sentences. Some of these variable
substitutions would yield sentences, but not significant statements.
For example, in the formula "*x* is a younger son", to substitute "Tom"
for "*x*" would yield a sentence that would have meaning and thus
could be used to make a significant statement, while substituting "the
square root of 2" for "*x*" would not.

In consequence, we can talk about the range of admissible values
for a variable, but, unlike formal logic, in ordinary language there are
no precise rules for what is admissible and what is not. Once again,
statements have a contextual component, and that lies beyond the
reach of formal logic.

The limitations of formal logic are also manifest in its use of symbols, particularly with "⊃", susceptible as it is to misinterpretation.
"If ... then ...", "not ... without ..." and "either ... or ..." *cannot* be
safely identified with "⊃", the strong temptation notwithstanding.
For consider "If it rains, the party will be a failure". That suggests
connections that are not logical or linguistic; they are instead connections in the world discovered by experience. Compare the connection in that sentence with the one in "If he is a younger son, then he
has a brother". And we can also distinguish between assertoric and
hypothetical conditionals, between "since ..." and "if ...". It is plain
that not all of such reasoning is simply deductive; sometimes the
connections are causal rather than logical. In general, using "if" to
link two clauses indicates that the first is a grounds or reason for the
second. We cannot rightfully claim that "⊃" necessarily indicates a
logical necessity, and that is why it is best to paraphrase "$p \supset q$" by
"$-(p \cdot -q)$", or by "$(-p \vee q)$". None of this is a call by Strawson for an
elimination of "⊃" from the logician's vocabulary. The symbol has its

convenience, but it is useful if we continue to bear in mind its limitations and its possible misinterpretations.

There is a still further factor that also limits what formal logic can do. When the logician chooses the patterns for his representative rules, he chooses *common* uses drawn from ordinary language. He then makes that *common* use serve as the *standard* use because he cannot allow ambiguity within his system. The logician thus imposes a rigidity that ordinary language does not have. The logician's limitations stem from the very nature of his appropriate task.

> The logician is not a lexicographer. He is not called upon to include in his books the general entailments created by every introduction of a new technical term into the language. This job is for the specialist: the job of making clear the meanings of the words peculiar to his special subject-matter. The logician's interest is wider. He is concerned with types of inconsistency, types of validity and invalidity, which are not confined to discussion of any one particular kind of subject, but may be found to occur in discussions of utterly heterogeneous topics. (ILT: 40–41)

The logician is concerned only with general principles. It is easy to provide examples of such principles: to assert, and to deny that assertion, is inconsistent – if all *f*s are *g*s, and *x* is an *f*, then *x* is a *g*. And it is also not difficult to notice certain characteristics of such general principles. They are indifferent to subject matter. They are second-order statements, behind which stand *linguistic* rules for the use of such expressions as "assert", "deny" and "inconsistent". Those statements are *logical* rather than overtly *linguistic*, hence they are not tied to the expressions of any particular language. But Strawson finds such principles "unwieldy" in the logician's efforts to do logic in terms of statements about statements instead of rules about representative expressions. The source of the difficulty here is that different expressions may, in some contexts, have the same use: "all", "the" and "a" may have the same use for the logician. And the same expression may have different uses: "not ... and not ..." may be variously used as a double negative, to emphasize or to show necessity. But the logician seeks to eliminate this complexity and clutter, incompatible with his system, and to impose a system's rules in order to cure the perceived deficiencies of ordinary language. What does not fit the system is eliminated from consideration, hence while the logician has a ready use for "all", and "some", and "not", he has no use for "most" or "few", even though those latter terms can obviously be used in ordinary reasoning.

Logic has a primary concern with recognizing analogies among inferences on widely varying topics, leading us to seeing them as having the same form. But consider:

- x is congruent with y, and y with z, hence x is congruent with z
- x is an ancestor of y, and y of z, hence x is an ancestor of z
- x entails y, and y entails z, hence x entails z

The resemblances among those inferences may lead us to recognize a common pattern (F)

xRy and yRz, hence xRz

and to proceed from this pattern to a logical rule of the form "F is a valid inference pattern". But if for R we substitute "loves", or "hates", or "amuses", then the consequent invalidity is evident. We can, of course, establish a criterion for distinguishing between valid and invalid inferences by giving a common name to all words or phrases that when substituted for R yield a valid inference formula. Such expressions are called "transitively relational". But we must not think that in so doing we have discovered some *general* principle for these valid entailments, because for that task we shall have to have recourse to the workings of ordinary language, to the work of the lexicographer and all the clutter and complexity that involves.

The claim of "On Referring" is that ordinary language has no exact logic, and a primary task of *Introduction to Logical Theory* is to provide in detail particular points of contrast and contact between the two. We have seen some of the ways in which Strawson challenges any claim for a sovereignty of formal logic over the workings of ordinary language. There are further difficulties, centred on the very notion of "logical form".

> The existence of logical formulae encourages us to talk of the *logical form* of sentences and statements; and perhaps we are inclined to think of the logical form of a statement as a sort of verbal skeleton which is left when all expressions, except those selected as logical constants, are eliminated from a sentence which might be used to make a statement, and replaced by appropriate variables. But there are all sorts of difficulties about this. (ILT: 49)

We may recall that a distinction between sentences and statements is at the root of "On Referring". Strawson now observes that there is a consequent distinction between the uses of "logical form" dependent on whether that notion is being applied to sentences or to statements. One sentence with its logical form may be used to make statements having differences of logical form. Thus the sentence "The cat is a hunter" might be used to make statements having different logical forms, for example, a statement about an individual cat and a general statement about cats. It is also true that the verbal form may mislead us with regard to its logical form.

For Strawson, the notion of "logical form" is viable, there are indeed analogies among inferences on widely varying topics, and they are frequently useful in our reasoning about things, but this should not keep us from recognizing that there are attendant pitfalls:

- It is a mistake to talk of *the* logical form of a statement. To speak of this form is in part to point towards certain valid inferences that may be made; but the statement may contain other classes of valid inference as well.
- It is a mistake to think that the logician's rules make those of the lexicographer superfluous.
- It is a mistake to think that logical features can be described without taking into account the subject matters involved.
- It is a mistake to say that inferences are valid *in virtue of* their formal powers. It is the other way about. Form depends on inference.

There is thus for Strawson an apparent rift between the rules of formal logic and the practices of ordinary language. It may be objected that this is a rift, and nothing more. Strawson's animadversions seem merely to point to the readily acknowledged truth that a word having a variety of uses in ordinary speech may be given a single standard use by the logician.

> From what I have said so far, one might think that the formal logician envisaged his task as that of compiling lists of highly general rules of inference or types of entailment; embodying these, where possible, in rules for representative formulae. We have seen that this step – the adoption of rules for representative formulae – represents the beginning of a rift between the logic of certain expressions, figuring as constants in the formulae, and the logic of these same expressions as they figure in ordinary speech; where they may be idiomatically be used in ways which conflict with the logician's rules. This does not mean that the logician's rules are incorrect, nor does it mean that ordinary language is

inconsistent. It means simply that a word which has different logical uses in ordinary speech may be assigned a single standard logical use in the logician's rules. (ILT: 56)

If that were the sum of it then, provided that the appropriate cautionary notes were kept in mind, the relation between ordinary language and formal logic might be seen minimally as one of peaceful coexistence, and more truly as a separation of powers that is both necessary and useful to both sides. For Strawson, what has turned this rift into a chasm is the ideal in modern logic of the construction of a *system*. The logician is no longer content with being consistent. He wants a connected system of principles. He seeks completeness.

Logicians saw early on that you can use a small number of valid inferences to provide a basis for *proving* the validity of a larger number of inferences. The original purpose in logic was simply to codify certain general principles within a second-order vocabulary. That original modest purpose has in modern logic very largely been supplanted by the ideal of systematization. One of the difficulties with that as an attainable ideal is that certain expressions in their ordinary use lack the closed boundaries of logical constants: "∨" notably defies one common ordinary use; disjunction may be inclusive or exclusive; "unless" has more than one mode of employment. These complexities run counter to a mathematical model taken as the paradigm for the whole of logic. The response of the modern to those complexities is to make rules that satisfy his needs, while ignoring the nuances that are an essential aspect of the ways in which we ordinarily communicate.

It is the *deductive* system in its mathematical mode that most appeals to the modern. Descartes saw the axiomatic method as the means whereby the mathematician had uniquely secured a sure way of proceeding from undeniable premises to equally undeniable conclusions. The extension of that methodology to the whole of philosophy and science became the accepted norm, notably for the logician. From a small number of rules, taken as analytic, further rules were derived by means of certain rules of inference, so that it would be inconsistent to accept the fundamental rules of the system and to refuse to accept the derived rules.

For Strawson, all that has an undeniable appeal. Its seduction is likely to mislead.

The intellectual charm of the deductive method of systematizing logic is the charm of any deductive system. It lies, partly, in the exhibition of the set of formulae in an ordered arrangement, each derived formula (or theorem) following from the ones before it; partly in a feeling of increased control and comprehension, a sense of having reduced a great mass of principles to a handful of premises and a couple of rules such that, by the application of these to those, the great mass can be re-erected as an orderly structure. A price is paid, however, for this intoxicating success, as I have suggested already and as we shall see more clearly hereafter. (ILT: 60–61)

The older logicians worked on general types of inconsistency, validity and invalidity as they occur in our ordinary use of ordinary language. The modern formal logicians try instead to establish a new language, one that for Strawson is well adapted to forming an elegant system, but not especially suitable for ordinary speech. The effort of the modern to find a correspondence between his symbols and some ordinary words already in common use is certainly subject to a critical review. On one view, the task of the modern may seem to be twofold: (a) to construct a *purely abstract* system of symbols in the service of "proofs"; (b) then to give those symbols an interpretation in ordinary language. But it is precisely that view that may mislead, since the logician always approaches the initial task of system construction with some particular kind of interpretation already in mind. We should instead recognize that ordinary language has an inalienable primacy.

Chapter 3: Truth-functions

On that note, Strawson turns next to the actual construction of logical systems. He first considers the familiar use of truth-tables. The system contains as variables the letters "p", "q", "r", "s", ...; and as constants the symbols "$-$", "$\cdot$", "$\vee$", "$\supset$" and "$\equiv$". Constants and variables can be combined to form truth-functional formulae. A truth-functional formula in any expression can be obtained by either writing "$-$" before any variable, or by writing any one of the constants with a variable on each side of it. Formulae obtained in this way are simple, for example, "$-q$", and "$p \supset q$", and these may be used to obtain complex formulae. The latter involve the use of parentheses to determine the scope of the constants, that is, the range of expressions they govern. In order to prevent ambiguity, it is then necessary to establish some way of indicating precedence. For example, the expression "$-p \vee q \cdot r$" taken as it stands has a variety of possible interpretations. To preclude any ambiguity, there is the common but "clumsy" use of brackets. Thus

$-p \vee (q \cdot r)$
$-[p \vee (q \cdot r)]$
$(-p \vee q) \cdot r$

are ways of establishing which interpretation is intended. Strawson will economize the use of brackets by ranking constants in an order of precedence, namely "$\equiv$", "$\supset$", "$\vee$", "$\cdot$" and "$-$". In this system, brackets always override precedence between constants, but in the absence of guiding brackets, precedence among constants prevails. Thus the common "$p \supset (q \vee r)$" can now be written more simply as "$p \supset q \vee r$".

The variables in this system as interpreted are groups of words that could occur as sentences usable for making statements. The truth or falsity of truth-functional statements is determined entirely by the truth or falsity of their constituent statements. The rules that determine that truth or falsity are the truth-functional constants and their meanings, and they can be summarized by means of the familiar truth-tables, for example:

p	q	$p \cdot q$	$p \vee q$
T	T	T	T
T	F	F	T
F	T	F	T
F	F	F	F

This system is a two-valued logic, that is, every statement is either true or false. There are of course other possibilities, for example, the many-valued logics as developed by Jan Łukasiewicz and Alfred Tarski, but they are irrelevant to Strawson's present purpose.

Truth-tables can also be used to determine the truth-values of complex formulae. Any such formula contains one major constant that has as its scope the formula taken as a whole. In constructing such a table we begin with the truth conditions for the smallest subordinate, that is, the constant with the smallest scope, and then proceed to the constants of ever wider scope, concluding with the major constant.

p	q	r	$(p \supset q)$	•	$(q \supset \mathrm{I})$	$\supset$	$(p \supset r)$
T	T	T	T	T	T	T	T
T	T	F	T	F	F	T	F
T	F	T	F	F	T	T	T
T	F	F	F	F	T	T	F
F	T	T	T	T	T	T	T
F	T	F	T	F	F	T	T
F	F	T	T	T	T	T	T
F	F	F	T	T	T	T	T

Thus equipped, we can readily compare the truth conditions of any two truth-functional formulae. Their relation may be one of entailment ($[(p \cdot q) \supset (p \vee q)]$); they may be logically equivalent ($[(p \supset q) \equiv (-p \vee q)]$); the two may be contradictories ("$p \vee q$" and "$-p \cdot -q$"); they may be contraries ("$p \cdot q$" and ("$-p \cdot -q$"); they may be subcontraries ("$p \vee q$" and "$-p \vee -q$").

Truth-tables also enable us easily to recognize certain laws, that is, truth-functional formulae that are analytic within the system.

(1) $p \supset q \equiv -(p \cdot -q)$
(2) $p \vee q \equiv -(-p \cdot -q)$
(3) $(p \equiv q) \equiv -(p \cdot -q) \cdot -(q \cdot -p)$
(4) $(p \cdot q) \cdot r \equiv p \cdot (q \cdot r)$
(5) $(p \vee q) \vee r \equiv p \vee (q \vee r)$

It is evident that the constants of the system are interdefinable, and Strawson (ILT: 76–7) lists a number of such laws.

The truth-table method of determining the logical status of any truth-functional formula can be applied to formulae of ever increasing complexity without loss of validity. But the method as thus far explicated does have its drawbacks.

It is evident that as truth-functional formulae increase in complexity, contain more and more variables, the use, without modification, of the tabular method of determining their status (as analytic, synthetic, or self-contradictory) becomes increasingly cumbersome. Great ingenuity has been devoted to framing sets of rules for swifter and more elegant methods of testing complex formulae [See, for example, Quine's *Methods of Logic* (1972)]. These I shall not describe. For my main concern is not with the craftsmanship of logic, pleasing as this can be, but with the fundamental character of logical systems and their relation to ordinary discourse. (ILT: 77–8)

It is useful at this point to recall the major purposes Strawson intends to serve in this *Introduction to Logical Theory*. His stated aims are twofold: to make clear at an introductory level the nature of formal logic, and to bring out points of contact and contrast between that logic and the logic of ordinary language. The two aims are obviously complementary; he certainly accomplishes the first. His account of formal logic is clear and concise: economical, rigorous, but also eminently accessible. He moves easily within the system, and his credentials as a logician are plainly established. His account is in accord with those found in many contemporary texts and treatises, and it is arguably better done than most. It is valuable in itself, but he sees it as ancillary to his second and main concern, namely, the relation between that logic and the logic of ordinary language. If we misunderstand that relation, there will be, for Strawson, consequences of a most profound sort for our study of epistemology and metaphysics, indeed for the whole of the philosophical enterprise.

Strawson's detailed consideration of that relation begins with an examination of the uses of the truth-functional constants and their putative identification with ordinary words. His argument throughout will be that this identification, common and unexamined as it is among modern logicians, is a prime source of misunderstanding. Today, many formal logicians all too easily identify "–" with "not" or "it is not the case that"; "·" with "and"; "... ∨ ..." with "either ... or ..."; "... ⊃ ..." with "if ... then ..."; "... ≡ ..." with "... if and only if ...".

> Of these identifications the first two are the least misleading. We shall find that the remainder are not only misleading, but definitely wrong. We shall be entitled to say that such an identification is definitely wrong, wherever we shall find that the ordinary conjunction, in its standard or primary use, does not conform to a logical rule which holds for the truth-functional constant with which it is identified, and whenever we find, conversely, that the truth-functional constant does not conform to a logical rule which holds for the ordinary conjunction in its standard or primary use. But we shall also find that even the most mistaken of these identifications has a point; we shall find not only some degree of formal parallelism (which could be noted independently of interpretation) but some degree of interpenetration of meanings of the interpreted expressions of the system and of ordinary speech respectively. We could not, of course, find the latter without the former. (ILT: 78)

The task of the formal logician is as legitimate as it is useful, and the care that Strawson takes in delineating that logic makes plain his attention to and his respect for that enterprise. The limitations he wishes to point out are therefore not a wholesale rejection. On his analogy, we cannot reproach the logician for his divorce from linguistic realities any more than we could rightly reproach the abstract painter for not being representational. Mischief could only arise if he were misleadingly to claim that he is in fact a representational artist.

Of all the identifications between the truth-functional constants and ordinary words, the least misleading are those of conjunction and negation. Even here there are limitations. "And" can perform many functions that "•" cannot: "•" couples only sentences or groups of words that may serve as sentences, whereas "and" may also be used to couple nouns, adjectives and adverbs, for example, "Tom and Mary came". Moreover, the order of the sentences in a paragraph written in formal logic is irrelevant, since by its laws "$p \cdot q$" is equivalent to "$q \cdot p$", whereas in the contexts of ordinary speech the order may be an essential part of the meaning.

Of all the identifications between truth-functional constants and ordinary words, "$\supset$" is the one most singled out by Strawson as particularly susceptible to being misleading or simply wrong. Consider the hypothetical sentence

"If the Germans had invaded England in 1940, they would have won the war."

In ordinary use, the pair of sentences used by a speaker to make statements *corresponding* to these two constituent subordinate clauses are ones about which we must assume the speaker either to be in doubt or to believe to be false:

"The Germans invaded England in 1940; they won the war."

In formal logic, those same sentences used for a statement of material implication can be framed this way.

"The Germans invaded England in 1940 $\supset$ they won the war."

There is thus apparent a radical difference between hypothetical statements and truth-functional statements. The falsity of the antecedent clause suffices in material implication for the truth of the statement, but not in the corresponding hypothetical statement. Even in cases where both the antecedent and the consequent of the hypothetical statement are true, it does not follow that a speaker making that statement is right, since the truth of the consequent may be fulfilled because of factors unconnected with the truth of the antecedent. The objections to the identification of "if *p* then *q*" with "*p* ⊃ *q*" hold doubly with the identification of "*p* if and only if *q*" with "*p* ≡ *q*".

There are indeed some parallel laws between the rules of hypothetical statements and the rules of material implication, for example, for the familiar *modus ponens*, "(if *p*, then *q*; and *p*) ⊃ *q*)", and *modus tollens*, "(if *p*, then *q*; and not *q*) ⊃ not *p*)", but there are also laws where there are no parallels, for example, for the law of material implication, "–*p* ⊃ (*p* ⊃ *q*)". The rules that latter cases are analytic are sometimes called "the paradoxes of implication", but if "⊃" is indeed taken as identical with "if ... then ...", then Strawson will say that the rules are not paradoxes at all; they are simply incorrect. The constants of the logical system are interdefinable; "·" and "–" are relatively less likely to mislead than "⊃", and so the safe way to read "*p* ⊃ *q*" may be "not both *p* and not *q*".

The final connector Strawson considers is alternation. The relationships between "∨" and "or" are both more distant than those between "·" and "and", and less distant than those between "⊃" and "if". A statement made by joining two subordinate clauses using "or" is an alternation. Talk about the relationship between the first and second alternatives (*p* or *q*) is analogous to the relationship between the antecedent and the consequent of a hypothetical statement (if *p* then *q*). The truth of either of the alternatives is no more a sufficient condition of the truth of the alternation than is the falsity of the antecedent a sufficient condition for the truth of the hypothetical statement, the usages of the formal logician notwithstanding. This is but one more of the cautionary flags raised by Strawson against a too easy identification of the uses of formal logic and those of ordinary language.

> Certain things should now be clear about the system of truth-functions. It should be clear that the constants of the system cannot be simply identified in meaning with those expressions of ordinary speech with which they are sometimes equated by writers of logic. It should be clear, too, that the decision on the meanings of the constants in the system ... is not just an odd caprice of the formal logician, but is dictated by the desire for systematic simplicity. For this characteristic, while admirably exemplified by the truth-functional system, is exemplified not at all by a veridical account of the maze of logical uses through which we unhesitatingly thread our way in our daily employment of the customarily related conjunctions. (ILT: 93)

Chapter 5: Predicative Formulae and Quantifiers

When Strawson turns to the workings of the class system of quantificational logic, he finds compounded the inherent difficulties in the relationships between ordinary language and truth-functional logic. The devices employed in quantificational logic include individual variables, predicative variables and existential and universal quantifiers. Strawson provides a wealth of illustrations found in the common usage of contemporary logic (ILT: 129–48). For example, the sentence "No one loves without suffering" may be paraphrased by "There is no one who loves and does not suffer" and expressed in formal logic by "$-(\exists x)(fx \cdot -gx)$" or by "$(x)(fx \supset gx)$". In the case of a relational predicate, as in the sentence "No one loves without *somebody* suffering", where there is no implication that lover and sufferer are the same, the expression in formal logic may be "$(x)(\exists y)(-fx \vee gy)$" or "$(x)(\exists y)(fx \supset gy)$".

Once we are informed about the symbolism of this predicative system, we are once again able to ask about the relation between the systems of formal logic and the practices of ordinary language. Roughly speaking, in making ordinary statements we refer to some particular person, object or place, and we then provide for that particular some description, ascription or classification, that is, we say something about something or someone. This primary and critical distinction between referring and describing looks back to "On Referring", but it also looks forward to Strawson's next major work, *Individuals: An Essay in Descriptive Metaphysics.*

All the laws that are *peculiar to* quantificational logic involve quantifiers. Any comparison of ordinary language with either modern quantificational logic or the older logic must therefore begin with an examination of the constants peculiar to quantificational logic, "(x)" and "$(\exists x)$", and their relation to expressions in ordinary language. The expressions corresponding to the quantifiers, for example, "for every instance of 'x'", "there is at least one 'x' such that", are themselves expressions that do not commonly occur in ordinary speech. That itself is noteworthy:

> And we might think it strange that the whole of modern formal logic, after it leaves the propositional logic and before it crosses the boundary into the analysis of mathematical concepts, should be confined to the elaboration of sets of rules giving the logical interrelations of formulae which, however complex, all begin with these few rather strained and awkward phrases.   (ILT: 147)

Critics of Strawson claim that he exaggerates the strangeness. He admits the exaggeration, but counters that the critics have minimized it and have therefore failed to recognize the real discrepancies between modern logic and ordinary speech. There is, of course, an alternative to the system of modern logic: the older class logic rooted in Aristotle. Modern orthodoxy claims that once the older system is appropriately cleaned up, it becomes simply a small part of quantificational logic. The merits of that claim rest on the assumption that the latter system is correct, an assumption that Strawson will next examine.

Chapter 6: Subjects, Predicates, and Existence

In the structure of Aristotelian logic, four forms or moods of propositions are recognized.

A   All *x* is *y*
E   No *x* is *y*
I   Some *x* is *y*
O   Some *x* is not *y*

These forms are not patterns to be strictly exemplified, they are instead representative; all of the sentences that exemplify the A-form have resemblances, but they are not rigidly defined by the form. Modern logic has an indefinitely large number of valid inference patterns, but the number admitted in the older system is notably small. All the laws of that system are contained in just three main groups: the laws of immediate inference,[2] the square of opposition and the syllogism. The doctrine of the syllogism is the major accomplishment of the older logic.

Each syllogism has three terms: two premises and a conclusion. The two premises and the conclusion each contain two terms. Each term of a syllogism has a form or mood: A, E, I or O. There are four figures, which are determined by the location of the middle term which is common to the two premises. Thus with *s* for subject, *p* for predicate and *m* for middle:

Figure	1	2	3	4
	m p	*p m*	*m p*	*p m*
	s m	*s m*	*m s*	*m s*
	s p	*s p*	*s p*	*s p*

Each of the four figures has 64 moods (all the permutations of the four moods over the four terms in the figure), so there are altogether 256 possible forms of the syllogism. Of these moods, only 24 are recognized as valid, six for each of the four figures.

It would be possible to present the whole body of laws of traditional logic as a system or calculus in the manner of modern logic. Such a system would need as axioms such laws as those of immediate inference and the square of opposition and at least one syllogistic law. It would need appropriate rules of inference and the theorems of the propositional calculus. That kind and degree of matching between tradition and modern is manifest.

The traditional logic has indeed its critics, but Strawson thinks that with only a few reservations the traditional rules do conform to the use of words in ordinary language. The significant standard criticisms of the older system centre on the question of existential import: that is, for the moods A, E, I and O, is there a commitment to the actual existence of the members of the terms? The modern assumption is that there is such a commitment for members of I and O, while for A and E whatever the traditionalist decides for one must also apply to the other. If so, then a dilemma follows: if A and E do have existential import, then one set of traditional laws goes, and if A and E lack that import, then another set of those laws will go. It is useful to spell out that dilemma in some detail. Consider the two alternatives:

- We can conjoin the negatively existential formula "$-(\exists x)(fx \cdot -gx)$" for the A form with the assertion of existence for the first term "$(\exists x)(fx)$". On this alternative, all 24 of the valid syllogisms in traditional logic are preserved. But whatever decision we make about the assertion of existence for the subject term must apply to both A and E forms. And so now a price must be paid for preserving the validity of all 24 syllogisms. In the tradition, one of the laws of immediate inference is conversion, in which subject and predicate terms exchange places. Conversion of the E form is said to be valid. But if we add, as now we must, the assertion of existence for the first term, then conversion of the E form fails the test of validity; to say "Nobody is both an architect and an angel, and there is at least one architect" is not the same as to say "Nobody is both an angel and an architect, and there is at least one angel".
- We can alternatively take the negatively existential formula simply by itself, without the assertion of existence for the first term. But in this case, while the validity of conversion for the E form is

preserved, nine of the syllogisms that traditional logic considers valid will fail, for example, AAI.

The dilemma then is a clear one. It rests upon the assumption that the only two unambiguous interpretations of the system for which its constants approximate in sense to their ordinary use are the two just considered. Unless this assumption can be shown to be mistaken, the conclusion must be accepted that there is no consistent and acceptable interpretation of the system as a whole.

(ILT: 170)

But for Strawson that conclusion and the assumptions on which it rests are false, since for all four of the forms – A, E, I and O – it is perfectly possible to find interpretations such that all of the laws of traditional logic remain valid. A significant way of doing that is to examine some of the features of ordinary language. The modern starts with the assumption that all four of these forms must be either positively or negatively existential. In ordinary usage, that is not true. Take as an example someone saying "All John's children are asleep". Obviously in any normal circumstance the speaker is assuming that John has children. But if John has no children, then the question of whether the statement is true or false simply does not come up. The existence of John's children is a *necessary precondition* of the statement being *either* true or false.

People hesitate to accept that analysis because of the familiar trichotomy "true, false or meaningless". That trichotomy is misleading because it contains a confusion between statement and sentence. The sentence "All John's children are asleep" is not meaningless, since there are contexts in which its utterance as a statement may be true or false. It may at one time be true, and at another time false, but it is senseless to ask whether the sentence itself is true or false. That confusion is the basis for the modern's charge that traditional logic is faced with a dilemma for which there is no resolution. Strawson has a suggestion that he thinks will enable the whole of the tradition to be preserved at a single stroke.

What I am proposing, then, is this. There are many ordinary sentences beginning with such phrases as "All ...", "All the ...", "No ...", "Some ...", "Some of the ...", "At least one ...", "At least one of the ...", [for which] the existence of the members of the subject-class is to be regarded as presupposed ... by statements made by the use of those sentences; to be regarded as a necessary condition, not of the truth simply, but of the truth or falsity, of such statements.   (ILT: 176)

The adoption of this suggestion saves the traditional rules because their breakdown came about from the non-existence of members of the subject class. Strawson's proposal would mean that such non-existence would keep a statement from being either true or false. We may then indeed correctly say that *if* the subject class does indeed have members, then if an A-form statement is true, then the statement of the I form must also be true. Parallel reasoning will preserve all of the valid syllogisms that tradition affirms.

That may appear to remove one of the horns of the dilemma with which the modern challenges tradition, but it would still leave in place the other horn, that is, if we assert existence for the first term, then the conversion of the E form fails the validity test; recall the case of architects and angels cited above, which Strawson has as an example. Thus xEy might be true, while yEx would be neither true nor false; that the first term must have existential import does not guarantee that the second term must also have existential import. But to remove that difficulty all we need is the provision that if both xEy and yEx are either true or false, then either both are true or both are false.

The question of existential import is not the only difficulty with which the modern taxes traditional logic. Tradition made "Caesar is dead" an A-form statement. Moderns assume on the other hand that statements in A form are all of them class inclusion statements, and that statements such as "Caesar is dead" are instead singular predicative statements, and that traditional logic therefore errs. Plainly there is a difference between "$(x)(fx \supset gx) \cdot (x)(gx \supset hx) \supset (x)(fx \supset hx)$" and "$fy \cdot (x)(fx \supset gx) \supset gy$". But while the statements are different, Strawson observes that they are also formally analogous. There are analogies between the premises and between the conclusions, and whether we are speaking about an individual or the members of a class makes no difference with regard to the validity of the inferences that are drawn. Strawson thinks it was not absurd for traditional logicians to note the analogy.

While there are limitations in the traditional account, Strawson finds that if we expect formal logic, whether old or new, to be reflective of ordinary usage, then there are also oddities in the modern's account. In quantificational logic, the words "all" and "no" have no existential import, while in ordinary language those words are often the referring or subject part of a subject–predicate statement in which the existence of the subject is *presupposed*. And consider three sentences that may be used to make statements: (1) "John Straw is happy"; (2) "Mary Straw is happy"; and (3) "All the Straws are happy". It seems odd and contrary to ordinary speech to say with quantificational logic that (1) and (2) may be used to make subject–predicate statements in which reference and description have distinct roles while denying that capacity to (3).

None of this is taken by Strawson to mean that traditional logic succeeds and the modern's quantificational logic fails. Plainly tradition gives a very limited account of the logical relations of subject–predicate statements. And while Strawson's remedying proposal may remove many of the objections that the modern raises against the tradition, there is no guarantee that a traditionalist will accept that proposal. Nonetheless, Strawson finds that quantification's urge for a systematic completeness and economy lead it to a rigidity that make it a poor and misleading fit for the complexities inherent in the logic of ordinary language.

Chapter 7: General Statements and Relations

Strawson would establish the existential presuppositions of A statements both as reflective of common usage in our ordinary speech, and as a means of saving traditional logic from many of the criticisms directed against it by modern logicians. To fortify his proposal, Strawson offers some further clarifications about general statements.

Consider the sentence "All trespassers on this land will be prosecuted". Here we have an apparent A form where there is no presupposition of the existence of members of the subject term. Strawson's riposte is that the sentence is not a prediction, but is instead a warning; it looks as though such sentences are used to make statements, but they are not. Or consider the sentence "All moving bodies not acted upon by external forces continue in a state of uniform motion in a straight line". While there are no bodies not acted upon by external forces, the sentence can be used to make a statement and the question of its truth or falsity can arise; the statement can be called true as part of a general theory that does have direct application, since there are moving bodies. Strawson concludes that there are all sorts of general statements, and contrary to the systematic simplicity that quantificational logic would impose, those statements defy any neat and tidy classifications.

It is possible to take examples of general sentences which clearly belong to sharply contrasting classes; e.g., analytic statements;

ideal law-statements; rules of games or of institutions; quite for-
tuitous collocations of fact. But the general sentences which can
be neatly classified under one or another of such headings are
probably the exception rather than the rule. The fact that general
statements are thus the confused meeting-place of many characters has both encouraged wrong assimilations ... and fostered
spurious distinctions.   (ILT: 201–2)

The same contrast between the rich complexities of ordinary language and the simplicities of quantification are found when we consider the treatment of relations. The logician's desire to codify all
relational predicates runs counter to the absence of common formal
features. Compare:

(a) x is a descendant of y • y is a descendant of z ∴ x is a descendant
 of z
(b) x loves y • y *loves* z ∴ x loves z
(c) x fathers y • y fathers z ∴ x fathers z

Example (a) is transitive, (b) is non-transitive and contingent, and
(c) is non-transitive and a contradiction. Of transitive relations, some
are symmetrical, some are asymmetrical, some are neither, and to
say that a relational predicate is symmetrical is to say that it is its
own converse. Classifications are indeed possible, yet we cannot say
that relational statements taken as a whole lend themselves to the
exhaustive system of classification that a formal logician might desire.
A dogmatic claim of completeness is ill-founded.

Chapter 8: Two Kinds of Logic

There are the entailment rules of formal logic, but side by side with
them are the referring rules of the logic of ordinary language. Formal
logic deals only with meanings that can be given by entailment rules,
and indeed only a small class of those rules are of interest to the logician. Entailment rules abstract from the time and place of utterance,
and from the identity of the utterer. These entailment rules must in
practice be supplemented by "referring rules", which lay down the
contextual requirements of what a statement presupposes, and not
what such a statement may assert.

The *formal* distinction between individual and predicative variables
reflects the *functional* distinction between referring and describing,

which in turn reflects the *grammatical* distinction between subject and predicate. To ignore those distinctions is in effect to ignore the distinction between sentence and statement, a distinction that has been central to Strawson's account of logical theory from its beginnings in "On Referring".

Practice comes before rules and anyone is at liberty to violate a rule if he can provide a good reason for doing so.

> The most important general lesson to be learnt from [the study of the logical features of ordinary speech] is that simple deductive relationships are not the only kind we have to consider if we wish to understand the logical workings of language. We have to think in many more dimensions than that of entailment and contradiction, and use many tools of analysis besides those which belong to formal logic .... Nor, in this study, are we confined to linguistic minutiae .... For in trying to discover the answers to questions of such forms as "What are the conditions under which we use such-and-such an expression or class of expressions?" ... we may find ourselves able to frame classifications or disclose differences broad and deep enough to satisfy the strongest appetite for generality. What we shall not find in our results is that character of elegance and system which belongs to the constructions of formal logic. It is none the less true that the logic of ordinary speech provides a field of intellectual study unsurpassed in richness, complexity, and the power to absorb.   (ILT: 231–2)

Chapter 9: Inductive Reasoning and Probability

Strawson at this point has concluded his investigation of the interrelations between the study of formal logic and the logical features of ordinary speech. In the book's concluding chapter, he turns to a brief consideration of non-deductive reasoning.

A deductive argument is either valid or it is not. But neither historians nor detectives are limited to that approach, and an argument not deductively valid may nonetheless be sound. This justifies inductive reasoning, where the question is not one of entailment but rather of the degree of support that is based on evidence, the best evidence being that which is conclusive. It is a fundamental misapprehension to suppose that entailment and support are competitors in the same field, with inductive arguments being regarded as "only probable". We use the word "probably" in two senses: either to indicate incomplete support for a "complete" generalization, or to indicate complete support for an "incomplete" generalization. In the latter case, incompleteness in generalization is a matter of degree, and so the hope has been that this degree can be put in terms of a mathematical ratio: that "odds" can be established. Up to a point that is viable, but this has led to the further thesis that here we have a *complete* account of probability and hence of support. That thesis is unacceptable because strength of support is a product of two factors: (a) the degree of completeness of the underlying generalization; (b) the degree of completeness of the support for that underlying generalization. Thus the generalization that most *f*s are *g*s is a matter of degree that may possibly be expressed as a mathematical ratio, but the evidence of the support is as good as our observations are numerous and made under a variety of conditions. There are no precise rules for evidence.

Granted that this is the nature of inductive reasoning, there may seem to be a residual question of its justification, of why we should place reliance on that procedure.

> Why should we suppose that the accumulation of instances of *A*s which are *B*s, however various the conditions in which they are observed, gives any good reason for expecting the next *A* we encounter to be a *B*? It is our habit to form expectations in this way; but can the habit be rationally justified? When this doubt has entered our minds it may be difficult to free ourselves from it.
>
> (ILT: 249)

If we raise the somewhat parallel question of a justification for deduction, we can see the absurdity of the request, since a "justification" would itself be deductive. The request for a justification for induction is also absurd, since it is in effect a demand that induction be justified by deductive criteria. Fantastic as that pursuit may be, the effort has been made to find some supreme premise for induction, but since we have no precise rules for the assessment of evidence, the choice of any such premise would be either arbitrary or uselessly vague. The demand for a justification for induction is senseless; it is like asking whether the law of the land taken as a whole is or is not legal.

Any successful way of finding out, of going from the observed to the unobserved, must have inductive support. That is not to say that induction is justified by its success in finding out, nor is it true that the validity of induction presupposes a universe that is uniform rather than chaotic. A chaotic universe is not one in which induction ceases to be rational; in such a world we would simply have inductive grounds for expecting irregularity.

***

Strawson's mastery of the major accomplishments of modern logic since 1900 is beyond challenge. For someone with his credentials to say that there are two kinds of logic – the entailment rules of formal logic and the referring rules of ordinary language – to say moreover that the two are interrelated and that both are necessary in human communication, and to reproach the establishment figures of modern logic with making for their construction of formal logic ill-founded claims of high autonomy and the role of sole and ultimate arbiter over all things linguistic – all that was bound to stir the hornet's nest and to provoke a strong and indeed heated response.

Richard W. Behling (1998) mounts a modern formalist's counter-attack on what he sees as Strawson's muddled effort to broaden logic's domain. Behling acknowledges that until 1900 the workings of ordinary language did indeed have a tie with logic. That was a logic dating back to Aristotle, in which there is a bond between logic and both the True and the False. But logic as it is understood today has long since enjoyed a divorce from that bond. Logic today does not use the terms "true" and "false" to characterize the axioms or starting-points used in an argument. Logic's interest is now confined to an enquiry into what follows from whatever is given. Behling admires the precision of the logician, and he concludes that the uses of ordinary language are so diverse that any search for its "referring rules" is illusory. Behling will credit Strawson with the discovery of pragmatics, but "logic is logic, and pragmatics is pragmatics". Strawson notwithstanding, there is but one kind of logic.

Behling's charge is that Strawson is not at liberty to use "logic" in just any revisionary way that suits his taste. Strawson's soft but deft reply (in Hahn 1998: 127–8) is that while we can indeed use "logic" in Behling's strict sense of confining it to the study of entailment rules, we may equally well take the term in a more liberal fashion, maintaining its link with the uses of ordinary language and thereby preserving the relevance of logic to rational discourse broadly conceived. There is a certain irony in these charges and counter-charges. There is the frequently expressed view of some of today's formalists that the logic of Aristotle at best expresses but one small part of the domain of entailment rules that is the sole proper concern of the logician. But it is certainly open to Strawson to counter that formalists such as Behling themselves express but one part of logic's proper concern with "truth" more broadly conceived. *Introduction to Logical Theory* is equally committed to a comprehensive and clear account of entailment rules themselves, and to the ways in which our referring statements made in ordinary language are bonded with those rules. If the charge of a revisionary use of "logic" must be made, then the charge may well be preferred against the modern formalist who would restrict it to the study of entailment rules. Traditional logic was concerned with such rules, but it also had a concern with "truth" that was broader than that of argument consistency, a concern that was rooted in Aristotle's distinctions in *Prior Analytics* and *Posterior Analytics*. Strawson's two logics certainly go far beyond anything found in the *Analytics*, but they have nonetheless a common concern.

Strawson's doctrine of two kinds of logic has a root in his seminal article "On Referring", with its distinction between sentence and statement. That root distinction also accounts for the longstanding disagreement between Strawson and Quine on singular terms and reference. For Quine, singular terms are at best superfluous, to be eliminated without loss:

> [T]he extrusion of singular terms is unaccompanied by any diminution in the power of the language. What the disappearance of singular terms does mean is that all reference to objects of any kind, concrete or abstract, is narrowed down now to one specific channel: variables of quantification. We can still say anything we like about any one object or all objects, but we say it always through the idioms of quantification: "There is an object x such that ..." and "Every object x is such that...". The objects whose existence is implied in our discourse are finally just the objects which must, for the truth of our assertions, be acknowledged as "values of variables" – i.e., be reckoned into the totality of objects over which variables of quantification range. To be is to be the value of a variable. (Quine 1972: 234)

Here is the great divide that on Strawson's account separates him from both Quine and Russell. Quine's concern that singular terms are ambiguous in their reference is set aside by Strawson on the grounds that singular terms in themselves do not refer at all, they are instead used by persons to make reference. If in that reference there is ambiguity, the responsibility lies with the statement-maker, not with the term. For that matter, ambiguity has its uses and indeed its occasional sweetness in the ordinary language of daily life.

These questions lead naturally enough to the further questions of how we go about identifying and reidentifying the particular individuals to whom we do make reference. There is the question of whether that reference can indeed be secured through the exclusive use of purely universal or general terms, or whether in every case the identification of particulars by a speaker making references rests ultimately on his own environment, and thus on the use of expressions with some demonstrative, or egocentric, or token-reflexive force. Those questions are addressed in Strawson's *Individuals: An Essay in Descriptive Metaphysics*, which followed on from his initial work in logic. It is that work to which we now turn.

Chapter 2

Individuals: An Essay in Descriptive Metaphysics: Towards a basic ontology

The central question raised by Strawson in Part I of *Individuals* concerns the ways in which reference to individuals and particulars is obtained in the practices of ordinary language. Anything whatsoever can be identifyingly referred to, can appear as a logical subject, can appear as an individual. Thus particulars such as historical events, material objects and persons are individuals, but so too are such non-particular individuals as qualities, properties, numbers and species. There is the further question of whether our reference to a particular can be secured through the exclusive use of purely universal or general terms, or whether in every case the identification of a particular by a speaker making references rests ultimately on his own environment, and thus on the use of expressions of a demonstrative, or egocentric, or token-reflexive sort. Part II is concerned with the linguistic complements to those metaphysical or ontological questions, and at the end with the perennial question of what things may properly be said to exist.

The distinction between singular reference and predication has also been central to Strawson's entire work. We have already seen how that distinction led him to mark out three parallel distinctions: the formal one between individual and predicative variables, the functional one between referring and describing, and the grammatical one between subject and predicate. To ignore those distinctions and parallels would be to ignore Strawson's root distinction in "On Referring" between sentence and statement. To maintain those distinctions and their parallels, on the other hand, leads directly and necessarily to the further question of just how that reference to these individuals or particulars is obtained in the practices of ordinary language. The referring terms and rules of ordinary language do indeed have an unavoidable note of approximation and a sometimes useful ambiguity, and that might seem to preclude the establishment of firm guidelines, but we have already seen that Strawson thinks that a loosening of the strict regularity that some formalists would require is simply the condition that must be met if we are to seek realistically an engagement between formal logic and the workings and the logic of ordinary language.

In pursuit of these issues in *Individuals*, a work that Strawson subtitles *An Essay in Descriptive Metaphysics*, he maintains a distinction between a descriptive metaphysics, which is content to give an account of the actual structure of the world of our experience, and a revisionary metaphysics, which attempts vainly to provide a better structure. Aristotle and Kant he finds descriptive, while Descartes, Leibniz and Berkeley are seen as revisionary. Revisionists are laudable for their partial visions, but Strawson will find his own home in an attempt to rethink the thoughts of Aristotle in contemporary terms.

We recall from "On Referring" that the singular terms of sentences do not in themselves refer; they are instead used by persons to make statements that do refer to objective particulars. Quine notwithstanding, those singular terms are not eliminable extrusions. We cannot simply say that to be is to be the value of a variable of quantification, since, as we shall see at length, the identification of a particular lies beyond that formalist reach. For Strawson, our ontology must include objective particulars or individuals as well as what it is that makes it possible for us to identify and reidentify them. Our ontology will doubtless include much besides those particulars, but they will always be present as basic to the entire structure. We are thus led to the broader ontological questions of the most general features of our thought about the world of our experience, and to those presuppositions that make the identification of particulars possible.

Individuals is divided into two parts. Part I, "Particulars", is concerned with the central and fundamental place of material bodies and persons among particulars in general. That is presupposed in Part II, "Logical Subjects", which then proceeds to consider the connection between the idea of a particular and the idea of an object of reference or logical subject. That link is found in the crucial idea of completeness. We may see Part I as metaphysical and Part II as grammatical or linguistic, but the practices of ordinary language are continuously present in both parts, and Strawson himself doubts whether either part can be completely understood without the other. We do well to follow the order that Strawson provides.

Part I: Particulars

Chapter 1: Bodies

The Identification of Particulars

Our account of things that exist comprises objective particulars as foundational. The general theoretical problem addressed in *Individuals* is how the identification of those particulars is secured. Strawson thinks that his own use of "particulars" is an ordinary one: "Historical occurrences, material objects, people and their shadows are all particulars; whereas qualities and properties, numbers and species are not" (IE: 15). A speaker making a statement may refer to some particular, and a hearer may or may not be able to identify the particular referred to. And, since we can think about a particular in an identifying way without speaking about it, the question of identification will not be directly dependent on the speaker–hearer relationship. Thus we come at the outset of our investigation to the general question of the conditions that make such identifications and reidentifications possible.

Certainly a sufficient although not a necessary condition for the successful identification of a particular is that the speaker be able to discriminate that particular from all others. Prime instances of such discriminations occur when the particular is sensibly present to the speaker and reference is made through the use of demonstratives. When the particular is not sensibly present, however, a speaker must ultimately depend on the use of descriptions. That would seem to raise the fundamental difficulty that a single description might equally well apply to different particulars located in different sectors of the universe. That for Strawson is a needless worry, since our knowledge of particulars takes place in a unified structure of a spatiotemporal character, and our use of this system turns fundamentally on our knowing our own place in it (IE: 23).[1] We accord this pre-eminence to spatiotemporal relations as a common point of reference because this system is peculiarly comprehensive and pervasive. We need not worry about there being two or more exactly similar networks that would make individuating descriptions impossible; the worry is groundless since we the speakers have each of us a unique time and place that provide points of reference within the network. A similarly groundless worry supposes that each "here" and "now" is altogether private and personal, with the result that there are as many networks as there are persons; this worry is also groundless because we are *in* the system, rather than having the system within us.

Strawson's claim that the identification of particulars necessarily rests on demonstratives will deny the possibility of "pure individuating descriptions", for example, "the first dog to be born at sea", or "quasi-pure individuating expressions", for example, "the tallest man who ever lived". There are indeed descriptions that begin with phrases such as "the first" or "the only" and thereby apparently proclaim the uniqueness of their application, and so it would seem that our individuating thoughts do not always need demonstratives and a single unified spatiotemporal framework of particulars. Strawson's rejoinder is that such expressions are not applicable when (a) there are no candidates for the title, or (b) when there are two equally good candidates for the title. Apparent remedies for such failures themselves fail: "We may indeed increase the improbability of the second kind of application-failure by adding to the detail of the description; but we thereby increase ... the probability of the first kind of application-failure" (IE: 28). Our only way out of this bind is to draw on the way we do indeed have an actual knowledge of particulars in our common spatiotemporal framework, that is, through the foundational use of demonstrative terms. For Strawson, any particular identified in purely descriptive terms would effectively be cut off from playing any effective role in our general scheme of knowledge.

In all of this the reader may properly be reminded of Strawson's root distinction between sentence and statement that lies at the heart of "On Referring".

Reidentification

One of the conditions of our use of this system of spatiotemporal identification is that we are able not only to identify but also to reidentify particulars. Both identification and reidentification involve thinking that some thing is *the same one*. Our criteria of reidentification must allow for discontinuities and for limits of observation. Our account leans heavily on "qualitative recurrences", that is, on the fact of repeated observational encounters with "the same pattern of objects". This latter phrase allows a confusing but helpful ambiguity between *qualitative* and *numerical* identity. Where we say "the same" of what is not continuously observed, we think we can make that qualitative–numerical distinction.

The sceptic will deny this and will say that in cases of non-continuous observation all we really have are different kinds of *qualitative* identity, that we have no warrant for saying that this particular is numerically the same as one previously encountered. For Strawson, the best reply is that our conceptual scheme simply *is* that of a single spatio-temporal system of material things, and a condition of that scheme is precisely the acceptance of particular-identity in at least some cases of non-continuous observation. Thus what the sceptic rejects, the sceptic tacitly accepts:

> [W]e should ... have the idea of a new, a different, spatial system for each new continuous stretch of observation .... Each new system would be wholly independent of every other. There would be no question of *doubt* about the identity of an item in one system with an item in another. For such a doubt makes sense only if the two systems are not independent, if they are parts, in some way related, of a single system which includes them both. But the condition of having such a system is precisely the condition that there should be satisfiable and commonly satisfied criteria for the identity of at least some items in one sub-system with some items in the other. [The sceptic] pretends to accept a conceptual scheme, but at the same time quietly rejects one of the conditions of its employment. Thus his doubts are unreal ...   (IE: 35)

There is a complex interplay between the reidentification of things and the reidentification of places. For Strawson, there is no mystery about their mutual dependence:

> [T]he reidentification of places is not something quite different from, and independent of, the reidentification of things. There is, rather, a complex and intricate interplay between the two. For on the one hand places are defined only by the relations of things; and, on the other, one of the requirements for the identity of a material thing is that its existence, as well as being continuous in time, should be continuous in space.   (IE: 36–7)

With this reference to this interplay of things and places, Strawson is revisiting familiar ground. John Locke held that it was not possible for two things of the same kind to exist in the same place at the same time, and that it is under this condition that we find the principle of individuation. Leibniz in reply thought that some further distinctions are required:

> In addition to the difference of time or of place there must always be an internal *principle of distinction*; although there may be many things of the same kind, it is still the case that none of them are ever exactly alike. Thus, although time and place (i.e., the relations to what lies outside) do distinguish for us things which

we could not easily tell apart by reference to themselves alone, things are nevertheless distinguishable in themselves. Thus, although diversity in things is accompanied by diversity of time or place, time and place do not constitute the core of identity and difference .... It is by means of things that we must distinguish one time or place from another, rather than *vice versa*; for times and places are in themselves perfectly alike ...

(Leibniz 1981: 230)

Further questions on the relationship between the spatiotemporal framework and the contents of that framework are precisely those ontological and epistemological issues that Strawson will later examine much more fully in its Kantian context in *The Bounds of Sense*.

Basic Particulars

We have at this point Strawson's account of how it is possible for us to identify and reidentify the particulars to which we refer in the statements we make. That account naturally allows us to raise the question of whether among the various kinds of particulars there is one class or category of particular that we necessarily regard as basic, that is, a class of particulars to which we make those identifying references without which references to other sorts of particulars would be impossible.

From the premise that identification and reidentification rest on location in a unitary spatiotemporal framework, we might conclude that the particular objects that constitute the content of that framework must be three-dimensional objects with some endurance through time. From this we could in turn conclude that *material bodies* must count as basic particulars.[2] Strawson is quick to agree that such an argument so simply put is at the same time so general and so vague that it is inadequate as a viable support for a general philosophical position. Consequently he sets out to develop a line of investigation that will be both more direct and more detailed, and which will thus provide a more adequate backing for according material bodies a primacy among particulars.

There are "private particulars" such as mental events and sense data which cannot count as basic particulars since they are clearly dependent on another more basic class of particulars, namely, persons. We may also find another class of "identification dependence" in the cases of theoretical constructs such as the particles of physics, which while *not* private are nonetheless also both unobservable and dependent for their identification on grosser larger bodies. Here we find a dependence of things that are unobservable on things that are not only observable but that are also objects of public perception, objects such that different people have sense experiences of them, ones that speaker and hearer alike can identify on a particular occasion of discourse. It is, of course, true that the publicly observable particulars available on any particular occasion do make up a severely limited field, and that successful identifying reference to items lying outside our immediate perception may be made only through the use of some category of particulars that is itself in turn identification-dependent, but that does not invalidate the claim of an ultimate primacy for material bodies.

What makes identification and reidentification possible is the basic particular that is publicly observable. Strawson's initial claim is that material bodies meet that requirement. But there might seem to be another class of particulars that would equally well meet the need, namely, particular events, processes, states or conditions. A particular flash or band of light might be identified as the first or the *n*th in a series of such things directly located by a speaker and a hearer but, of course, our reference to it is made by way of a reference to a particular of a different sort, for example, to a place or a material body. We may also think of a series no member of which can be solitary, for example, day and night, or the succession of years, but even in such cases reference is made by situating it in relation to the present spatiotemporal moment.

Thus far it seems that material bodies and their spatiotemporal locations remain basic. Against this we might object that such a criterion is inadequate in the face of simultaneous events, but Strawson can easily respond that simultaneity does not preclude spatial difference. A further objection has ties to longstanding metaphysical contentions. Every birth event is indeed the birth of some particular creature. But we could then argue that every creature is tied to a particular birth, and so there might seem to be a mutual identification dependence between the event and the material body, and in that case the material body no longer has an exclusive claim to be the basic particular. That is an argument Strawson rejects. A large class of events or processes such as being born is necessarily conceived of as predicated of particulars of another type, namely, material bodies. There is a general and one-way relation between the material bodies, persons and places on the one hand, and events on the other. We can refer to Socrates without referring to a particular event in his life, but we cannot refer to the particular event without referring to Socrates and thus there is a real asymmetry. Material bodies, persons and places may be referred to without reference to particulars of types other than their own. They uniquely provide one single common and extendable framework. They alone are basic to particular identification of whatever sort.

This unique role of material bodies is further confirmed when we consider the question of reidentification, that is, our ability to identify either bodies or events as the same as ones previously identified. If bodies are basic to identification, they must also be basic to reidentification. In the cases of a break in the continuity of observation, that reidentification is dependent on a continuity of existence in space, that is, a common spatiotemporal framework. Again, we can see that bodies alone are competent to provide that framework, since they alone are relatively enduring occupiers of space.

It has been objected that this conclusion rests on an untenable distinction between material bodies or persons and processes. It may be argued that "Caesar" is simply the name of a series of events, that crossing into Britain and crossing the Rubicon are members of a series of events, effectively and in sum a biography, and that the basic reference is to "process-things". The conclusion is that there is no justification for a fundamental distinction of category between things and processes. Strawson's reply is that such "process-things" are a category of four-dimensional things for which we have neither an accepted use nor a systematic need. In practice, we do in fact distinguish between an object and its history, a person and his biography, and the terms we use to talk about persons and things are simply fundamentally different from the terms we use when talking about processes and events. We do not use the category of "process-things" when talking about either. It might be objected to this rejoinder that there are neither bodies nor persons who have no histories or biographies, that none of Strawson's particulars are "bare particulars", that bodies and persons in fact are unavoidably tied to processes. But it would be open to Strawson to accept this and nonetheless to maintain that there is an identification dependence of events and processes on bodies and persons, but not vice versa. Bodies and persons are the basic particulars.

Strawson considers a final objection. How do all of these theoretical arguments for the primacy of material bodies bear on and relate to the ways in which in our actual speaking we commonly go about the business of identification and reidentification? And if a firm tie between practice and theory cannot be secured, then what is the use or the justification for the theory? Strawson grants the force of this objection. It is closely parallel to an objection he himself has made against the claims of the modern formalist logician whose concern with systematic completeness and consistency has made him impervious to the practices of ordinary language. For Strawson, it would indeed be possible to attempt to spell out in great detail all the complex ways in which his general theory fits with our actual practice, but to do so would be to erode progressively the possibility of any general theory at all, and, in any event, Strawson finds that his efforts are not completely in vain. We do not in our ordinary conversation make explicit use of the referential framework that bodies alone can provide, but we do in practice use a device that is close kin to that framework:

> The place of the explicit relational framework is taken in part by that linguistic device which has so often and so justly absorbed the attention of logicians – the proper name. Demonstratives or quasi-demonstratives apart, it is proper names which tend to be the resting-places of reference to particulars .... Now, among particulars, the bearers *par excellence* of proper names are persons and places. It is a conceptual truth ... that places are defined by the relation of material bodies; and it is also a conceptual truth, of which we shall see the significance more fully hereafter, that persons have material bodies. (IE: 58)

For Strawson, the primacy of material bodies in that identification and reidentification of particulars, which is foundational to ordinary language, is secure.

Chapter 2: Sounds

Material bodies are then basic and prior in the identification of other kinds of particulars. Strawson does not make the claim that this ontological priority of bodies justifies more ambitious claims such that only bodies are real, or that all particulars are reducible to bodies. Such claims may be understandable in the light of the priority that material bodies do have, but they are claims that Strawson carefully and emphatically rejects.

A question and a challenge remain. While we may carefully restrict the priority claims for body to particular identification, it might seem that this apparently modest claim might still be challenged, since even if we grant the primacy of bodies in a spatiotemporal framework in our ordinary identification of particulars, it might seem that there could be other kinds of frameworks that could equally well claim that power. The question thus arises of whether we can make intelligible to ourselves some other conceptual scheme, that is, one in which material bodies in a spatiotemporal framework are not the sole basic particulars.

Strawson begins his examination of this question by noting two distinctions that have been central up to this point, namely, the distinction between identification and reidentification, and the distinction between speaker and hearer. The two distinctions have so far been closely tied. This is a tie that Strawson now wishes to loosen. This is apparently plausible, since thinking is not essentially different when we intend to communicate to another than when we do not. Plainly we can think in an identifying way about particulars without talking about them.

Consider then simply within the contents of consciousness those particulars that are only states of consciousness of one's own, and those particulars regarded as having actual or possible *objects* of those experiences. Refer to the latter as "objective particulars". In the context of this terminology we may now ask whether bodies as basic particulars are a necessary condition of the knowledge of objective particulars. The claim thus far that bodies are basic is deduced from the fact that our schema for the reidentification of objective particulars is a unified system of both space and time. One way to look for a schema in which bodies are not the basic particulars would be to entertain the notion of a non-spatial conceptual scheme that would nonetheless provide for the reidentification of objective particulars.

For that purpose, Strawson suggests that we explore this notion of a no-space world, one that by definition would be a world without bodies. Which of our five senses would we have to eliminate to arrive at a bodiless no-space world? Eliminate the "trivial senses" of taste and smell. Touch and sight must also be eliminated since their fields are necessarily extended and hence spatial. A purely auditory world, a world in which sounds are the only sensory input, would on the other hand not allow for any spatial dimension. Thus we arrive at the fruitful question of whether a person whose sensory experiences are sounds and sounds alone could have a conceptual scheme that would provide for objective particulars. If sounds are thus to be public objective particulars, we need the notion of other people, other observers. Thus the issue comes to these two closely allied questions:

"Can the conditions of a non-solipsistic consciousness be fulfilled for a purely auditory experience? ... Can we, in purely auditory terms, find room for the concept of identifiable and re-identifiable particulars at all?" (IE: 69). A positive answer to the second question is a necessary condition for a positive answer to the first, since the very notion of reidentification requires the continuous existence of an *unobserved* particular, a requirement unavailable for a solipsistic consciousness.

What sense could we give in a purely auditory world to the question whether this particular sound can be identified as the same sound heard at another time? We can certainly say that the G major chord heard in this performance of Bach's Mass in B Minor is the same chord that we heard in a previous performance, but in this case we can say that it is the same chord only as a universal or type, and not as the same particular chord. Strawson concludes that our familiar notion of an unobserved particular reidentified across time requires the idea of such particulars also having a particular place in a spatial system whose entirety is not revealed at any particular moment, and that this spatial system provides differentiating locations, places that house not only spatialized objects but also such particulars as sounds that are not essentially spatial. This enabling notion of place is one that is not available in the no-space world of the purely audible.

Gareth Evans's article "Things Without the Mind – A Commentary upon Chapter Two of Strawson's *Individuals*" (1980) provides a detailed and probing account of some of Strawson's assumptions and conclusions in *Individuals*. While Evans is frequently critical of Strawson, he nonetheless praises and joins him in their common effort to consider imaginatively alternative and possible accounts of the concepts that are commonly accepted as part of the human conceptual scheme. We have seen a primary example of that enterprise in Strawson's attempt in *Individuals* to fill in the details of the world of a subject having only the auditory sense, a subject in a no-space world.

For Evans, one way of considering such possibilities is to compare the worlds of a subject having hearing only, henceforth Hero, and a subject having seeing only, henceforth Seer. At the beginning of *Individuals*, Strawson proposes that spatiotemporal material bodies are the basic particulars in our conceptual scheme, but he is then prepared to ask whether such particulars are a necessary condition of any scheme at all that provides for the knowledge of objective particulars. It is this that leads to the question of the possibilities that may be inherent in Hero's no-space world. That leads Strawson to consider the question of whether it is so much as possible that Hero could have a conceptual scheme that would "in purely auditory terms, find room for the concept of identifiable and re-identifiable particulars at all". There is the further question of whether the conditions of a non-solipsistic consciousness could be met by Hero. Despite a valiant effort, Strawson inconclusively concludes that continuing to explore the fantasy world of Hero is both tedious and unpromising. His modest purpose throughout has simply been to explore the issue of the very intelligibility of a conceptual scheme that, while devoid of material bodies, would nonetheless provide for the identification and reidentification of objective particulars.

While Evans is broadly critical of the main line of approach that Strawson has taken in exploring the possible viability of Hero's world, a criticism that, with minor exceptions, Strawson accepts, Evans nonetheless finds it promising to consider another and more promising line of approach that is at least implicit in *Individuals*. Evans approaches the questions of whether Hero's conceptual scheme allows for the identification and reidentification of objective particulars and whether it allows for a non-solipsistic consciousness by testing the very provisional hypothesis that Hero would at least understand two mutually dependent conditions: (a) that the phenomena he perceives may occur unperceived, with the change or maintenance of their relative "positions" in some quasi-spatial dimension; and (b) that a change or maintenance of his own position may occur. For Evans, that understanding is more than can be provided for by a purely auditory experience, and he concludes that in the absence of some further support, it is virtually impossible for Hero to have the conception of an objective world existing independently of his experience.

For Strawson, Evans's hypothesis has two mutually dependent but distinguishable aspects: (i) objectivity, the thesis that there are processes independent of Hero's experience of them, and (ii) spatiality, the thesis that Hero's perceptible objects are ordered in a spatial manner allowing for the simultaneous existence of distinct processes (objects) of that kind. Strawson thinks that if Evans's argument is sound, this would strengthen what is, after all, the major point of *Individuals*, namely, the primacy of spatiality in our identification and reidentification of material bodies.

Evans's argument has two major lines, the causal ground argument and the simultaneity argument. The causal ground argument holds that if there is to be an objective world existing independent of a subject's experience, then the perceiver's perceptible objects must have sensible properties that themselves require a persisting causal ground distinct from themselves. Our human experience does have such a ground in our concept of space-occupying material bodies. No set of properties constructed from sense experience alone could provide the concept of such a ground. Hero has only sense qualities and relations, and thus lacks the resource needed for the concept of an objective world existing independent of his experience.

That argument is supplemented by the simultaneity argument. What is needed for an objective world is the idea of distinct although possibly qualitatively identical things existing simultaneously in spatial relationships. Blind persons do have that concept despite their lack of sight, but their situation is not that of Hero, who lacks any opportunity for the direct application of simultaneous spatial concepts.

Strawson thinks that Evans is right in holding that "simultaneous spatial concepts" are a necessary condition for the idea of an objective world. It is not quite clear to Strawson whether Evans also thinks that it is a sufficient condition. Consider the case of Seer, a subject who has only visual experience. Seer does indeed have the requisite simultaneous spatial concepts and, if having such concepts are sufficient to provide objectivity, he lacks nothing. It seems to Strawson that Evans would be no more willing to grant the concept of objectivity to Seer than to Hero, but for the reason why this is so, it is necessary to return to the major causal ground argument.

Strawson assumes that, for Evans, while such properties as colours and visual shapes are commonly considered objective properties, they are dispositional properties of objects, having other non-sensory properties that make them space-occupiers, thus providing the causal ground of the sensory properties themselves. Strawson agrees that no objective world can be constructed out of those sense experiences alone. We ordinarily take the experience of visual properties such as shape and colour to be things in an objective spatial world. We cannot take such properties to be merely dispositional; they need some persisting categorical base of a character different from themselves. We apparently need some non-sensory theoretical properties such as force, mass and charge. The difficulty is that these properties are themselves dispositional, and thus that the categorical base for objectivity is yet to be found.

The resolution of this difficulty is complex. Strawson has addressed it in "Perception and its Objects" (1979). In this reply to Evans, he gives at least a hint:

Fundamentally, the question is whether we are to retain our hold on a direct realist view of perception, such as can plausibly be ascribed to unreflective common sense, or to embrace an exclusively representative theory. If we do retain our hold on the former, then we are released from the grip of the belief that sensory properties, conceived of as objective, must therefore be conceived of as merely dispositional, as requiring a categorical base of a different character from themselves. It may be asked how if we do retain our hold on the uncritical realism of common sense, we can simultaneously entertain, without contradiction, the scientific worldview – a view which, taken alone, is necessarily associated with a representative view of perception and, if held with a consistent exclusiveness, inevitably runs into the difficulty just described. The answer lies in recognizing a certain irreducible relativity in our view of the world and in acknowledging our capacity to shift our standpoint from one standpoint to another, while retaining our grasp of the identity of what we thus variously view from different standpoints. Self-consciousness on this point is what saves us from self-contradiction; though not, necessarily, from intellectual discomfort.   (Strawson 1979: 280–81)

Strawson never assumes the real possibility of either a purely auditory experience or a solipsistic consciousness. Any further pursuit of the no-space fantasy he finds both difficult and tedious, but its investigation does serve to confirm the thesis that in a descriptive metaphysics, material bodies in a common spatiotemporal network are the basic particulars. He now abandons his investigation of the purely auditory world and turns his attention to the issues raised by an apparent possibility of a solipsistic consciousness in the world of our ordinary human experience. Our concern in that world is with the identification and reidentification of three sorts of particulars: material bodies, places and persons. Material bodies are indeed the *basic* particulars, but in fact they and places are said to have a mutual dependence, and the very notion of persons is said to entail embodiment. A fuller explication of the notion of persons in its relation to material bodies and to the very possibility of solipsism is therefore in order.

Chapter 3: Persons

Among particulars, material bodies are for Strawson uniquely basic in the sense that they alone can be identified and reidentified without reference to any other sort of particular. He finds this confirmed by the apparent impossibility of finding a place for a reidentifiable particular in the fantasy no-space world of a purely auditory experience, since in a sounds-only world there is no readily apparent way in which a distinction can be made between oneself and what is not oneself. The conditions of a non-solipsistic consciousness would thus be unavailable.

But how then *are* the conditions of a non-solipsistic consciousness produced in our ordinary human experience? It is here that keeping in mind the purely auditory experience will help us to see the strangeness of what we as a matter of fact do. In the world in which sounds alone exist, what possible place could there be for the distinction between the hearer and the heard? It would seem utterly strange for the hearer to think of himself as a sound among sounds, the notion of a sound having the experience of other sounds.

This brings into sharper focus the question of what makes possible in the first place the distinction between the hearer and the heard, between the perceiver and his perceptions, a distinction we commonly make in our experience of the world. Strawson begins his investigation by thinking of some of the ways in which we commonly talk about ourselves. We ascribe to ourselves characteristics that we ascribe to material bodies such as height, colouring, shape and weight. But we also ascribe to ourselves other characteristics that we would not ascribe to material bodies, characteristics such as actions and intentions, sensations, thoughts and feelings, perceptions and memories. That distinction suggests at least two related questions: why are one's states of consciousness ascribed to anything at all and why are they ascribed to the same thing to which we also ascribe physical characteristics?

The answers to those questions may appear to be satisfied by the fact that in our actual human condition a person's body plays a unique role in his perceptual experience. Take visual experience. Consider (a) eyelids and all that is known by ophthalmic surgeons, (b) the orientations of the person's eyes and (c) the location of the person's body. For each person there is just one body that occupies uniquely a particular causal position with regard to his perceptual experience of both other things and himself. That fact does account for the particular attachment I feel for my own body, but it does not explain why I should ascribe my thoughts and my feelings to anything at all: why there should be a concept of *myself* at all. And even if those thoughts and feelings are ascribed to a something, the fact of the unique role of body in perceptual experience still does not in itself account for our attributing events in consciousness to the very same thing to which we attribute the corporeal characteristics of the favoured body. In sum, we have yet to account for the use we make of "I": for the notion we have of a person. Historically, one response to these apparent puzzles has been the claim that they rest on linguistic confusion. That claim has been shared by the Cartesians and by the no-ownership view held at a certain time by Wittgenstein and perhaps by Schlick.

For the Cartesian, the essence of mind is to think and the essence of body is to be extended, and the two are radically both distinguishable and separable substances. When we refer to a person, we are referring to that person's mind or to his body or to both, but we never attribute consciousness to the very same thing to which we attribute corporeal characteristics. That dualism seems to avoid at least for the moment the question of why we ascribe consciousness to the same thing to which we ascribe physical characteristics, but it does not escape the question of why we ascribe conscious events to anything at all.

For Strawson, the no-ownership view does indeed address that latter question. Both Wittgenstein and Schlick found support for this view in Lichtenberg's dictum that instead of saying "I think" I ought simply to say "There is a thought". The statement "It is raining now" does not require the existence of an "It" presently engaged in the process of raining. The no-ownership theory presumably begins with a consideration of the unique causal position of a particular material body in a person's experience. It is the uniqueness of this body that gives rise to the linguistic confusion of supposing that one's experiences are owned by that particular body. That would make some kind of sense if we continued to think of the body itself as the owner, but we slide from that acceptable sense to the view that the ownership belongs to something else called an ego whose sole function is to provide that ownership. But the very notion of ownership supposes that what is owned may be transferred, and since this is clearly not true in the case of mental events, the whole notion of an Ego to which states of consciousness may be ascribed is an illusion.

For Strawson, that view of things is incoherent, since the no-ownership theorist is using the very sense of ownership that his theory denies. He begins his account with some such contingent statement as "All *my* experiences are uniquely dependent on the state of body B". Any effort on his part to be rid of the troublesome "my" would inevitably lead to saying something like "*All* experiences are causally dependent on body B", and that statement is clearly contingently false. Experiences owe their identity as particulars to the fact that they are experiences of a particular person. If experiences are to be the identifiable particulars that they are, then it must be logically impossible for an experience ascribed to one person to be alternatively assigned to another. What the no-ownership theorist would deny, he must admit.

Both the no-ownership theory and Strawson's rejection of that theory have a history that has been usefully articulated by Roderick Chisholm (1969). He reminds us that the theory in one form was defended by Hume: "As our idea of any body, a peach, for instance, is only that of a particular taste, color, figure, size. consistency, etc., so our idea of any mind is only that of particular perceptions without the notion of anything we call substance, either simple or compound" (Hume 1955a: 194).[3] Locke had already described the notion of substance as that of an unknown and unknowable substratum and, granted Ockham's razor, Hume's conclusion was bound to come. The no-ownership theory continues to have its supporters in the present age, and Chisholm cites instances in which this is evident on both sides of the great divide between continental and Anglophone philosophers. Thus Sartre makes a basic distinction between being-in-itself (*en-soi*), things presented to the consciousness, and being-for-itself (*pour-soi*), the conscious self to which those things are manifest, and it is impossible for us to make of the self an *en-soi*, something known as it is in itself.[4] Russell said that the self is not "empirically discoverable" (1956: 305), and Carnap said that the given is subjectless (2003 [1928]: 103–6).

Support for the no-ownership theory thus occurs across time, but so does opposition. Chisholm (1969) cites Brentano's remark about the concept of substance: "Those who say that this concept is not included in any perception are very much mistaken. Rather it is given in every perception, as Aristotle had said ..." (Brentano 1925: 30). And to the extent that Hume's position is anticipated in Locke, then Leibniz had already provided a counter:

> [F]rom the beginning we conceive several predicates in a single subject, and that is all there is to these metaphorical words "support" and "substratum". So I do not see why it is made out to be a problem. On the contrary, what comes into our mind is the *concretum* conceived as wise, warm, shining, rather than ... *abstractions* or qualities such as wisdom, warmth, light, etc., which are much harder to grasp .... So to treat qualities or other abstract terms as though they were the least problematic, and concrete ones as very troublesome is ... to put things back to front.
>
> (Leibniz 1981: 217)

To free ourselves from the problems inherent in a no-ownership view, Strawson finds a need to recognize the primitiveness of the concept of a *person*, that is, "a type of entity such that *both* predicates ascribing states of consciousness *and* predicates ascribing corporeal characteristics, a physical situation etc. are equally applicable to a single individual of that single type" (IE: 101–2). Descartes made a radical distinction and separation between mind and body, between thought and extension, and thus bequeathed to modern philosophy the task of showing how those two primitive notions could be related. The difficulty is that we cannot come to the concept of individual different consciousnesses, other minds, if we attempt to make that concept primitive. Strawson's counter is to make the concept of person primitive, and to make ego a secondary concept to be analysed only in the comprising concept of person. I can distinguish between the contents of a person's consciousness and his corporeal characteristics, but at base they cannot be separated and made primitive.

For Strawson, making the concept of person primitive is also an effective reply to the no-ownership theorist. It was inevitable that from his starting-point, Hume would come to a no-ownership view:

> For my part, when I enter most intimately into what I call *myself*, I always stumble on some particular perception or other, of heat or cold, light or shade, love or hatred, pain or pleasure. I never can catch *myself* at any time without a perception, and never can observe any thing but the perception.   (Hume 1955b: I IV vi, 84)

For Chisholm, what Hume denies, Hume presupposes. Chisholm wonders how Hume can say he does not find himself if he finds himself to be stumbling, and if he finds himself to have certain perceptions and to lack others. For Strawson, Hume sought, or pretended to seek, the illusory primary concept of the unity of a pure consciousness, the ego-substance. His search was in vain because that unity can only be found if there is simultaneously a way to differentiate among individual consciousnesses, but apart from the corporeal characteristics of a person, no such way exists. Where there is no principle of differentiation there can be no principle of unity.

> The concept of a person is logically prior to that of the individual consciousness. The concept of a person is not to be analyzed as that of an animated body or of an embodied anima .... A person is not an embodied ego, but an ego might be a disembodied person, retaining the logical benefit of individuality from having been a person.   (IE: 103)

For Strawson, we cannot argue, in the manner of Hume, "from my own case", because I can have no idea of "my own self" without already having the idea of "other self". To have this idea of "other self" requires that I be able to identify individuals of that type, and that identification in turn requires that those other selves have both states of consciousness *and* corporeal characteristics, that is, that they be persons.

From a linguistic point of view, Strawson thus makes a rough distinction between the M-predicates and the P-predicates of a person. The M-predicates of a person are those that are also applied to those material bodies to which we would never ascribe predicates ascribing states of consciousness. M-predicates would thus include having a certain weight, or being in a certain location. P-predicates are all the other predicates we apply to persons. Learning to apply P-predicates is simultaneously learning how to apply them to others and how to apply them to oneself.

It might seem that ascribing P-predicates to another is necessarily rooted in observation, while ascribing them to oneself is not. This is the source of the idea that the only things we know apart from observation or inference are purely private experiences, and this would seem to drive a wedge between the concept I have of myself and the concept I have of another. In reply, Strawson asks us to consider those actions such as playing a ball game or going for a walk that involve bodily movement but that also clearly imply intention or at least some general state of consciousness. In such cases I do not hesitate to concede that the actions of myself and those of another are of the same sort, and I understand them both in terms of a common intention. Self and others as persons are thus inextricably joined in a common human nature.

While there is a common human nature, one condition of our actual conceptual scheme is that this nature is not that of a community nature – of what has sometimes been referred to as a "group mind". Those who have attempted to talk of such a mind have inevitably done so in analogy to our talk about individual persons. We do indeed sometimes talk of groups such as armies and teams having intentions and goals, but we do this some of the time, not all of the time, and we do well to remember that this is an analogy with definite limitations. If instead of talking in analogy of a group's having such person-charactertistics as intentions *some* of the time, we were to say that they have them *all* of the time, we should no longer be speaking in terms of an analogy. In this manner of speaking, there would then remain no way of making an identifying reference to any individual consciousness within the group, and we will thus have eliminated the very condition that seemed to make the hypothesis of a primary "group mind" possible. We are brought back to a description of our actual linguistic practice when we recall the "startling ambiguity" of the phrase "a body and its members".

To be a person is to have both M-predicates and P-predicates. This concept of person is primary, but it is possible to think of a separate pure individual consciousness in a secondary and derivative way. We could entertain the notion of a disembodied person, a former person, surviving bodily death. Strawson does not find it difficult to conjure up such a possibility. He thinks that we have only to think of ourselves as having visual and auditory and perhaps some organic sensations, as we do at the present, while having no perception of our own bodies and having no power of initiating any changes in the physical world. But then two unappealing consequences follow:

> The first is that the strictly disembodied individual is strictly soli-
> tary .... The other ... is that in order to retain his idea of himself as
> an individual, he must always think of himself as *dis*embodied, as
> a *former* person .... In proportion as the memories fades, and this
> vicarious living palls, to that degree his concept of himself as an
> individual becomes attenuated. At the limit of attenuation there
> is, *from the point of view of his survival as an individual*, no dif-
> ference between the continuation of experience and its cessation
> .... No doubt it is for this reason that the orthodox have wisely
> insisted on the resurrection of the body.   (IE: 115–16)

Chapter 4: Monads

We can now see that a central issue for Strawson is the relationship between the problem of the individual consciousness with the general topic of identification. He turns now for comparative and clarifying purposes to a consideration of Leibniz's system, a system he takes to be in marked contrast to his own point of view. He is not concerned with whether his account of Leibniz is in all detail historically accurate. Strawson's purpose here is simply to use his description of Leibniz's system as a way to make clear his own very different perspective.

There are two important ways in which Leibniz's system appear to run counter to positions that are fundamental to Strawson's approach. For Strawson, the identification of particulars rests ultimately for us on the use of terms with some demonstrative force, on the use of a spatiotemporal system in which each of us has a particular location. Hence for Strawson it follows that a system that does not allow for temporal or spatiotemporal entities cannot be a system that allows for particulars at all. Kant is correct in saying that space and time are our only forms of intuition.

In contrast, for Leibniz the basic individuals are monads. The nature of these monads comes under the principle of the identity of indiscernibles as a necessary truth, so that each monad has a unique complete individual concept: "some description in purely universal, or general, terms, such that only that individual answers to that description" (IE: 120). Leibniz evidently thought that he could specify that *type* of description, but that only an omniscient God could give the actual description for each particular individual, that is, a complete individual notion, a description of the entire universe from one certain "point of view". The number of possible points of view is greater than any assignable number, each point of view is universally exhaustive, and, under the principle of the identity of indiscernibles, each must be unique.

For Leibniz, the models for these basic individuals or monads are minds. Monads can therefore be individuated without reference to material bodies or persons, thus in terms of the states of consciousness alone. To take "point of view" literally would be to think of the monad as representing a common world of spatially extended objects. Even on that literal interpretation, the identification of a particular becomes impossible. Think of the squares of a chessboard. The "point of view" from c3 is qualitatively indistingishable from the view from f6. But for Strawson that literal interpretation is not faithful to Leibniz, since in his system all that is real are the monads, that is, mind-like consciousnesses and their states. For Leibniz, there is no public space, only the private spaces of the individual monads, among which there are certain correspondences. But, in the absence of a public space, a plurality of monads with the same "point of view" is logically possible. Leibniz thus far fails to provide for the identification of individuals.

For Strawson, Leibniz is now reduced to the following unappealing alternatives:

(a) Reduce the identity of indiscernibles from a necessary truth for all possible worlds to a contingent truth for our actual world. But the system then becomes capriciously theological: the free choice of a God who apparently does not care for redundancy.

(b) Make "complete individual concepts" rather than minds the basic individuals of the system, and let the system be altogether concerned with the relations of concepts and concept sets. Logical purity is then retained, and a number of principles that characterize Leibniz's system are guaranteed, namely: the identity of indiscernibles; the principle that monads are neither spatial nor temporal; the requirement that the predicate inheres in the subject of every singular proposition; pre-established harmony; and a maximum of diversity in phenomena combined with a maximum of simplicity in natural laws in the best of all possible worlds. As a logical construct this is all admirable; the difficulty is that it tells us nothing about the empirical reality with which we are familiar.

(c) To remedy that difficulty, we might continue to make "complete individual concepts" rather than minds the basic individuals of the system, but nonetheless allow each concept to have an instantiation "at least something like the creation of a unitary series of perceptual and other states of consciousness – a private view of a possible world" (IE: 130). For such an instantiation to yield results satisfactory to Leibniz, the identity of indiscernibles and other key doctrines must be made contingent. Strawson finds this mixed interpretation truest to the historical Leibniz. The basic individuals of the system are neither spatial nor temporal, but the system is not totally divorced from empirical reality. The logical impurities are thus admitted, although at one remove.

Strawson thinks that if we start along with Leibniz with the notion of a consciousness and its states as the primary individuals, then we are going to be faced with the insoluble problem of the possibility of a number of individuals being indistinguishable from one another, and the identification of particular individuals impossible. For Strawson, the problem is not one to be solved; rather, it is to be dissolved by making person rather than consciousness the basic particular. Person is primary, and the person's M-predicates and P-predicates are secondary terms, distinguishable but inseparable. For each one of us in our actual use of language, there is just one *person* to whom ascribing consciousness does not depend on observed behaviour. That person is oneself.

Strawson's account of Leibniz's system does serve as a useful foil for his own account of the identification of particulars. The contrasts are indeed clarifying, and it is evident why Strawson classifies the metaphysics of Leibniz as revisionary set over against his own descriptive metaphysics. For Strawson, it matters little whether his account is historically accurate. Strawson is certainly entitled to his foil, and the use of Leibniz as a foil has a long history going back to Voltaire and continuing unabated down through our own time. A scholarly concern about actual detail in texts may in this context seem beside the point, yet a consideration of possible differences between Strawson's account of Leibniz and the texts themselves may be in some measure enlightening. Indeed, it can be argued that a closer consideration of Leibniz's own texts shows him in many ways to be supportive of Strawson's own position.[5] Here are some particular instances.

For Strawson, all that is real in Leibniz's system are consciousnesses and their states. The monad is neither temporal nor spatial in any public sense. But for Leibniz, each finite monad expresses its own body's changes and viewpoint and thereby all other things, and there is thus a sense in which each finite monad is both spatial and temporal. Every change has its place and time, and each finite monad has a certain ordered relation of coexistence with all the others. Leibniz does *not* think "that any finite substances exist apart from a body and that they therefore lack a position or an order in relation to the other things coexisting in the universe" (Leibniz 1970: 531).[6] In the world that Leibniz himself thinks actual, there would be no sensation without body; indeed, there would be no thought of any kind, since ultimately self-consciousness itself is dependent on the experiencing of sense particulars (1981: 212).

Strawson also claims that for Leibniz there are infinitely many possible worlds, each separately capable of being described in universal terms without contradiction, and that for Leibniz the instantiation of one possible world does not logically entail either the creation or the non-creation of other possible worlds (IE: 130). That effectively voids a distinction between possibility and compossibility. But there are texts in which Leibniz clearly maintains that distinction. The universe is not a collection of all possibles, since not all possibles are compossible (Leibniz 1970: 662).[7] For Leibniz, there are many possible universes, each being a collection of compossibles, and he forcibly rejects as the "first falsehood" the claims of Descartes, Spinoza and Hobbes that everything that is possible is either past or present or future (*ibid.*: 273).[8] Jaakko Hintikka (1972) has argued that if Leibniz's logically based distinction between possibility and compossibility is to hold, then irreducible relations must necessarily obtain among the individual substances constituting an actual world.

Strawson explicitly denies his Leibniz the irreducible relations that characterize a single common world: there are private spaces, but no public space. But in a text that is not isolated, Leibniz himself maintains the reality of a single actual world:

> The mutual connection ... of all created things to each other ... causes each simple substance to have relations which express all the others and consequently to be a perpetual living mirror of the universe .... The infinite multitude of simple substances, which seem to be so many different universes, are nevertheless only the perspectives of a single universe according to the different points of view of each monad. (1970: 648)[9]

Like Strawson, Leibniz acknowledges the possibility of disembodied consciousness, but also in accord with Strawson he does not recognize separated consciousness entirely detached from any body. The finite monad is indeed the primary individual, and the further distinctions between mind and body are secondary.

In *Individuals*, Strawson is not primarily concerned with whether his Leibniz corresponds in all detail to the texts. His Leibniz is intended only to serve as a clarifying foil. It is true that from the voluminous body of Leibniz's writings it is possible to make more than one selection of texts and claim that this selection represents Leibniz's actual system, and Strawson is fully entitled to his own interpretation. It also seems true that there is another Leibniz, whose stance on the identity of individuals is in some ways not completely dissimilar to Strawson's own.

Part II: Logical Subjects

Chapter 5: Subject and Predicate (I): Two Criteria

To this point, Strawson has argued for the primary place of material bodies and persons among the particulars to which we make an identifying reference, with other kinds of particulars seen as secondary. He now sets out on a further investigation of the apparent connection between the idea of particulars in general and the idea of an object of reference or a logical subject. The initiating difficulty is that anything at all can be identifyingly referred to, can appear as a logical subject, can appear as an individual. It is necessary at the outset to keep in mind Strawson's distinct uses for "individual" and "particular". Particulars are individuals, but so are a vast variety of individuals other than particulars; for example, categories such as "quality", "characteristic", "relation", "sort", "species", "number" and so on are also individuals (IE: 227). We thus make identifying references to both particulars and categories as individuals. We may accept the uniqueness and the primacy of material bodies and persons among particulars, but there is the further question of whether particulars in general hold some special position among objects of reference or logical subjects.

The traditional doctrine that Strawson wishes to investigate holds that particulars such as "John", and universals such as "being married", and universals-with-particulars such as "being married to John", can all be identified through the use of referring expressions, and can all be logical subjects, while only universals and universals-with-particulars, and never particulars alone, can be predicated through the use of predicative expressions. If so, then there is thus an asymmetry of use between particulars and universals, and a functional antithesis between subject and predicate in propositions with two terms copulated. That antithesis has been forcibly denied, notably by Ramsey, for whom there is no essential distinction between the subject of a proposition and its predicate.[10] Strawson articulates Ramsey's objection, and then attempts to sort out the differences between that objection and the traditional doctrine.

That task requires a preliminary consideration of the subject–predicate distinction itself. Strawson will find two different criteria for making that distinction, the grammatical and the category, and between those two criteria he will find both tensions and affinities. If we can both find and explain a correspondence between the two, then we will have found the rationale for the traditional doctrine that Ramsey rejects.

The "Grammatical" Criterion

The traditional doctrine is that some terms can appear only as subjects while others can appear either as subjects or as predicates, and that in no proposition can the act of referring to something be an act of predicating that thing. Strawson's investigation of the merits of that thesis begins by listing certain distinctions between the two kinds of elements that combine to form a singular proposition of a fundamental sort. Those distinctions may be made in more than one way:

I. The functional distinction between (A) indicating something and (B) ascribing something to that something.

These two functions can be assigned to the linguistic parts of a statement, and that in turn yields:

II. The distinction of linguistic parts between (A) subject expressions and (B) ascriptive-expressions.

Distinctions I and II taken together suggest a further and *non-linguistic* distinction:

III. The distinction of propositional constituents between (A) subjects and (B) predicates.

The elements or roles in Lists I and II are exclusive, that is, the act of referring to something cannot be the act of describing it. In contrast, some of the elements of III can appear in either role in Lists I and II.

Strawson considers next the possibility of a List IV, in which the division exclusions of Lists I and II are preserved, while at the same time the elements on this new list are non-linguistic and in that sense correspond to the elements of List III. The distinction in List IV is thus a non-linguistic counterpart of the distinctions in List II. Borrowing Frege's terminology, the parallel distinction on List IV is between (A) object and (B) concept; a proper name can never be a predicative expression, although it may be part of one, for example, "is married to John".

Thus armed, Strawson begins the task of drawing an overtly grammatical distinction between A-expressions and B-expressions. Both kinds of expressions introduce terms, but they do so in distinctive ways. B-expressions introduce their terms in a propositional or assertive way. What such terms are introduced into is a proposition. In contrast, the terms introduced by A-expressions have no such implication; they are, for example, the forms we use if we simply want to make a *list* of terms, with no assertive aspect. Frege characterized the distinction between A-expressions and B-espressions on List IV by means of a metaphor. Objects are complete or "saturated", concepts are incomplete or "unsaturated", and at least one part of a thought must be incomplete or predicative if the parts are to hold together (IE: 152–3).[11]

It is only because the sense of "B-expressions" is incomplete that they are capable of serving as a link in a proposition. "B-expressions" appear fragmentary because they suggest a particular kind of completion, while "As" look non-fragmentary because they carry no such suggestion. It is essential in all of this to recall that the distinction made is between the styles of the introduction of terms, between assertion and non-assertion, and that nothing has been said up to this point about the distinction between particulars and universals.

A further qualification is necessary. A-expressions and B-expressions alike must introduce a term, that is, an A-expression or a B-expression must have the intention of distinguishing that term from all others, of identifying it. Compare "Peter struck a philosopher" to "Peter struck the philosopher". The expression "the philosopher" does distinguish and therefore counts as a singular term, but not so for "a philosopher". Thus indefinite descriptions such as "a philosopher" are excluded, as are the substantives of quantification, "everything" and "something".

The distinction thus made is between B-expressions, which are assertive and incomplete and that serve therefore as a link in a proposition, and A-expressions, which have none of those characteristics. But the distinction thus made seems to encourage precisely the scepticism of someone like Ramsey. It seems that we might undermine the whole distinction between A-expressions and B-expressions by simply assigning the linking function to something both conventional and separate from those terms, for example, by simply enclosing the subject and predicate terms within parentheses, that is "(Socrates Wisdom)". With that move, the essential difference between A-expressions and B-expressions is removed, and with Ramsey we might move to the conclusion that no fundamental distinction between universals and particulars can be made on the basis of an essential difference between subject and predicate. While Ramsey's scepticism may rest on simple instances of the subject–predicate distinction that do not adequately address the full complexities of our ordinary language, that scepticism does serve the function of requiring us to look beyond the grammatical distinction if we are to find a proper basis for the traditional doctrine, namely, that a particular can never serve as a predicate. That further search leads us to an investigation of the category criterion.

The Category Criterion

The grammatical version of the subject–predicate distinction holds that what is predicated is introduced by a part of the sentence that has a unique assertive role. It takes no direct account of a difference of type or category of terms. The category version is in contrast based on a difference of category or type of terms, notably the differences between universals and particulars.

Any term, universal or particular, can be assertively tied to another term to form a proposition. Any term can thus be thought of as a principle of collection for other terms, and it collects just those terms that, when it is assertively tied to any one of them, results in a true proposition. Strawson carefully distinguishes three types of assertive tying, ones in which the speaker:

(a) *instances* something as such and such, for example, "Fido is a dog".
(b) *characterizes* a subject as such-and-such, for example, "Socrates is wise".
(c) *attributes* something to something else, for example, "Plato is the teacher of Socrates".

Assertive ties may bind particulars to universals, universals to universals, and particulars to particulars. For the binding of particulars to universals, there is a distinction between instantial and characterizing universals, and hence between instantial and characterizing ties.

Instantial universals distinguish and count the individual particulars they collect, and do not provide any method for individuating those particulars. "Dogs" and "vertebrates" are universals for distinct sorts, but those terms do not themselves individuate the particulars they collect. This kind of universal is generally introduced by certain common nouns. *Characterizing* universals group and count only those individual particulars that are already distinguishable by some antecedent method. This kind of universal applicable to particulars is introduced by verbs or adjectives, for example, "smiles" or "angry". The power of characterizing universals to supply principles of grouping for particulars already distinguishable by some antecedent method is, however, a power they share with particulars themselves. Thus "utterances" can be further characterized or grouped by a universal, for example, "wise utterances", but they may also be characterized or grouped by a particular, for example, "Socrates' utterances". Socrates, like wisdom, can serve as a principle for grouping particulars. Strawson now assigns the name "the attributive tie" to those assertive ties that bind particulars to particulars.

With these distinctions in hand, Strawson is prepared to compare some of the ways in which terms collect each other. We find that one particular may be instantially tied to different sortal universals, for example, Fido is a dog, an animal, a terrier; and, in turn, the sortal universal dog collects Coco and Rover as well as Fido. One particular may also be characteristically tied to different characterizing universals, for example, Socrates is wise, warm, fights and talks, and, in turn, the characterizing universal "warm" collects particulars other than Socrates.

The attributive tie is different. Thus "Socrates" collects by characterizing ties a great number of universals: he is smiling, he is orating. By the attributive ties he also collects a great number of particulars: a particular smile, a particular oration. But while the universals "smiling" and "orating" can in turn collect, by the characterizing tie, many particulars of the same kind as Socrates, the particulars "Socrates' smiling" and "Socrates' orating" cannot collect, by the attributive tie, any other particulars of the same kind as Socrates:

> Let us express this feature of attributive ties by speaking of the dependent member and the independent member of any such tie; the independent member may in general collect many particulars similar to the dependent member, but the dependent member cannot collect any other particulars similar to the independent member. (IE: 170)

Strawson concludes that we may rule that universals can be predicated of particulars, but particulars cannot be predicated of universals. Universals can be either subjects or predicates, while particulars can be subjects but never predicates, although they can be parts of what is predicated, for example, "married to John".

Strawson's investigation of the distinction between subjects and predicates began with a consideration of the threefold grammatical criterion for that distinction: the predicate is introduced by an assertive symbolism, there is no assertive symbolism for the subject, and no category distinction is made between universal and particular terms. The investigation has now proceeded through the category criterion for which the distinction between universal and particular is central, no particular can appear as a predicate, and in which there is no reference to the location of the assertive symbolism. The grammatical and category criteria therefore appear independent, but there are affinities, since they seem to yield similar conclusions. If we can both find and explain a correspondence between these criteria, we will have a rationale for the traditional doctrine that particulars can appear in discourse as subjects only, and never as predicates, while universals can appear as either subjects or as predicates.

Strawson thinks that he can find and explain that correspondence, and that the general lines of his argument are clear and indisputable. He also warns us that its detailed explication is a subtle matter of great difficulty. The key to the correspondence between the grammatical and category criteria is found in the ways in which terms are introduced into propositions. Strawson begins by considering first the introduction of individual particulars into *propositions* and then the introduction of *kinds* of particulars into discourse.

The introduction of terms into propositions involves the idea of identification, that is, the question of which particular term or which universal term it is that is being introduced. For speaker and hearer alike, for an identifying reference to a particular to be made, there must be some true *empirical* proposition such that there is but one particular that answers to that description. Thus John may be identifyingly referred to by name and, if need be, both speaker and hearer must be prepared to substitute some true empirical proposition, which will be a description of John as a unique particular. That description may include demonstrative terms and, indeed, ultimately it must do so, since Strawson has argued that in the end a description made in purely universal terms cannot satisfy the condition that a successfully identifying reference must refer to just one particular.

There is no such demonstrative requirement for the introduction of a universal term. Knowing which universal is being referred to does not require knowledge of an empirical fact; it requires only knowing the language. And now we have a new criterion for the subject–predicate distinction, one that harmonizes with both the grammatical and the category criteria:

> We ... propose ... a new, or mediating, criterion for the subject–predicate distinction. A subject-expression ... presents a fact in its own right and is to that extent complete. A predicate-expression is one which in no sense presents a fact in its own right and is to that extent incomplete .... This new criterion harmonizes ... with the grammatical criterion .... We find an additional depth in Frege's metaphor of the saturated and unsaturated constituents .... The new criterion ... also harmonizes ... with the category criterion .... These considerations ... explain the traditional, persistent link in our philosophy between the particular–universal distinction and the subject–predicate (reference–predication) distinction. (IE: 187–8)

The crucial point for the whole of Part II of *Individuals*, and thus for a real understanding of the entire work, is thus found in the notion of completeness. It is here that we find the link between the idea of a particular and the idea of an object of reference or logical subject (IE: 12). Strawson concedes that the crucial idea of completeness remains vague, but he argues that expressions that introduce particulars must always carry with them some presupposition of empirical fact. Quine has argued in opposition that all "subject expressions" are superfluous because they can always be replaced by quantificational variables and predicative expressions, with the consequent elimination of all singular terms. Strawson finds Quine's argument circular in that it effectively presupposes precisely what it is intended to deny. Quine would eliminate all singular terms for particulars and have "their place" taken by the bound variables of existential quantification, but it makes no sense to say that those variables have the place they have if there is in fact no such place.

Chapter 6: Subject and Predicate (II): Logical Subjects and Particular Objects

The Introduction of Particulars into Discourse

For Strawson, the introduction of an individual particular into a proposition presupposes an empirical fact that itself involves the introduction or identifying reference to some particular. This introduction of particulars into a proposition is clearly set off against the introduction of universals into a proposition, where there is no presupposition of an empirical fact. We may now also attempt to think of a *general* theory for the introduction of *kinds* of particulars, or particulars in general, into our *customary* discourse.

Just as the introduction of a particular has a presupposition, so too does the introduction of a kind of particular. Every introduction of a particular carries a presupposition of empirical fact. The introduction of certain kinds of particulars has as its parallel condition the existence of facts of a presupposed kind, but the statement of those facts cannot in the end introduce any sortal or characterizing universals at all. At this point, the asymmetry between particulars and universals that was an essential characteristic of the presuppositions of individual particulars may appear to have been lost.

This confronts us with the question of how the theory that governs the introduction of particulars can complement the theory that governs the introduction of kinds of particulars while at the same time preserving the asymmetry between particulars and universals.

For the introduction of kinds of particulars, we shall have to find universals that are neither sortal nor characterizing. Strawson thinks there are such universals, termed *"feature-universals"*, for example, terms such as snow, coal, gold and water:

> *Snow, water, coal* and *gold* ... do not function as characterizing universals .... [They] are general kinds of stuff, not properties or characteristics of particulars; though *being made of snow* or *being made of gold* are characteristics of particulars. Nor are [these] universal terms sortal universals. No one of them of itself provides a principle for distinguishing, enumerating and reidentifying particulars of a sort. (IE: 202)

Such a phrase as "lump of coal" does introduce a sortal universal, but "coal" taken by itself does not. Thus while "coal" does not introduce a particular, it does provide the basis for such an introduction.

Strawson thinks that his argument about the introduction of *kinds* of particulars or particulars in general into discourse has a "speculative and uncertain character", from which his earlier argument about the introduction of particulars into propositions is happily both independent and free. But if we are prepared to accept both arguments, then they can be brought together to give us a certain logico-metaphysical picture. Here once again Strawson's basic view will be that particulars are complete in a way in which universals are not. There are both right and wrong ways of showing this.

A wrong way is to attempt to separate the unitary thought of a particular into the idea of the particular itself and the idea of a universal that it instantiates. In this way, "Socrates" is separated off as a "bare particular" for which there are innumerably many descriptions in universal terms. This way of the bare particular is the way of Locke, the path that leads to the notion of the particular subject as an unknown and unknowable substratum. This leads in turn to Hume's vain search for himself. For Strawson, the contrasting right way is to see once again that the introduction of particulars into propositions and into discourse depends on some empirical fact, while the introduction of a universal does not. The proposition taken *as a whole* individuates the particular, but does not introduce it. This individuation of the introduced particular is obtained by describing it as either (a) uniquely related to some other identified particular, or (b) uniquely exemplifying some combination of universal and demonstrative terms. We still need a theory to account for the introduction of *kinds* of particulars. We need a resolution that will exclude sortal and characterizing universals. Strawson finds this in the facts of a feature-placing kind that underlie our talk about the basic particulars, namely, about material bodies and persons.

Strawson's aim throughout Part II has been to find some basis for the subject–predicate distinction in the antithesis between "completeness" and "incompleteness", an antithesis that would serve to show the basis for the traditional association of the subject–predicate distinction with the particular–universal distinction. He is now prepared to sum up:

> We set up, as a paradigm for reference, as a paradigm for the introduction of a subject, the use of an expression to introduce a particular ... [namely] something which is both complete for thought in that it unfolds into a fact, and incomplete in that, so introduced, it is thought of as a constituent of a further fact .... We set up as a paradigm of description, of the introduction of a predicate, the use of an expression to introduce a universal ... [namely] something which has the same kind of incompleteness as the particular but lacks its completeness. (IE: 212)

It is evident that in our ordinary language about the world of our experience, the introduction of the ordinary concrete particular has a primary importance. Strawson has argued above that there are occasions in our ordinary discourse when we do dispense with particulars and their predicates and all sortal and characterizing universals in favour of corresponding feature concepts. Since we do this some of the time, we may well ask whether it would be possible to do it all of the time. That is to ask whether, consistent with our continuing to be able to converse about the world as we commonly experience it, a language without particulars is possible. It is evident to Strawson that this would require an enormous inflation of needed expressions and tortuous constructions. One particularly acute problem that would arise early in our search would be finding a way to provide these features with a particular location in space and in time. There may be such a way, but Strawson is content to leave the task to someone whose taste for ingenuity for its own sake exceeds his own. We come in the end to the not surprising conclusion that if we wish to say the things that we do say, then the introduction of ordinary concrete particulars into our language has huge advantages.

Chapter 8: Logical Subjects and Existence

Anything whatever can be identifyingly referred to; anything can appear as an individual. Particulars are individuals, but so are all manner of categories: qualities, properties, classes, kinds, numbers, propositions and so on. The variety is endless. Anything can be a logical subject.

A grammatical index of the appearance of an individual or subject in a proposition is the presence of some singular definite substantial expression, for example, a proper name, the name of a universal or a definite description. That raises immediately the question of the manner in which such expressions may also be said to exist, a question that reflects the ancient but evergreen debate between nominalists and realists.[12]

Consider "the man in the moon". We may say "The man in the moon does not exist", or "The man in the moon does exist". By the grammatical index, there appears to be a reference to an individual, along with an explicit affirmation or denial of that individual's existence. But the grammatical index is not infallible, since we cannot take "the man in the moon" as truly a referring expression, since that would presuppose precisely what the content of the proposition affirms or denies. Consider instead "The man in the moon lives on cheese". In this case, the grammatical index is not misleading. Here the reference is to an individual for whom there is no explicit denial or affirmation of existence, it is instead simply a *fact* that no such particular exists. So the first case, in which the existence of the man in the moon is explicitly affirmed or denied, is the interesting exception to the use of the grammatical index for the appearance of a singular definite substantial expression as an individual. There is no problem from a logical perspective in glossing that exception by construing the proposition as referring to nothing, and as saying merely that there is, or is not, just one man in the moon. We may conclude that while the grammatical index is not quite infallible, it is nonetheless generally a good guide. We need only use caution in exceptional cases.

Strawson agrees, however, that such an approach is likely to meet resistance from empirically or nominalistically inclined philosophers. The nominalist is opposed to allowing non-particulars to be individuals, to be logical subjects. He seeks to have his way by a reductionist programme in which we replace reference to non-particulars by quantification over particulars. In this programme, (a) "Anger impairs judgement" is replaced by (b) "People are generally less capable of arriving at sound judgements when they are angry than when they are not". In this case, the replacement seems natural enough. Thus states such as "anger" are poorly entrenched against the nominalist programme. So too are qualities (bravery), relations (fatherhood), activities (swimming) and even species (man). There are, however, other kinds of non-particular individuals that seem well-entrenched that are resistant to reduction. Strawson instances types:

> I have in mind, for example: works of art, such as musical and literary compositions ..., makes of thing, e.g. makes of motor-car, such as the 1957 Cadillac, of which there are many particular instances but which is itself a non-particular; and more generally other things of which the instances are made or produced to a certain design, and which, or some of which, bear what one is strongly inclined to call a proper name, e.g. flags such as the Union Jack. (IE: 231)

Those non-particulars that are types support a remarkable analogy to particulars themselves. Consider the instance of the Union Jack, which we may see as a *model particular*, a prototype serving as a standard for the production of other particulars. This way of seeing things tends quickly enough in the direction of a Platonic realism, in which the Idea is the model particular for all of the particular imitations in the sensible order. It is a direction that for Strawson has constraining limits, since if it is generalized to cover all non-particulars, it becomes "absurdly inappropriate".

While Strawson is no advocate of a Platonic realism, nor is he an advocate of an opposing nominalism. He has argued throughout for particulars to be taken as paradigm logical subjects, and that may seem to lean him in a nominalist direction, but once again there are constraining limits. There is a Platonist zeal, and there is a nominalist zeal, and Strawson rejects them both. He is thus brought in the end to questions that have been with philosophy since its earliest days: should non-particulars have the status of logical subjects? Do such entities exist? Here the apparatus of contemporary logic may seem to provide some immediate help. That logic reconstructs the question of existence and its association with logical subjects through the means of quantification. Thus, from "Socrates is wise" the explicitly existential statement "There exists something that is wise" can be inferred; "Fx", hence "$(\exists x)Fx$". The conclusion follows that whatever can be referred to by a subject expression may be said to exist, and conversely.

Reflection may enable us to see that this approach is too simple. It initially invites the question of why the apparatus of quantification should always be applied to subject expressions and never to predicate expressions. The logician would have it that a number of subjects are said to have a single constant predicate. What keeps us from an alternative structure in which a number of predicates are said to have a constant subject? What possible justification is there for the logician's preference? Following Russell, we can see an answer to this question by considering the ways in which the subject and predicate terms of a proposition are introduced. Consider a statement: "Socrates is wise". Why do we have

(1) "(... is wise) is sometimes true"

but not

(2) "(Socrates ...) is sometimes true"?

Recall now the different ways in which subject and predicate terms are introduced into a proposition. The predicate term "is wise" does not have an empirical presupposition. We understand the term quite aside from whether we think anyone is wise or not. It follows that (1) is a functioning part of a proposition, which as a whole does convey empirical information. But that in turn requires that the term "Socrates", performing its role as subject, presupposes an empirical fact known by both speaker and hearer. But in (2), there is no way in which "Socrates" can be a referring expression:

> To put the point crudely. That an already identified item, of whatever type, has *some* (unspecified) property or other, i.e., falls under *some* (unspecified) principle or other of collection of like things, is never news; that something or other unspecified has an already identified property, i.e., falls under an already identified principle of collection of things, is always news.   (IE: 237)

Acceptance of this conclusion gives rise directly to another fundamental question. When I say that Socrates is wise, why am I committed to the view that there exists such a thing as a wise man, rather than to the view that wisdom exists? The way to an unrestrained Platonism seems to lie open. The proper approach to that possibility is once again the comparison of the contrasting ways in which subject and predicate terms are introduced into propositions. If we simply concentrate on what *follows from* subject–predicate propositions in the way of existence claims, we get no reason for preference. But if we concentrate on what is *presupposed* by the use of these term-introducing parts of a proposition, the situation changes. A subject expression introducing a particular presupposes some empirical fact; a predicate expression introducing a universal does not.

A difficulty still remains. Particulars are indeed the paradigm for logical subjects, and now with Locke we may be tempted to adopt the view that the *only* things that exist are particulars. A resolutely reductionist programme would eliminate the presence of any non-particular individuals. If we take this path, however, an unrestrained Platonism is escaped only by the adoption of a similarly unrestrained nominalism. That is a path Strawson is unwilling to take, since he thinks that no programme to eliminate all non-particulars as subjects can be successful. He finds an alternative way, one that for him escapes the dilemma between Platonism and nominalism. Recall the statements that the man in the moon exists or that he does not exist. We have seen that the attempt to take "the man in the moon" as an identifying reference to a particular necessarily fails. By use of the idioms of existential quantification, we can avoid the snares that follow from such misleading attempts. The benefit of this approach is that it gives us an effective means to say that particulars exist without having to say that existence is a predicate of particulars. Every subject–predicate proposition entails one in which the subject expression is replaced by the existential claim "There exists something which ..." – "$\exists x$ ...". The converse is also true, that is, in every case of a true statement made through the apparatus of an existential claim, a true statement could be framed in which a term-identifying subject expression replaces the existential quantifier. To take this approach is to allow for the introduction of non-particular individuals into our discourse. Every existentially quantified statement can be reconstructed as a subject–predicate proposition in which the subject is a *property* or a *concept*, and the predicate term either affirms or denies its instantiation.

Summary

The central questions addressed in Part I of *Individuals* concern the ways in which reference to individuals and particulars is obtained in the practices of ordinary language. Anything whatsoever can be identifyingly referred to, can appear as a logical subject, as an individual. Thus particulars such as historical events, material objects and persons are individuals, but so too are such non-particulars as qualities, properties, numbers and species. Among particulars, material bodies and persons hold a central position, since they are basic from the standpoint of identification and reidentification. The notion of persons as primitive and underived is a necessary condition for the maintenance of our common membership in a non-solipsistic, spatiotemporal world of particulars.

Part II of *Individuals* is concerned with the linguistic complements to those metaphysical or ontological theses. Particulars are found to hold a primary place among individuals because they are paradigms for logical subjects. A joint consideration of the grammatical and category criteria for the introduction of subject and predicate terms into a proposition provides support for according a central place among individuals to material bodies and persons, and to saying that they are what primarily exist. That belief is one that is widely held among persons who are not deeply reflective: by the common man in the street. Strawson concludes that if metaphysics is the finding of reasons for what we instinctively believe, then what he has done is metaphysics.

Some critiques of Strawson's positions

One of the best early notices of *Individuals* is that by J. O. Urmson (1961). The issues he raises have remained central in the evaluation of Strawson's work, and time has justified Urmson's claim that *Individuals* was a book that would continue to influence philosophical discussion for some time to come. I also think that Urmson is correct in saying both that *Individuals* is a difficult book, and that it is made more so "by many sentences which, while logically and grammatically impeccable, are unnecessarily complicated in structure". At the same time, I also think that Strawson's prose is not always turgid, and indeed that at critical junctures there is a pithy directness, a helpful metaphor, and not infrequently a certain elegance of style.

Urmson finds Chapter 3, "Persons", both rewarding and inconclusive. He finds that, for Strawson, the notion of person is primitive, that is, there is a logically irreducible category of things to which certain predicates (thought, pain, perception) can be applied by the criterion of either the observation of others or one's own experience. But, for Urmson, there cannot be predicates "*P*" such that each of these two criteria can be a sufficient condition for applying "*P*" while at the same time holding that the two criteria are not equivalent. Strawson has rejected both Cartesian dualism and the no-ownership theory as accounts of mind and other mind, but Urmson finds Strawson's arguments in this regard unpersuasive, since there are many concepts for the application of which we have, illogically, two independent sets of criteria or sufficient conditions. Urmson instances personal identity, for which we sometimes use memory, and sometimes body-continuity. Normally, both conditions are satisfied, but conflict may arise, and we may well be puzzled. We shall presently see Strawson himself in *Freedom and Responsibility* reflecting on the ways in which we attempt to bring together ostensibly conflicting criteria.

In "The Primitiveness of the Concept of a Person" (1980), Hidé Ishiguro further investigates the two concepts of "person" and "primitive" as they are employed in *Individuals*.[13] On her interpretations, to say that "person" is a primitive concept is not to say that it is simple; it is rather to say that it is indispensable. To say that a concept is primitive is, moreover, not to say that it is absolute; its use is, instead, relative to some other concept, for example, the concept of a person is relative to the concepts of a mind and a body.

In considering this concept of person, Ishiguro finds helpful Leibniz's earlier distinctions among clear, confused and distinct ideas (Leibniz 1970: 91–4).[14] For Leibniz, an idea is clear if it suffices to allow us to recognize the thing represented. Clear knowledge is either confused or distinct. It is confused if we are unable to enumerate the various marks that distinguish the thing from other things, even though it may have such marks. This is the way we know colours and odours and all of the other objects of the senses. We cannot explain red to a blind person, nor may an artist be able to explain why this particular note or ending is the "right one". Distinct knowledge, in contrast, does enable us to enumerate the distinguishing marks; compare the contrasting ways in which a miner and a chemist identify the metal gold. For Ishiguro, our knowledge of persons may be similarly clear but confused in that sense. We are thus obliged to consider a person a person whether we like it or not; nor does this have to wait for the time when we recognize them as material bodies having certain M-predicates.

The fact that some people think they can talk with plants, fish or dogs does not for Ishiguro establish those things as persons. She thinks that a minimum condition of personhood involves the possibility of entering into a *mutual* relationship of that kind. She finds that in *Freedom and Resentment* Strawson calls such features of human life "shared reactive attitudes". Ishiguro would link such "shared reactive attitudes" with her idea that the concept of person is primitive in relation to the concept of a material body. She proposes to accomplish this in three steps:

1. We get the very concept of *person* by considering ourselves *and* other beings of the same sort as persons.
2. Thus we distinguish persons from other things without having to bother with saying what kind of material objects they are by means of some neutral physical features.
3. And it is in this *indispensable* way that we have the sortal concept of a person.

In reply, Strawson finds Ishiguro's most interesting point on the concept of person is her observation that in order to *be* a person, one must see oneself *and* others as persons, a point that he did not have in mind in *Individuals,* but one on which he thinks she is right.

Ishiguro makes one other point that Strawson also finds important. One of Strawson's purposes in *Individuals* had been to oppose the reductionism of the Cartesian dualist. Strawson thinks that while that reductionism is not in vogue at the present, there is another one that is both more popular and more plausible, namely, the view that we may reduce the notion of "person" to that of "living human body". But Ishiguro plainly holds that while the only persons we human beings have personal relations with are other human beings, the concept "person" does not in itself commit us to saying what kind of material object a person is by means of some neutral physical features. If we accept that, Strawson observes, then of course instead of identifying "person" with "living human body" we ought at least to have it identifying with "living personal body". In that event, "personal body" is plainly itself derivative from the primary concept "person". That would lend additional support to Strawson's campaign against the more popular and more plausible reductionism of the present.

Individuals was first published in 1959, and it was based on lectures given at Duke University, North Carolina, in the academic year 1954–55. The work has indeed stood the test of time in the sense that towards the end of his career, Strawson continued to support its major lines of argument and to see them as fundamental for his entire work. That is evident from his response to Chung M. Tse's article "Strawson's Theory of Subject and Predicate" (1998), written in November 1997.

> Professor Chung M. Tse shows great discernment in identifying what he calls "the soul" of my philosophy. Certainly, if any single

issue, or cluster of issues, can be said to be central to my thought,
it is precisely that of the metaphysical and epistemological foundations of the familiar logico-grammatical distinction between
reference and predication or subject and predicate.

(Hahn 1998: 383)

Chung's summary repeatedly cites *Individuals,* where Strawson has
argued both that the ontological distinction between particular and
universal provides the foundation of the logical distinction between
subject and predicate, and that among spacetime particulars, it is
enduring space-occupants that are primary. Universals taken as individuals may be identifyingly referred to, and if we take reference to be
the mark of existence, then on Chung's reading, Strawson's position
is that universals as well as particulars may be said to exist, "though
not in the same *sense* of existence" (*ibid.*: 384). Strawson's response
is to disclaim the reservation, since for him there is but one sense
of existence, although the vast differences between particulars and
universals may reflect a correspondingly great difference between the
implications of the two categories. In the end, Strawson himself recognizes the actual existence of two categories of entity: particulars and
universals. The existence of a particular requires having a particular
spacetime location; the existence of a universal requires no more than
the possibility of its instantiation.

The link to Kant

In *Individuals,* we see that, in the pursuit of an adequately descriptive general ontology, questions of formal logic, epistemology and the
practices of ordinary language are all inextricably tied together. The
whole work is a sustained effort on Strawson's part to search out the
presuppositions of the knowledge and experience that we undoubtedly
do have. That same touchstone of presuppositions is one that underlies all three of Kant's critiques, and so it was altogether natural that
in the years following the publication of *Individuals,* Strawson began
to lecture regularly on the *Critique of Pure Reason.* A consequence
of those lectures was his publication in 1961 of *The Bounds of Sense.*
This is a work in which the major themes of *Individuals* remain in
place, while Strawson continues to search for yet deeper insights into
the limits of what we can conceive of as a possible general structure
of our human experience.

Chapter 3

The Bounds of Sense: Kant's first Critique under analysis

The Bounds of Sense: An Essay on Kant's Critique of Pure Reason (1966a) builds on the questions and the answers that are central to Strawson's *Individuals*. In *Individuals*, Strawson had attempted to establish the conditions that are presupposed by the knowledge and experience we plainly do have. As we have seen, *Individuals* has its roots in the earlier *Introduction of Logical Theory* and "On Referring". In "On Referring", the use of the sentence "The king of France is wise" as a statement at this present time is neither true nor false, since its *presupposition* that there is a present king of France is false. Presupposition is thus carefully distinguished from both assertion and entailment, and in this way the critically misleading trichotomy framework of Russell's theory of definite descriptions is avoided. Taking into account the notion of presupposition in this way is a key to any properly descriptive account of our human experience; it is useless to argue for a point which is presupposed by the argument itself. This attention to the use of presupposition underlies all three of Kant's critiques, and so it was altogether natural that in Strawson's continuing reflection on the issues that he raises in *Individuals,* he found it rewarding to reconsider the major lines of the *Critique of Pure Reason*, and to offer an assessment of the strengths and weaknesses of Kant's work in the light of our contemporary analytic tradition.

The Bounds of Sense is a product of that reflection. Strawson makes no claim that this work is one of historical-philosophical scholarship. He observes that he has been both enlightened and mystified by Kant's effort to draw those bounds, and that he is seeking in the present work only to present a "clear, uncluttered, unified interpretation" of what he regards as the greatest single work of modern Western philosophy. To accomplish that, he provides an articulation of the *Critique*'s framework, and attempts to show both how its parts can be separately considered and how Kant himself conceives them to be related. Kant argues for a certain structure of presuppositions that he finds essential to any coherent and adequate account of our cognitive experience, and for the consequent incoherence of any attempt on our part to transcend our bounds of sense. In so doing, Kant intends to show the inadequacies of both his rationalist and his empiricist forerunners. Strawson will attempt a modification or reconstruction of Kant's basic lines of argument to make them more acceptable to those schooled in our contemporary analytic tradition. Strawson also finds that Kant's arguments are developed within the framework of a comprising set of doctrines that appear to violate Kant's own principles.

It is well to keep in mind Kant's own structure for the *Critique*:

- First Part: Transcendental Aesthetic
  Space and time identified as the forms of all of our intuitions
- Second Part: Transcendental Logic
- First Division: Transcendental Analytic
  Here the deduction of the concepts of the understanding is for Strawson both the heart and the most difficult section of the entire *Critique*. The concepts arise with the intuitions in establishing the bounds of sense, and thus the bounds of our possible experience. For Strawson, this is the constructive and positive face of the *Critique*.
- Second Division: Transcendental Dialectic
  This is Kant's dismantling of the illusions of traditional metaphysics. For Strawson, this is also Kant's attempt to transcend the bounds established in the Analytic.

In what follows, the section "Strawson's general review of Kant's *Critique*" is concerned with Strawson's general review of the entire work, the section "The Analytic: reconstruction and affirmation" is concerned with the "Transcendental Aesthetic" and the "Transcendental Analytic", and the section "The Dialectic: some illusions dispelled" is concerned with the "Transcendental Dialectic".

Strawson's general review of Kant's *Critique*

Kant had contrasted the steady and surefooted advance of knowledge in mathematics and the natural sciences with the results that had been attained in philosophy down to his time, the kind of contrast that had already been drawn by Descartes. Kant thought that the cure for philosophy's pretensions could only be found in the recognition that, while we can imagine worlds very different from our own, there are limits to what we can make intelligible to ourselves as a possible general structure of our actual experience. To set those limits is to hold that there can be no use of concepts that have no relation to the empirical conditions of their application. Concepts without their applicability to what is immediately given in sense experience are meaningless. Thus the long history of a transcendent metaphysics that would claim the knowledge of the world as it is in itself beyond the bounds of sense is simply a delusion. For Kant, a proper metaphysics will be one concerned instead with that conceptual structure that is *presupposed* by all empirical investigations. A critical philosophy must first set the limits on what it can hope to accomplish.

Strawson thinks that Kant is here close to the tradition of classical empiricism of Berkeley and Hume, one most clearly expressed in our times by Ayer. But that empiricism is a picture of a world of fleeting sense impressions, not Kant's view that the empiricist conception of experience makes sense only in the context of a general framework that includes the application to sense experience of concepts of an objective world. Philosophers as diverse as Descartes and Hume invite us to justify our common belief in an objective world by working outwards from the private data of individual consciousness; they have failed to grasp at the outset of their search the presuppositions of the very possibility of experience of any sort.

Strawson thinks that Kant's joint rejection of the classical forms of both rationalism and empiricism is "the blander, more acceptable face of the *Critique*" (BS: 29). But that acceptable face is accompanied by a set of more questionable assumptions. All of the presupposed limits that Kant would impose on our empirical knowledge are based on a strained analogy. We can make intelligible to ourselves the idea of our experience of the world only in the terms by which Kant draws his analogy between the particular forms of the human cognitive apparatus and the fundamental structure of those ideas. The idiom of the entire work is thus a psychological idiom.

For Kant, there is a duality between the forms of the sensuous intuitions of our immediate experience and the concepts under which those intuitions are subsumed. If any item is to enter our conscious experience, then we must be able to classify it in some way. We must have general concepts in order that empirical knowledge be possible. It is just as evident that if those general concepts are ever to be used, we must have material on which to use them. "Thoughts without content are empty, intuitions without concepts are blind" (*Critique*: A 51/B 75).[1] We experience a spatiotemporal world, and our time-oriented inner experience no more gives a knowledge of ourselves as we are in ourselves than does our space-ordered outer experience give us a knowledge of other things as they are in themselves. We have no knowledge of things as they are in themselves as contrasted with things as they appear to us. Our necessary ignorance of the supersensible from the standpoint of pure reason has, for Kant, the great merit of safeguarding the interests of morality and religion from scepticism.

Kant thinks that it is because our objects of experience must conform to the constitution of our minds that we can have the kind of *a priori* knowledge of the nature of experience that is demonstrated in the *Critique*. Strawson will find that while Kant certainly believed all of this in earnest, these doctrines are obstacles to our sympathetic understanding. Further obstacles include Kant's beliefs in the absolute nature of Euclidian geometry, Newtonian physics and Aristotelian logic, all reflections of the temper of his times. But Strawson thinks that Kant has much to teach us, and that we are able to dismiss those obstacles without anxiety.

Strawson finds both the heart and the most difficult passages of the *Critique* in the "Transcendental Analytic". There Kant tries to show the limiting features of any intelligible notion of our experience, and within this attempt Strawson distinguishes six general theses:

(a) the temporality thesis: experience essentially shows temporal succession;

(b) the necessary unity of consciousness thesis: there must be among our temporally extended series of experiences the unity that is needed for the possibility of self-consciousness;

(c) the objectivity thesis: experience must include an awareness of objects distinguishable from our experiences of them, that is, what is true of those objects regardless of our particular subjective experiences of them;

(d) the spatiality thesis: the objects referred to in (c) are essentially spatial;

(e) the spatiotemporal unity thesis: there is one unified framework for all experience and its objects;

(f) the analogies thesis: in the world of things in space, certain principles of permanence and causality must be preserved.

Strawson has varying judgements on the viability of these theses, but he thinks that the second thesis is in effect the premise of the Transcendental Deduction of the Categories, that section of the whole *Critique* that for Kant and for us is most difficult, but which is also one of the most impressive and exciting arguments in the whole of philosophy.

> The essential premise of the Analytic is ... the thesis of the necessary unity of consciousness .... [Kant] is concerned ... with the general conditions of the employment of concepts, of the recognition of the particular contents of experience as having some general character; and he regards these conditions as being at the same time the fundamental conditions of the possibility of ordinary or empirical self-consciousness. (BS: 26)

Strawson thinks this second thesis on the necessary unity of self-consciousness is surely acceptable, and that Kant's genius is nowhere more evident than in his making a fundamental condition of that unity the ability to distinguish between the temporal order of our subjective perceptions and the order that those objects of our perceptions independently have. Thus Kant's insistence on a general connection between an objective order and the necessary unity of consciousness was surely correct.

Kant took seriously both the duality of understanding and sensibility and the necessity of their cooperation in our experience, and he also thought that the general functions of understanding can be considered apart from sensibility. This led him to the "metaphysical deduction" of the categories. But in order to consider the ways in which those categories are applied in our experience, they must be interpreted in terms of the forms of our sensuous intuitions in space and time. That interpretation is provided in "The Schematism of the Pure Concepts of the Understanding". For Strawson, a modest knowledge of formal logic is enough to make us critical of both Kant's list of forms and his whole concept of their consequent derivation. It requires no logic at all to be astonished by most of the transitions from form to category, but unfortunately the list of the twelve categories remains to impose its artificialities on what follows in the *Critique*.

Strawson finds a further difficulty. Kant regards the necessary unity and connectedness of experience as a synthesis that is the product of the mind's own operations. But we can have no empirical knowledge of the truth of that claim. That would be to claim empirical knowledge of a condition of empirical knowledge, and Strawson finds this an aberration to which Kant was led by his explanatory model.

We can dispense with that model, and, on Strawson's reckoning still be left at the end of the Analytic with two commonplace theses following from what had already been said:

- the unified items of our experience are simply the experiences we ordinarily report about what we see, feel and so on, and no faithful report is possible without the concepts;
- the unity of those experiences is found in the general coherence or *consistency* of our ordinary descriptions of what we sense.

After construction comes demolition, and so after Kant's "Transcendental Analytic" comes his "Transcendental Dialectic", a section Strawson finds substantially easier to understand. Here we find Kant's exposure of what he regards as the metaphysical illusions of past philosophy. Kant argued that those illusions have a certain usefulness if they are regarded as "regulative": thought of "as if" they were actually so. Strawson thinks that argument implausible, although the general structure of the Dialectic enables us to see why Kant held this view.

Kant's exposure of those illusions has a systematic structure, one that allows him to engage in his favoured activity of architectonics or structure-building. We find this in "The Antinomy of Pure Reason" (B 454–89), where the claims of the classical forms of both rationalism and empiricism are discredited. Kant finds it characteristic of scientific investigation that it raises questions such that an answer immediately gives rise to another question of the same general sort. In itself, that is all very well, but the notion of a series of questions gives rise to the notion of the series being necessarily either finite or infinite, and that disjunction is the source of illusions of the antinomies. In the process of this dismantling, Kant also thinks that he finds a confirmation of his argument against the possibility of our knowing things-in-themselves as they are apart from the bounds of sense. Strawson thinks, however, that at this point Kant is closer to Berkeley than he realized.

In the antinomies, Kant finds "conflicts of pure reason with itself": conflicts between thesis and antithesis, between the claims of the rationalist and those of the empiricist. For Strawson, the validity of Kant's arguments used to derive the contradictions is questionable in the light of advances made in the physical sciences since Kant's time. Nonetheless, for the first two antinomies – on the beginning or the eternity of space and time, and on whether there are or are not simples in Nature – there is merit in Kant's idea of the regulative idea of an unlimited series setting a task that can never be completed. On the last two antinomies – on whether there is freedom, and on whether a necessary being exists – Strawson finds Kant less successful.

Kant draws a contrast between the phenomenal world of our experience within the bounds of sense and the noumenal world of things as they are in themselves apart from our experience. Strawson finds that thesis often unintelligible; Kant appears to be saying both that there is a supersensible reality, and that we can have no knowledge of it. But Strawson again finds merit in a negative sense of noumenon. A positive sense of noumenon would be the unintelligible claim that we are affected by a reality that is absolutely unknowable. A negative sense would be the salutary reminder that reality is not completely comprehended by our conceptual scheme.

Strawson concludes that in the end it is possible to disentangle Kant's metaphysical idealism from his brilliant setting of the bounds of experience, a setting that has not been bettered:

> In order to set limits to coherent thinking, it is not necessary, as Kant, despite his disclaimers, attempted to do, to think both sides of those limits. It is enough to think up to them. No philosopher in any book has come nearer to achieving this strenuous aim than Kant himself in the *Critique of Pure Reason*.   (BS: 44)

We come next to a consideration of Strawson's treatment on the Analytic, Kant's positive or constructive metaphysics of experience.

The Analytic: reconstruction and affirmation

Part II.I: Space and Time

Strawson observes that four great dualities dominate Kant's theory of our human experience: appearances and things as they are in themselves; intuitions and concepts; the *a priori* and the empirical; inner and outer. All four appear in the "Transcendental Aesthetic", but the second or epistemological duality of intuition and concept is the dominant one. In Kant's terminology, intuitions are direct or immediate experiences. Our empirical knowledge will comprise intuitions of particulars that, through concepts, we classify as instances of general kinds or characteristics. Intuitions without concepts are blind, and concepts without intuitions are empty. Thus the cooperation of both intuitions and concepts is necessary for our empirical knowledge. That leads Kant directly to his doctrine that space and time are exclusively the forms of our intuitions, that is, our immediate experiences, since any particular instances of any general concept will occur "*somewhen*", and any instances that can be found will be found *somewhere*. Spatio-temporal location provides the way in which we are able to distinguish between two particulars of the same general category or type.

With this analysis of the relation between intuition and concept in hand, Strawson turns next to Kant's duality of *a priori* and empirical. If there is a set of ideas that enters indispensably into the structure of any account of experience we could make intelligible to ourselves, then that set is *a priori*. The set of less general ideas that are not indispensable for all of our experiences is the empirical.

Kant's doctrine holds not only that space and time are the forms of our intuitions, but that they are *a priori* forms as well. That may seem subject to challenge since, while the claim that all of our experience has a temporal aspect appears to be beyond question, we may well wonder whether a similar priority is necessarily assigned to the spatial. But Strawson recalls the chapter on a "sounds-only, no-space world" in Chapter 2 of his *Individuals*, and the extraordinary difficulties we would face in any attempt to make intelligible to ourselves such a framework for the knowledge that we undeniably do have. He notes that while in the "Transcendental Aesthetic" Kant does not argue for or explicitly assert the necessity of a spatial ordering of our experience, he will later assert it in the "Refutation of Idealism" and the "General Note on the System of Principles". Kant's arguments for that position are not, in Strawson's judgement, wholly satisfactory. He thinks it is better to argue simply that the possibility of our experience requires at least *some* mode of sensible ordering other than the temporal, and that in the end we have no viable alternative to the spatial.

The account of the "Transcendental Aesthetic" given thus far constitutes what Strawson calls "the austere interpretation" (BS: 47) in which there is a modest and restricted use of the term "*a priori*". A central purpose of *The Bounds of Sense* is to separate what Strawson regards as sound doctrine in the *Critique* from the doctrinal fantasies of "transcendental idealism". To effect that distinction, Strawson considers Kant's claim that "the spatial and the temporal are the modes in which we become aware of particular instances of general concepts as ordered in relation to each other" (BS: 52). Taken in itself, that statement reveals a telling ambiguity. It may mean that space and time are how instances are ordered, and *hence* the way in which *we* are aware of them. Or it may mean that space and time are *our* ways of becoming aware of instances, and *hence* the ways in which they are ordered. Plainly, the second alternative leans heavily in the direction of subjectivity.

For Strawson, we ordinarily say that in our intuitions or direct experiences we are affected by objects. We are in this way accustomed to distinguish between our perceptions and the objects on which they are dependent. So far, so good, but Kant wants more. He would have it that space and time are *nothing but* our forms of intuition. We have no knowledge of things as they are in themselves other than that they are not spatiotemporal. At this point, the sober statement that space and time are how the instances of our experience are ordered gives way to the startling claim that space and time are simply our ways of becoming aware of particulars.

We might argue against Kant that while we may know nothing of objects as they are in themselves, surely we do know directly the events of our own consciousness. Kant's counter is that we know nothing of ourselves or our minds as they are in themselves, and that time is just the form of our inner experience as space is the form of our outer experience. We may properly speak of an empirical self-consciousness, under the condition that it is no more than the mere appearance of ourselves as we really are. "[Time] is the immediate condition of inner appearances (of our souls) and thereby the mediate condition of outer appearances .... All appearances ... whatever necessarily stand in time-relations" (A34/B50–51).

Strawson finds that the ambiguity in Kant's account now comes clearly into focus. Kant holds both to the transcendental ideality of the forms of space and time and to their empirical reality. Space and time are the presuppositions of all of our experience, and they have no application to things as they are in themselves. Kant claims to find here the basis of what distinguishes his account from that of Berkeley, for whom "bodies are mere illusion" (B71), but Strawson finds instead that Kant's distinction is not as clear as he thinks. Kant may seem to be claiming that space and time are on an equal footing, both being effects of things in themselves, but on Strawson's reading, Kant's real doctrine is that they are *not* on an equal footing:

> Rather, *all* the actual effects of these transactions between things-in-themselves are temporally ordered states of consciousness; but these include ... states of consciousness that we rate as perceptions of bodies in space. So space and time, bodies and states of consciousness, are not really on the same footing at all. The point

> may be obscured for us (and for Kant) by his insistence that all things in space and time are equally appearances; but ... states of consciousness, ordered in time, are appearances because they are merely effects of things as they are in themselves and not of some such things (ourselves) as they (we) really, atemporally, are. But bodies in space, ... are not even effects of things as they are in themselves. It is simply that among the effects of [those] things are some states of consciousness which we are constrained to regard as perceptions of bodies in space; and apart from these perceptions bodies are nothing at all.   (BS: 56–7)

What arguments does Kant provide to support the "doctrinal fantasies of transcendental idealism"? Strawson finds the provided arguments both elliptical and weak. Kant's argument is basically derived from his view of the nature of geometry, what he calls "the mathematics of space", with his argument about time being simply a fainter parallel of his view about space. Kant sought to free himself from the Newtonian encumbrances of space and time as independent existences (A39–41/B56–8) by regarding them as systems of relations among the particulars of our experience. Kant argued that to avoid the unacceptable conclusion that it is merely contingent that the propositions of geometry hold for space-ordered objects, it is necessary to conclude that space and time have their source in our minds alone. For Strawson, Kant is ultimately able to claim only that space and time are the modes in which we become aware of the particulars of our experience as they are related to each other, a claim that leaves us with the ambiguity of interpretation on which Strawson has already remarked.

Strawson finds Kant also declaring that there is only one space and one time, and that both are infinite. To that we might object that clearly we can form the notion of different spaces, for example, the space of a bottle in my mind's eye compared to the space to which that bottle belongs, but that objection would miss Kant's point. For him, the class of spatially related items, all of which are related to each other in a single comprehensive system, is the class of public physical bodies, and a parallel argument can be made for the unity of time. We have thus the notion of a single spatiotemporal system that comprises all that happens and all that physically exists. Kant claims that space and time are *a priori* intuitions but, for Strawson, the claim again rests ultimately on an unsatisfactory argument from geometry.

Strawson concludes that the "Transcendental Aesthetic" does include a number of theses that we may readily accept: (a) particular states of consciousness are temporally ordered; (b) those states include perceptions of items conceived of as existing independent of those states and ordered both spatially and temporally: (c) space and time are unitary. Those unexceptional theses are intertwined by Kant in a transcendental idealism with its unsatisfactory claim that space and time are said to be *a priori* intuitions.

Part II.II: Objectivity and Unity

The cooperation of sensibility and understanding is necessary for our human experience, as is the excitement of those faculties by things as they are in themselves. Kant has provided in the "Transcendental Aesthetic" an account of the *a priori* forms of sensibility, and now in the "Transcendental Logic" he attempts to provide those of understanding, that is, "the form of the thought of an object in general" (BS: 73, referring to A51/B75). The word "object" here is critically important. For Kant, there must be types of general concepts, and these types are the categories, the pure concepts of the understanding. Thus "object" here means more than merely a particular instance of a general concept, it carries instead the connotations of "objectivity".

In pursuit of those categories, Kant looks first to structures of formal logic. Strawson finds this approach initially attractive, but one that collapses on closer examination. Kant's starting-point in the Logic is again the observation that all empirical knowledge requires the cooperation of sensibility and understanding. That knowledge is expressible in propositions that are either true or false. Each of these propositions must have some of the general forms of formal logic, but those forms abstract from all content of empirical knowledge. Formal logic concerns the relation of any knowledge to other knowledge, not the relation between its forms and objects. "Transcendental Logic" will deal with the latter.

At this point in the argument, the space and time forms of sensibility are not invoked. But we do bring to the objects given in sensibility "forms of particularity", or general concepts, all given in a vocabulary parallel to that of formal logic, namely, of true and false, and of the traditional quantificational modes. In this way, we come to the twelve categories of the understanding, all arranged in triads under the headings "quantity", "quality", "relation" and "modality".

Strawson notes that Kant's approach has some fundamental limitations. Kant claimed a complete list of primitive or underived pure concepts, but the logician's choice of what is primitive and what is derivative *is* a choice. For example, while the general idea of quantification cannot be defined in the terms of propositional logic alone, there is a choice between universal and existential quantifiers as primitive or defined.

Our current logic places a high value on parsimony, and so Strawson thinks we are not likely to go far astray if we take that logic as the guide in a search not for fundamental logical forms, but for fundamental logical ideas. For our logic today, there are two fundamental ideas – truth-functional composition and quantification – but *how* those ideas are employed in concepts remains an open question. All the special forms of truth-functional composition can indeed be derived from the notion that a proposition is either true or false but not both, while quantification can be arrived at through the use of one of the two quantifiers together with that truth-functional composition. However, at this point a fundamental difficulty of application becomes apparent:

> "[R]eferring" [these two] general notions of truth-functional composition and of quantification "to the conditions of determining judgements as objectively valid" can yield nothing in the way of "*a priori* concepts of an object in general" *which is not already contained in the notion of a singular subject-predicate proposition,* i.e. a formally atomic proposition in which a one-or-more-place predicate is applied to one or more specified objects of reference. If, then, we are to make *any* use of the clue provided by formal logic, it is to this single notion we must turn .... Following the clue from logic ... will consist in asking the following question: How in general must we conceive of objects if we are to make empirical judgements, determinable as true or false, in which we predicate concepts of identified objects of reference? What in general must be true of a world of objects of which we make such judgements? (BS: 81–2)

It now becomes apparent that we have thus far made no progress towards answering the very question with which our investigation began: how are we able to make judgements of true or false about objects of reference? Our consideration of the forms of logic as a likely source has yielded nothing. However, this is not for Strawson a counsel of despair. Whatever the shortcomings of Kant's effort to secure a "metaphysical deduction" of the categories from the forms of logic alone, it remains worthwhile to consider the next move that Kant makes in his overall approach, and to consider sympathetically what we might yet be able to learn from him. That brings us directly to the "Transcendental Deduction of the Categories".

The Deduction is not so much an argument as it is an explanation, a description, a story. For Kant, the space and time forms of our sensuous intuitions and the categories of our understanding need no arguments to support their reality. Our awareness of objects must be spatiotemporal, and our thinking about those objects must be in accordance with those categories, simply because that is how we human beings are constituted. Kant's purpose in the Deduction is not to argue for what is evidently so; rather, he proposes to give an explanation that will make comprehensible both the relation of understanding to sensibility and the objective validity of the categories.

We begin with the distinction between a merely subjective awareness of objects and our awareness of objects we commonly think of as having an existence of their own apart from our awareness of them. For Kant, we cannot be aware of noumenal objects, things as they are in themselves; we can experience only their appearances. And so, to maintain the distinction between subjective and objective appearances, we will need a surrogate for the noumenal, and this Kant finds in the notion of connectedness among the appearances of sense experience. While we have "unruly" perceptions, ones that break the unity that prevails among our other perceptions, we also have perceptions that cohere with the general run of experience, ones that we take as informing us about how the world objectively is. The notion of our *experience of objects* can have neither more nor less meaning than this. Moreover, Kant thinks that experience without such connectedness is not so much as possible, and he bases that contention on the tautology that experience belonging to a single consciousness must indeed satisfy the conditions of belonging to a single consciousness. Strawson concludes that the burden for Kant's entire argument is thus placed on the notion of the necessary unity of consciousness.

Kant sometimes expresses that necessity by saying simply that it must be possible for "I think" to accompany all of my perceptions if they are to count as mine. That unity of consciousness is not ordinary empirical self-consciousness taken as a given fact; instead our proper concern here is to search out the conditions that would establish *the very possibility* of such a consciousness. If different experiences are to be said to belong to the same consciousness, then there must indeed be the possibility of *self*-consciousness: a single consciousness performs the acts of synthesizing by means of the concepts of the understanding, and the identity of this consciousness must be known to the subject of the experience. But to say that is to state the problem, not to solve it. We still need an explanation of *how* it is possible for a series of diverse experiences to belong to a single consciousness aware of its own identity. Strawson thinks that in the Deduction Kant fails to provide that explanation. Kant's thesis of synthesis rests ultimately on his distinction between the roles of sensitivity and understanding in our empirical knowledge. For him, sense data in themselves are without connection, and all connection is provided by the imagination under the control of the concepts of the understanding. Strawson finds the validity of those claims surely open to challenge:

> It is useless to puzzle over the status of these propositions. They belong neither to empirical (including physiological) psychology nor to an analytic philosophy of mind, *though some of them may have near or remote analogies in both*. They belong to the imaginary subject of transcendental psychology. (BS: 97)

Setting the claims of transcendental psychology aside, Strawson remains open to the possibility that we may yet gain insight from Kant's synthesis thesis: from the claim that for a series of appearances to belong to a single consciousness, they must be connected in a way that constitutes a unified objective world. For Kant, a single consciousness must have the ongoing possibility of saying that all of his ongoing experiences are *his* experiences, and in this way "unitary consciousness" is linked with "self-consciousness". That experience, that empirical knowledge, is in turn possible only if objectively valid judgements are possible. Kant's position may evidently be challenged, since we might maintain that no distinction can be drawn between the order and arrangement of objects and the order and arrangements of a subject's experience of them, so that impressions neither require nor permit being "united in the concept of an object". Strawson finds that what Kant himself saw as his way out of this difficulty is plain enough:

> The way out is to acknowledge that the recognitional component, necessary to experience, can be present in experience only because of the *possibility* of referring different experiences to one identical subject of them all. Recognition implies the *potential* acknowledgement of the experience into which recognition necessarily enters as being one's own, as sharing with others this relation to the identical self. It is the fact that this potentiality is implicit in recognition that saves the recognitional component in a particular experience from absorption into the item recognized (and hence saves the character of the particular experience as an *experience*)

even when that item cannot be conceived of as having an existence independent of the particular experience of it.   (BS: 101)

Kant's argument is intended to support both the necessity of the "I think", which is capable of accompanying all of the perceptions of a single consciousness, and the necessary objectivity of experience. The very notion of *experience* requires us to make a distinction between "this is how it seems to me" and "this is how things are", the distinction between the subjective and the objective, and that distinction requires both a unitary knowing subject and an objective order. For Strawson, the merit of the argument is that it is detached from Kant's synthesis thesis and the imaginary subject of his transcendental psychology.

It might be objected that this self-ascription of experience needs a criterion of identity for such subjects and hence that it makes them objects of intuition, objects perceptibly belonging to a common world. Strawson observes that this need in practice is met by the fact that each of us is in fact a corporeal object. We may be reminded here of Strawson's position in *Individuals* of the primacy of the concept of *person* as an individual having both corporeal and mental characteristics. Kant does not make use of this concept. His reply to the objection is instead to observe that this very need of a criterion of identity makes it necessary that each knowing subject should have *his* own experience of the world, and this notion of a diversity of subject experiences is possible only because of the attendant notion of an objective order. There is thus a necessary duality here, a doubleness that connects the two notions of self consciousness and the objectivity condition. While Strawson has no faith in either Kant's derivation of a list of categories from the forms of judgement or his theory of synthesis, Strawson does find reason to entertain favourably the general conclusion that whatever is a *necessary* feature of experience is so because of the *subjectivity* of its source. Fortifying that general conclusion will have to depend on arguments less abstract than those of the "Transcendental Deduction" but, with a fairly definite hope, Strawson next turns his attention to the "Analytic of Principles".

Part II.III: Permanence and Causality

Part II.III.3: Permanence

There are philosophers who would deny the very possibility of what Strawson hopes to find in the Principles. It has been argued that Kant's entire enterprise rests on his assumption of the Newtonian physical science of his day, an assumption not shared by the quantum and relativity physics of our age. While Kant can be seen as exemplary in the way that he made explicit the presuppositions of the physics and indeed the social and moral customs of his age, thus serving well as a model for the metaphysician of today, there is no way in which his Principles can give us detailed and intelligible statements for those generally necessary conditions that make possible any experience of an objective reality. Strawson argues in reply to those philosophers that even if we grant that Kant wrongly assumed the scientific thinking of his day as the condition of thinking in general, it does not follow that there are no such conditions, nor that Kant did not come close to realizing them. A consideration of the Principles in that light remains a viable and hopeful proposal.

In the Deduction Kant has argued for the necessity of some connection among experiences to make of them the experiences of an objective world. The section of the Principles that affords the single best exposition of this thesis is found in the "Analogies of Experience", where the general principle is that "experience is possible only through the representation of a necessary connection of perceptions" (B 218). Two other sections in the Principles are also helpful. The "Refutation of Idealism" contains the anti-Cartesian thesis that self-consciousness is possible only through the perception of outer objects, and the "General Note on the System of the Principles" argues similarly that any use of the notions of substance, cause and community must be able to apply them to outer or spatial objects.

In the Analogies, Kant seeks to place this necessary connection of perceptions in a spatiotemporal order. That order is not one assumed as a premise drawn from the argument of the "Transcendental Aesthetic"; rather, it is now freshly argued for. Strawson thinks that Kant has here the remarkable insight that what is needed fundamentally is a way to distinguish between objective and subjective time-relations, between the time-relations among the objects of our perceptions and the time-relations among the perceptions themselves. If that distinction fails, so too does the distinction between subject and object, with the attendant collapse of the possibility of an empirical self-consciousness and thus the very notion of experience itself. If the distinction *can* be made, then the conditions of that distinction are necessarily the conditions of the possibility of experience. For Strawson, it is promising to consider what elements of this line of argument remain viable.

His investigation begins with Kant's "Refutation of Idealism", with his anti-Cartesian thesis that self-consciousness is possible only through the perception of outer objects. Kant's announced purpose here is to prove a conservation principle that would make the quantum of substance in Nature a constant, but Strawson sees that as no more than an unsupportable gloss on Kant's underlying, promising and indeed viable contention of the necessity of something permanent in perception.

We distinguish between subjective time-relations and the objective time-relations in which the objects themselves have the relation of coexistence or succession, which are independent of our perception of them. We must perceive some of those spatially ordered objects as *enduring* objects, hence the framework is by necessity spatiotemporal. The objects endure, even if our perceptions of them do not. We are able to identify objects as numerically the same in the absence of our continuing perception of them. In this we have the concept of permanence. Kant's own exposition of this argument is apparently one with which he was not happy. Strawson attempts to make the main point more cogently. Think of a series of representations, the members of which are temporally ordered with each other. That in itself is not enough to make intelligible the idea of *the subject's awareness of himself as having this experience* at this particular time.

> To give content to this idea we need, at least, the idea of a system of temporal relations which comprehends more than those experiences themselves. But there is, for the subject himself, no access to this wider system of temporal relations except through his own experiences. Those experiences, therefore, or some of them, must be taken by him to be experiences *of* things (other than the experiences themselves) which possess among themselves the temporal relations of this wider system. But there is only one way in which perceived things or processes can supply a system of temporal relations independent of the order of the subject's perceptions of them ... viz. by *lasting* and being *re*-encounterable in temporally different perceptual experiences. Awareness of permanent things distinct from myself is therefore indispensable to my assigning experiences to myself.... (BS: 127)

In the reconstructed argument thus far given, there is no indication that the objective order must be spatial as well as temporal. But Kant may reasonably say that we have no alternative, that our experience must include not only "here" but also "now". There are also Strawson's own familiar arguments against the viability of a "no-space" world.

For all that to be possible, we need in turn empirically applicable concepts of persistence and identity for objects we do not continuously observe. We may choose to call such concepts "concepts of substances".

Part II.III.4: Causality

Only if it is possible to distinguish between objective and subjective time-relations can we have that notion of an objective permanence that alone can make intelligible the very idea of experience. For Kant, time-relations of whatever sort are fundamentally of two kinds: relations of succession and relations of coexistence. This raises the question of whether successive perceptions could have occurred in the reverse order. Apparently they could not: the succession is *not* order-indifferent. In contrast, if a persisting things has parts, then our successive perceptions of the parts *is* order-indifferent. Kant thinks that the distinction between order difference and order indifference is the only criterion for the distinction between succession and coexistence. Strawson thinks that while Kant's distinctions do seem to hold both for the perception of successive objective events and for the perception of coexistent objects, the use that he makes of those distinctions in the service of the concept of causality is plainly open to challenge.

In the second analogy of experience – "The Principle of Succession in Time, in accordance with the Law of Causality" – Kant advances the idea that we could not have these empirically applicable concepts of objective change and coexistence without the notions of order necessity and order indifference, and that those notions in turn have no application unless the relevant causal principles are in place. Strawson can only find in the argument of the second analogy a "numbing grossness". Here Kant shifts the application of the word "necessary" and he alters its sense by substituting one kind of necessity for another. The argument of the third analogy is even less satisfactory. Strawson finds here only "a disreputable play": with the notions of reciprocity and mutual determination.

Despite Kant's failures, Strawson remains hopeful that out of all this something can be salvaged from the materials Kant provides, since it is surely true that some of his theses are right. The very notion of experience does indeed require the distinction between subjective and objective time-relations. This in turn requires that there are currently unobserved objects of *possible* perception coexisting with objects of *actual* perception, that there is an identity of sometimes unperceived objects across time. For Strawson, it is also right that such objects are ordered in a framework of relations that alone can give sense to the notion of the particular identity of an object, and that the only such viable framework will be spatial. Thus established is the need for concepts of persistence and the existence of *re*identifiable objects in a common spatial framework. We may add to the idea of *unperceived* objective coexistence the idea of *perceived* objective existence or *change*. Change is, however, recognizable only against a background of persistence, since without some persistencies we would have a change *of* objects rather than a change *in* objects. Change differs from succession.

The very idea of experience requires a distinction between objective and subjective time-relations, and we can now see that this distinction in turn requires that our concepts of objects must provide for the idea of change. Thus there are limits that must be reflected in the concepts we have of objects, and these concepts are linked with sets of conditional expectations. For every kind of object, the note of persistence is struck when we expect that an object will not change unless ..., or that it will change unless ..., and that is to say that our concepts of objects are linked with sets of conditional expectations. Concepts of objects are always compendia of causal law-likeness conditions, and without these compendia no experience of an objective world is possible, and without that objective world the very notion of experience falls.

On that basis, Kant argued invalidly for the law of universal causality, a set of strictly sufficient conditions for every change that we can recognize. In opposition, Strawson argues that we can retain the idea of an objective world even in the case of an object in which there is a change that is inexplicable under the law-like expectations contained in our concept of the object. We cannot maintain Kant's iron-clad law of universal causality, but Strawson thinks we can retain conditions that are less rigorous and yet indispensable:

> The most that we can say about these two absolute thoughts – of *strictly sufficient* conditions for *every* objective change – is not that they are necessary thoughts, but that they are natural hopes. They do not represent, in our equipment of concepts, absolutely indispensable elements in terms of which we must see the world if we are to see an objective world at all. They represent, rather, a heightening, an elevation, a pressing to the limit of those truly indispensable but altogether looser conditions which I have argued for. (BS: 146)

Central to Kant's refutation of Berkeley's idealism is his distinction between the phenomenal world of our experience and the noumenal world of things as they are in themselves. Strawson finds merit in Kant's notion of a negative noumenon taken as a salutary reminder that reality is not completely comprehended by the human conceptual schema.

The implications and difficulties of this Kantian thesis that from the standpoint of pure reason we are and must remain ignorant of things as they are in themselves has understandably been open to a wide variety of interpretations. Strawson is well aware of interpretations other than his own, and he has often responded to them. A notable example occurs in his note on Rae Langton's *Kantian Humility* (1997), a work that he finds "a most interesting, impressive, and scholarly exercise in Kantian interpretation" (Strawson 2003a: 9).[2]

On Strawson's reading, Langton sees the source of Kant's humility in his steadfast conviction that there does exist a phenomenal world of things as they are in themselves, things about which we remain necessarily in an ignorance we may vainly regret. Our vanity would dispense altogether with that reality beyond the bounds of sense. On Langton's interpretation of Kant, those things in themselves do affect our sensibility, indeed they are what make the knowledge we have possible, but they do so only by way of their *extrinsic*, causal, relational properties, not by their *intrinsic* properties. We remain, without vanity, in an ignorance of those intrinsic properties.

Langton admits a difficulty in her interpretation. Kant makes space ideal; it is the mind itself that contributes the form of our sensuous intuitions of things external to the mind. If that claim is accepted, then we are faced with a ready challenge to the actual existence of an objective material world independent of our experience. If that challenge is in turn upheld, then we are apparently reduced to Berkeley's idealism, and that is a doctrine that Kant himself explicitly and forcefully rejects. Langton has a favoured response to the challenge:

> The solution she finds most satisfactory consists in drawing a distinction: the dynamical forces that constitute bodies are genuinely objective properties, but relational not intrinsic properties, of things as they are in themselves; space, though its source is subjective and hence spatial relations are ideal, is simply the *form* in which we have intuitive awareness of real dynamical relations; *spatial* relations are ideal, but they make *experience* of real dynamical relations possible. (*Ibid.*: 10)

Strawson thinks that there is a further difficulty in Langton's interpretation, one that she does not address. Her concern is with space as the form of the objects of our outer sense, but she does not take into account the question of *time* as the form of the objects of our *inner* sense. The contents of the flow of our perceptions are certainly not intrinsic properties of anything as it is in itself, neither can those contents have those properties of things of the outer sense that are the subject matter of the physical sciences, and yet without those contents of perception no *experience* of the world external to the mind is possible. For Langton's interpretation to succeed, she would need to find in addition to the dynamic properties of bodies some real but extrinsic properties of things in themselves that could constitute minds. Strawson thinks that no such properties are forthcoming.

As we have seen above, Strawson himself does not fail to address the question of subjective and objective time-ordering in their relation to mind or empirical consciousness, and what is for him the consequent viable contention of the necessity of something permanent in perception.

With the conclusion of the "Transcendental Logic", the constructive aspect of the *Critique* comes to an end. In the Aesthetic and the Logic, Kant attempts to set forth the necessary framework of our thinking about the world of empirical reality. What follows in the "Transcendental Dialectic" is his matching destruction of metaphysical illusion. Before turning to an account of that demolition project, it is useful to consider in sum Strawson's evaluation of Kant's constructive effort. That evaluation may well be seen as both a destruction and a reconstruction. We have seen that Strawson finds much of Kant's argument to be built on both unwarranted assumptions and grossly mistaken reasoning. But after much sifting, Strawson also finds in the *Critique* a residue of positions that in both viability and foundational significance establish its place at the summit of modern philosophy.

That residue includes at least the following. All of our experience takes place in temporal and spatial orderings that are unitary. The very notion of "experience" requires a distinction between subjective and objective spatiotemporal relations. That in turn requires concepts that provide persistencies for objects conceived as having an identity across time that is independent of our perceptions of them. Those persistencies are rooted not in a Kantian ironclad rule of causality, but rather in our law-like expectations, which are sufficient to maintain the needed distinction between the objective and the subjective.

The Dialectic: some illusions dispelled

Part III.I: The Logic of Illusion

The Dialectic is in the first place a demolition project, concerned to make plain the illusions of a transcendental metaphysics. Strawson finds that Kant wants more than demolition. In the Dialectic he is attempting to support four further theses: the rejecting of materialism and atheism; the establishing of a basis in morality of what speculative enquiry cannot provide; the regulative use of some of the ideas we cannot know for the direction of our enquiries about sensible experience; and a new proof of transcendental idealism. But Strawson will in the end conclude that all Kant is able to accomplish is the demolition of the illusions of transcendental metaphysics, and that his efforts to secure the four additional theses are implausible and fallacious.

Kant locates the source of the illusions in the three syllogistic forms of traditional logic: categorical, hypothetical and disjunctive. According to Kant, we have in each case a natural tendency to look for completeness in the series of conditions for a given conclusion. We see each member of the series as conditioned by the next member, but to see the series *as a whole* means identifying something that is not itself conditioned by any other member of the series. It is natural to assume that the unconditioned is an ultimate member of the series. The alternative and less natural assumption is the unconditioned totality of an *infinite* series. Thus either there is a final term or there is not, but with either alternative we allow ourselves the further and unwarranted assumption of an actual application for the concept of *the series as a whole*. This is the idea of the absolutely unconditioned, and it is this idea which is the source of our metaphysical illusions.

In describing the dialectical process in this way, Strawson restricts his description to Kant's four antinomies, and effectively to just the first two, namely, on whether with regard to space and time the world is finite or infinite, and on whether there are or are not simples. Strawson thinks that Kant finds in these antinomies four features that range over all of our metaphysical illusions: (a) we are *inevitably* led to the ideas of the series as a whole; (b) these ideas have an *absoluteness* or *ultimacy*; (c) these ideas are *transcendent* of any possible experience, there are no empirical grounds to choose between finite and infinite; and (d) these ideas have nonetheless a *regulative* power to direct empirical enquiries that will never be complete.

Kant thought that he could extend the application of those four features from the cosmological field of the first two antinomies to the ideas of rational psychology and speculative theology in the third and fourth antinomies. For Strawson, Kant's argument for a parallel between the cosmological and the psychological makes virtually no headway. It is true that the Cartesian conception of soul is without empirical foundation, but Kant fails utterly to show how that is parallel to reason's demand for series completeness; nor can he show how the idea has any directive utility. Kant's argument for a parallel between the cosmological and the theological fares a little better. The idea of God provides scope for the notions of the absolute and the ultimate, but we are neither *inevitably* led to this idea by the search for systematic unity nor is the enterprise of natural science *necessarily* conducted in its light.

Strawson sees in Kant's Dialectic both success and failure. In the demolition of the illusions of transcendental metaphysics, he provides us with positions that in both viability and foundational significance place it at the summit of modern philosophy. In his efforts to secure new and fruitful alternatives, he fails. Strawson now proceeds in specific detail to measure the degrees of success and the failure in the three critical areas of rational psychology, cosmology, and speculative theology.

Part III.II: Soul

Descartes's starting-point, which he assumed to be beyond all possible doubt, is the thinking self, an immaterial and persisting substance, completely independent of body or matter. Kant's counter-claim is that all of our experience arises with sensuous intuition, and such an intuition of a persisting immaterial subject of experience is unavailable. This is the source of the illusion of rational psychology. The Cartesian psychologist confuses the unity of experience with the experience of a unity. We have seen that Kant has argued earlier in the *Critique* that the very notion of experience requires a unity of a temporally extended series of experiences. That requirement is no warrant for the existence of a unitary subject of those experiences. The Cartesian self is without foundation in our empirical experience.

Strawson finds that while Kant's exposure of the illusions of a Cartesian self is brilliant and profound, it needs some serious supplementing, a reconstruction that Strawson now attempts to provide in schema.

1. The possibility of an empirical self-consciousness requires that a temporally connected series of experiences should have the unity and connectedness secured by the distinction between the subjective and the objective. A unified *objective* world makes possible one *subjective* or experiential route through that world, an autobiography.

2. The empirical concept of such a subject of experience is that of a *person*. Strawson thinks that, while it is implicit in Kant's position that any use of the concept of a subject retaining identity across time requires an empirically applicable criterion of identity, he barely alludes to the fact that our notion of *personal* identity carries with it an essential reference to the human body. The allusion occurs in B 415: "Its [the soul's] permanence during life is of course evident, since the thinking being (as man) is itself likewise an object of the outer senses".

   In a footnote (BS: 164), Strawson drily observes that the topic of personal identity has been well discussed in recent philosophy, and that he takes the matter to be well understood. Readers of *Individuals* will recall Strawson's own stress on the primitiveness of the concept of a person:

   > [A] type of entity such that *both* predicates ascribing states of consciousness *and* predicates ascribing corporeal characteristics, a physical situation &c. are equally applicable to a single individual of that type. (IE: 101–2)

3. In cases of immediate self-ascription, no criteria of self-identity are ever invoked; for example, it would make no sense to say "This feeling is anger, but is it I who am feeling it?"

4. In such cases, "I" can be used without criteria and nonetheless still be a subject since in practice the links with empirical criteria are not completely severed.

5. While the links are not in practice severed, in philosophical reflection there is a temptation to do so. Kant sees clearly that we may succumb to the temptation of attending only to the inner contents of consciousness and thereby come to the illusion of a Cartesian self.

6. Strawson agrees that Kant makes a merely minimal reference to the empirical criteria for subject-identity, and that he says instead that the delusive use of "I" *expresses* that transcendental unity of apperception that the whole notion of experience requires. Strawson thinks that in his own present reconstruc-

tion he has remedied a flaw in Kant's argument. He also thinks that Kant's use of "expresses" does have a measure of viability. Kant can indeed hold that there are necessary conditions of self-consciousness without saying what all of those conditions are, and the delusive thought of a Cartesian self does retain the idea that there are in fact such conditions.

7. Strawson concludes that Kant has delivered the *coup de grâce* to Cartesianism, and that the attack might go further than Kant has taken it. For example, why might there not be a plurality of consciousnesses that, in the absence of outer criteria, might all have the same content and thus be indiscernible? Here once again we can hear an echo of Strawson's *Individuals*, in his account of Leibniz's monads (IE: 17–36).

Strawson thinks that Kant's successful attack on Cartesianism can be accepted without reference to Kant's transcendental idealism and its absolute division of noumena and phenomena. Kant thinks instead that the two are tied, and that his exposure of the illusions of rational psychology would be blocked if we could indeed in this case step beyond the phenomenal and enter the noumenal.

A challenge to Kant's position may be raised. To say that the spatial and temporal things of our experience are appearances only is in effect to say that they are dependent on things as they are in themselves, apart from our experience of them. But if supersensible realities are completely unknown, then how is it possible for Kant to speak of outer objects as they are in themselves, and of ourselves as we are in ourselves? Kant's rejoinder is that *within* phenomena a necessary distinction is drawn between bodies in space and the successive experiences we count as states of ourselves. There is indeed a dependence of both bodies and states of consciousness on the supersensible, but that distinction between the outer and the inner is proper to the phenomenal world only. The world of things as they are in themselves may very well be homogeneous.

For Strawson, further consideration makes the weakness of that response evident. What Kant intends in the "I think" of the unity of apperception is not just the connectedness of our experiences, it is also the point of contact between things in themselves and the phenomenal. For Kant, each human subject is the source not only of the categories but also of our sensibilities, the source of all the world's structures is in *us*, but for Strawson that makes sense only if that subject is somehow connected with what we ordinarily understand by ourselves. It seems therefore that a good bit *can* be known about the noumenal self, although it is not what the rational psychologist had supposed:

> In a quite extraordinary clause Kant writes: "The being that thinks in us is under the impression that it knows itself through pure categories and precisely through those categories which (in every type of category) express absolute unity" (B 402). To that extent the "being that thinks in us" appears to be deluded. But if the being that thinks in us is under the impression that its understanding affects its sensibility in the production of a temporal succession of connected perceptions, feelings and thoughts (including this one), then, apparently, the being that thinks in us is not deluded at all, but absolutely right! (BS: 174)

Part III.III: Cosmos

In "The Antinomy of Pure Reason", Kant attempts to show "the conflicts of reason with itself". For each of the four antinomies, he provides a thesis and an antithesis: purportedly valid arguments that are seemingly exhaustive alternatives and at the same time mutually exclusive. In the first two antinomies, the ones dealing with the cosmological issues of space and time and simples, the consequence that pure reason seems thus divided against itself is taken by Kant to be the result of an attempt to transcend the bounds of sense through an entry into the noumenal. This provides an indirect argument in support of the thesis of transcendental idealism, the pivotal distinction between phenomena and noumena.

In the first antinomy, the thesis holds that the world has a beginning in time and is spatially finite, while the antithesis holds that the world is infinite in both time and space. Kant pledges himself to the correctness of the proofs offered, but Strawson finds those arguments plainly invalid. On that basis, Kant's antinomy must fail in its purpose.

Kant's thesis argument for time having a beginning is rooted in the unjustified assumption that counting must have a start. The argument that the world is spatially finite is similarly deficient. The antithesis arguments are no more satisfactory. The claim here is that the world must be finite in time, since if it had a beginning, there could be no reason for its beginning at one time rather than another. For

Strawson, that antithesis claim rests on the unwarranted assumption that the critical question of why the world began when it did is in principle answerable.

The question "Why did it begin when it did?" allows for a variety of interpretations. When asked about an ordinary course of events, the question has two external characteristics. Consider the question, "Why did the Civil War begin when it did?" The question of "when" is placed within an external framework of the history of a nation or a world, and it seeks a reason why it occurred at this time rather than earlier or later in that framework. In his presentation of the antithesis claim, Kant exploits the idea that if we are talking about the existence of the world taken as a whole, no such external criteria are available, and hence that it correctly follows that the world is infinite in time. Thus there are formally valid proofs for both thesis and antithesis, and pure reason in its illusory attempt is faced with the antinomy.

For Strawson, the absence of any external criteria in response to the question of why the world began when it did has led Kant to an unwarranted conclusion:

> It is tempting to conclude at once that the supposition that it might have begun at some other time is as empty of meaning as the supposition that its external temporal relations might have been different; that it is, indeed, just the same as this empty supposition. This would indeed confirm the Kantian point that there can be no explanation of the world's beginning when it did and not at some other time. But it would confirm it by showing that there is nothing to explain; and thus deprive the point of any force it might seem to possess. (BS: 179)

The second part of the antithesis of the first antinomy argues that if the world were *spatially* finite, it would be limited by a surrounding empty space, but "empty space" is meaningless: the world is spatially infinite. That argument deserves little comment, since to say that the world *in* space has some relation *to* space is senseless.

For the second antinomy, the thesis holds that every composite, every space-occupying material thing, is made up of simples, while the antithesis holds that there is nowhere anything simple. The argument for the thesis is based on the unwarranted assumption that for material composites the composition must be theoretically removable. The argument for the antithesis is weaker still. It assumes that whatever is extended is not simple, and that whatever occupies a space is extended.

If we were to take Kant's arguments for the theses and the antitheses to be valid, then we would be drawn to the conclusion that the legitimate cosmological questions of mutually exclusive alternatives that they raise can never find a solution in our empirical experience (A 484/B 512). For Strawson the arguments are themselves invalid, but he constructs four possible interpretations of those arguments with the hope once again of finding from Kant's efforts a residue that will have some contemporary viability.

For the general form of Kant's own stated solution to the problem of the antinomies, Strawson identifies four propositions, where each of the first two is false, and each of the last two is true:

(1) The series exists as a limited whole.
(2) The series exists as an infinite whole.
(3) If the series existed as a whole, it would exist as a limited whole.
(4) If the series existed as a whole, it would exist as an infinite whole.

For Kant, it will follow that things in space or time must be appearances only and not things in themselves, and this will in itself constitute an indirect proof of his transcendental idealism. Strawson notes that this summary account of Kant's position is ambiguous. He has deliberately made it so to allow for all of the three interpretations that he will now consider.

(a) On a strong interpretation, it only seems that there are things in time and space at all. It is not just that there are no series existing as either a limited or infinite whole, it is more radically the case that there are no series at all. Strawson finds this strong interpretation so distant from Kant's text and intent that it merits no further consideration.

(b) On a weak interpretation, to say that things in space and time are only appearances is *not* to say, as does the strong interpretation, that there only appear to be space and time things. There are in fact such things. The point in saying that in their being they are only appearances is to avoid saying that they have characteristics "in themselves" quite apart from any that appear to us. This is Kant's familiar distinction between the phenomenal and the supersensible. Moreover, these things may indeed appear in a space or time ordering as members of a series. I may meaningfully talk in an empirical way about the series of stones in the path that leads to my front door, or the temporal series of Plantagenet kings. There *is* in our empirical experience serial ordering, and the illusion comes only from our supposing that because we have the concept of a series, we have in *every* case the concept of a whole series. There are cases where we know the series to be terminal and hence finite, but the world *taken as a whole* in not such a case. Here the thoughts of both finite and infinite wholes are equally empty. Such concepts cannot be given in our experience no matter how extensive that experience may be.

The illusion of the antinomy thesis comes from emptying the legitimate class of a finite series from all possible empirical content. The illusion of the antinomy antithesis comes from applying the concept of an infinite series in mathematics to the world of empirical subject matter. To search in science for ever more remote members of a series is a legitimate activity, but to suppose that the series must be either finite or infinite is illusory. Therefore, on the weak interpretation, propositions (1) and (2) are false, or, more precisely, they are empty of content.

If and only if we vainly free ourselves of restriction and take the view that things in space and time are things as they are in themselves do the disjuncts of finite and infinite in propositions (3) and (4) become irresistible in their incompatibility. Strawson finds Kant's claim that (3) and (4) are true to be merely capricious.

This weak interpretation is attractive, and we might well wish that it were Kant's, but Strawson thinks that it is not. It secures Kant's central thesis of transcendental idealism only by weakening it.

(c) The third or mixed interpretation has a certain affinity with the idealism of Berkeley. The central thesis of this interpretation is that there is one temporal series that is real: that of our inner states. Our representations have no outer existence of their own; they are nothing over and above our perceptions. If serial orderings of things in space or time did exist external to us, they would indeed be either finite or infinite. However, in the successive perceptions of our empirical investigations they do not so exist, and we may conclude that in our experience a series is finite only if we can experience the end, and infinite only if we can explore infinitely far, but we can do neither.

Strawson finds this mixed interpretation very close to Kant's intention in the Antinomies. Nothing, apart from the unknown and unknowable world of things in themselves, exists apart from our perceptions. However, this interpretation does not fit in with the Analytic, and it presents two further problems. The first concerns the need for a justification for the central thesis that our perceptions are real and exist in themselves, a thesis the strong interpretation rejects. The second concerns the need for a justification for the view that past generations also had perceptions, a justification that would not simultaneously be evidence of the existence of the generations themselves in space and in time apart from out perceptions of them. The absence of such a justification would bring us to the brink of solipsism. That is a doctrine Kant does not accept, but we are nonetheless, on this interpretation, led to that brink.

Kant supposed that these cosmological questions raised the problems and led to the solutions given in the Antinomies. Having surveyed Kant's failures, Strawson is now prepared in conclusion to consider the questions in their own right. For Kant, the problems arise out of attempts to settle the issue of whether the series involved in the cosmological questions are finite or infinite. Kant thinks these questions are empirically undecidable, and he concludes that they must be dealt with philosophically.

One counter to that approach is to hold that the questions are *not* empirically undecidable, and in that light to advance revisable theories that can be submitted to empirical tests. A second counter would be simply to declare that the series *is* indeed finite or infinite, but that we shall never know which is the case because the universe is independent of our means of observation of it. Both of these counters see the alternatives of finite and infinite as genuine alternatives. A third counter would side with Kant in rejecting these alternatives, but, in opposition to Kant, it will do so in the following way. Suppose that for the series involved we fix on some definite unit of measurement for distance or duration, and then ask the question about the spatial extent or temporal duration of the universe in terms of those units. As far as *a priori* possibilities are concerned, there would be an infinite number of possibly true answers. That would *not* be to say that a possible answer would be "an infinite number". That answer would be senseless, while an infinite number of answers done in terms of finite units would be possibly true. This third counter agrees with Kant on the emptiness of the infinity alternative, but, *contra* Kant, no member of the set of possible answers is senseless, since all members are subject to empirical disconfirmation. And now, Kant's antinomy is gone:

The two-limbed finite-infinite disjunction disappears: the finite limb is as empty as the infinite limb, for no limit is set to the possibilities in declaring the cosmological series to be finite. In its place we have the infinite disjunction with no empty limbs at all. On the question whether an answer corresponding to one of its limbs might not be, in principle, empirically confirmable as well as empirically refutable, the upholder of this doctrine is not, as such, required to take up a position. He could consistently adopt either view. (BS: 202)

The actual advances of science since Kant's day show further limits to his approach. Today's sub-atomic physicist does not assume that every "simple" is subject to a further and progressive "decomposition". Theoretical advances in physics do not have to take the series molecule–atom–electron as the only model. The effort to find an improved theory to cover empirical facts might instead find a complete reconceptualization more satisfactory. Again, Kant's assumption that the geometry of physical space is Euclidean is questioned today. It may well be that our empirical observations are best accommodated by a theory making the geometry of physical space non-Euclidean, so that physical space is finite, with the consequence that the universe in space is also finite. In the light of those scientific advances, Strawson sets these three counters to Kant's position alongside the "weak interpretation" of Kant's own solution, and concludes that, from this perspective, no one of the three counters can claim unqualified support from the facts.

The weak interpretation is one that Strawson thinks we might have hoped, vainly, to be Kant's own. A central issue here is the relation of Kant's transcendental idealism to what Strawson refers to as Kant's principle of significance. Kant's idealism holds that the whole of Nature, including states of consciousness, is merely appearance. In comparison, his principle of significance holds simply that there can be no meaningful use of concepts that does not relate them to the empirical condition of application. A consequence of the weak interpretation is that Kant's idealism is reduced to an affirmation of the principle of significance, and that is a reduction that Strawson thinks Kant himself would not accept, since Kant had mistakenly held the opposite view: that the principle of significance is a consequence of transcendental idealism.

Perhaps we should say that the cosmological questions, as framed by Kant, neither have a clear meaning nor are completely devoid of meaning. They serve to hold open the field of empirical inquiry, though not, or not only, in the way in which Kant supposed they did. They leave it open for the framing of testable theories of kinds unforeseen by him, which might in a sense be said to embody answers to the questions, but only by quite transforming the look of them. Kant offers ... complementary impossible tasks to the imagination and draws far-reaching metaphysical conclusions from their impossibility. Yet physical theory may transformingly occupy ... the field of those impossible tasks. From the standpoint of the philosophical critic, one thing at least is clear: Kant was mistaken in his belief that it was a field on which a decisive battle could be fought, and decisive victory won, for the doctrines of transcendental idealism. (BS: 205–6)

Part III.IV: God

Strawson turns next to the fourth antinomy in which the conflict is between "the thesis [that] there belongs to the world, either as its part or as its cause, a being that is absolutely necessary, [and] the antithesis [that] an absolutely necessary being exists nowhere in the world, nor does it exist outside the world as its cause" (A 452).

In the first two, or mathematical, antinomies, Kant finds that the thesis and antithesis, as incompatible, are both false, since both wrongly presuppose that the involved series exist as wholes. In the third and fourth, or dynamical, antinomies, there is a significant difference. Here the thesis also is false since it wrongly presupposes the involved series to be whole, but the antithesis does not make that presupposition. From this, we might expect Kant to conclude that the antithesis is true: that there is no freedom and that there is no necessary being. That is not Kant's conclusion. Instead, he claims that when correctly interpreted, both the thesis and the antithesis may be true. In the third antinomy, that all is nature is true for phenomena, but that there is freedom may be true for the transcendental ground. Similarly in the fourth antinomy, that there is no first cause is true for the phenomenal, but that there is a being that is absolutely necessary may be true for the transcendental.

Kant's rationale for coming to this solution lies in his commitment to his transcendental idealism with its critical insistence on a distinction between the phenomenal and the noumenal. For Kant, the appearances of the phenomenal world must have a noumenal ground:

If ... we ask ... whether there is anything distinct from the world which contains the ground of the order of the world ... the answer is that there *undoubtedly* is. For the world is the sum of appearances and there must therefore be some transcendental ground of the appearances, that is, a ground which is thinkable only by the pure understanding. (A 695–6/B 723–4)

For the first two, or mathematical, antinomies, which deal with questions of the size of temporal or spatial extent, if the unconditioned is to be found anywhere, it must be found in the sensible phenomenal world. But for the third and fourth, or dynamical, antinomies, we may be properly concerned with the transcendental and unconditioned ground of the sensible order itself. For Strawson, this Kantian solution to the problem of the dynamical antinomies must fail. For the third antinomy, from Kant's own standpoint in the "Analytic of Principles", "cause" is indissolubly bound up with time, so that any application of that concept to the transcendental is systematically impossible. For the fourth antinomy, from Kant's own standpoint in the "Postulates of Empirical Thought in General", "material necessity in existence" is applicable only to what is causally determined by empirical laws. Thus, for Strawson, Kant's argument is "preposterous ... redundant and irrelevant" (BS: 212).

The solution we might have expected for the dynamical antinomies is plain enough, namely, that the thesis is false since it wrongly presupposes the involved series to be complete, while the antithesis does not make that presupposition, so that the antithesis is true, with the consequence that there is no freedom and that there is no necessary being. We have not far to look for the source of Kant's deviation from that solution. It has nothing to do with the demands of pure reason; it is instead rooted in the interests of practical reason, that is, morality, where Kant finds the absolute categorical imperative presupposing both freedom and an unconditioned God.

Morality aside, what of Kant's effort to produce a metamorphosis from "cosmological" to "transcendent" ideas, to claim the legitimacy of referring to the non-sensible as a way of satisfying the understandable if misguided "demand of reason for the unconditioned" (BS: 219)? For Strawson, Kant cannot expect to reconcile directly the claims of thesis and antithesis in the third and fourth antinomies; he must instead attempt to divert the demands of the thesis so that a form of accommodation between the two becomes at least possible. Thus, Kant is not saying that from the standpoint of pure reason the demand can actually be met; he is saying only that the possibility exists.

Kant holds that this ideal of pure reason is characteristically sought in two ways. We first think of all the particular existing objects in our world as not only belonging to some class of things but also as having a sum of individual properties that go beyond class identification. We think of the sum total of all the properties of all the objects, and then we think of an unlimited super-reality that corresponds to that sum, a reality that is the ground and source of all.

The aims of natural science have the same tendency. We are served and receive direction by thinking of the world *as if* it owed its existence to a supreme intelligence acting in accordance with wise purposes. This idea has a regulative or heuristic purpose only:

> We misapprehend the meaning of this idea if we regard it as the assertion or even the assumption of a real being to which we may proceed to ascribe the ground of the systematic order of the world. On the contrary what this ground which eludes our concepts may be in its own inherent constitution is left entirely undetermined. (A 678–9/B 706–7)

Kant is now ready to expose the source of the illusions of transcendent philosophical theology as they are manifest in three traditional arguments: cosmological, ontological and teleological. In the cosmological argument, the idea of a non-contingent ground of contingent existence is the main power behind the claimed knowledge of God's existence. Kant is indeed committed to the claim that there exists a being free from causal dependence on anything else, but he is firmly opposed to the cosmological argument that would support the notion of a first cause, since it attempts to advance the powers of pure reason beyond the sensible.

The ontological argument seeks to overcome the inadequacy of the cosmological argument by replacing the distinction between contingent and non-contingent existence by a distinction drawn from the logical modalities of existential propositions. In a familiar form of the ontological argument, only that whose existence cannot be denied without self-contradiction is necessary, the concept of the supremely real includes existence, hence the supremely real or God necessarily exists. Strawson finds Kant's rejection of this form of the argument conclusive. Kant effectively argues that to form a concept is one thing, but to call it instantiated is quite another. No concept can guarantee its instantiation.

There remains the teleological argument: the argument from design. Kant shows a "tenderness" for this attempt, but it too fails.

We find in works of art a unity in variety, the harmonious subordination of parts to a whole, we know this to be the product of an intelligence invested with power, and by analogy we apply what we know about human works of art to the structure of nature itself. Kant finds this a suspect analogy but, even if accepted, at most it would show an intelligence and a power ordering *given* materials in accordance with *given* laws. It would thus yield not a creator God, but only an "architect of the world".

With the failures of these three arguments of transcendent metaphysics, Kant will have recourse in the second *Critique*, the *Critique of Pure Practical Reason*, to the presuppositions of the moral law as the way to establish a theology of reason. Kant thus finds that his treatment of the illusions of traditional philosophical theology is more than just a demolition. The removal of the old structure simultaneously opens ground for the new. Pure reason as foundational for our empirical knowledge is secure within the bounds of sense, but what it cannot affirm beyond those bounds, it also cannot deny. Its systematic separation from the demands of morality provide for their peaceful coexistence.

In an evaluative vein, Strawson would set aside whatever demands morality may be said to make on questions of a philosophical theology. He would also set aside the claims of Kant's transcendental idealism, its notions of a transcendental non-sensible ground of all sensible appearance, its unitive divine purposive intelligence and power, and its particular version of an "absolutely necessary" existence. With that considerable pruning in hand, Kant's treatment of the issues in the Dialectic would centre on two main ideas: (a) the ideal of completeness and systematic unity in scientific explanation; and (b) the concept of empirically unconditioned or non-contingent existence.

The first of these ideas Strawson finds profoundly authentic. This is for Kant a regulative principle only, used with the hope of continuously approaching but never finally achieving completeness and systematic unity. With regard to the second idea, we may advance the idea that everything in the world may be contingent on some other thing, but the world *as a whole* cannot itself be contingent, since with the rejection of transcendental idealism, there is nothing for it to be dependent on. Adopting this point of view would answer any felt need to support the attitude engendered by the notion of a unitive divine purpose:

> Once transcendental idealism has been laid aside, there is no
> obstacle to accepting Nature or the world-whole itself – empirically

unconditioned existence, all-embracing reality – as the object of such an attitude. How could enquiring human reason find a more appropriate object for its admiring and humbly emulative devotion than that which is at once the inexhaustible topic of its questions and the source of its endlessly provisional answers?

(BS: 230)

Strawson notes that Kant himself seems to show some sympathy with this idea, but that he would surely find a fully developed version in the manner of Spinoza alien to his own thought and perhaps morally repulsive as well.

Strawson's own conclusion is that any attempt to see from the standpoint of reason the idea of an extra-mundane world-directing intelligence is simply a pardonable indulgence based on a kind of fatigue of reason or a reversion to a comforting model. Of course, whatever the merits of the arguments and counter-arguments may be, the reader may well wonder whether such other-minded philosophers as Alvin Plantinga would find themselves either fatigued or comforted.

Part IV: The Metaphysics of Transcendental Idealism

At the end of this lengthy and closely detailed account of the first *Critique*, having identified in the Analytic Kant's enduring and foundational insights, Strawson is now prepared to complete his own *coup de grâce* to the illusions of transcendental metaphysics as they appear throughout the Dialectic. This demolition is unqualified and ruthless.

To this end, Strawson now raises questions about a number of interconnected doctrines of that idealism. Are these doctrines mutually inconsistent, or are they inconsistent with other parts of the *Critique*? Are they "perversions" of more intelligible positions? Does Kant in effect successfully avoid the pitfalls of the phenomenological idealism of Berkeley while establishing the viability of his own empirical realism? Can all of these doctrines of transcendental metaphysics be jettisoned while preserving the valued insights of the Analytic?

Strawson identifies eight such doctrines.

- There exists the supersensible world of things as they exist in themselves. We are affected by that world, and the outcome is experience.

- That experience has two elements: the matter-producing and the form-producing.
- The physical world is nothing apart from our perceptions.
- Experience yields empirical knowledge of physical nature and empirical knowledge of the states of oneself.
- The contents of experience are the *appearances* of things as they are in themselves.
- We have no *knowledge* of things as they are in themselves.
- We do have a non-empirical knowledge of things as they are in themselves in so far as that is independent of the particular contributions of the matter-producing element. Thus we have the geometrical knowledge of space and bodies in space, and the requirements of conceptualization-in-general of temporal data.
- That non-empirical knowledge is only of *appearances*.

For Kant, these doctrines are supportive of further claims. He thinks they support the demands of morality, since the discrediting of all claims to an empirical knowledge of the transcendental ground of appearances cuts two ways: pure reason can neither affirm nor deny statements about that supersensible world. On Kant's view, that leaves room for morally based convictions about that world rooted in pure practical reason. Strawson counters that few will think that the ideal of moral justice is an adequate basis for that belief.

The principle of significance requires no use of the concepts of the understanding apart from the empirical conditions of their application. Kant claims that this principle is a consequence of that doctrine of transcendental idealism that holds that the physical world is nothing apart from our perceptions. Strawson observes that this one particular doctrine, taken simply in itself, is properly called phenomenalistic idealism. Strawson's counter to Kant's claim is that the principle of significance, which he finds admirable, is one that may be held by philosophers who accept a phenomenalistic idealism apart from Kant's transcendental excrescences, or by philosophers who have no commitment to a supersensible reality or its supposed effects.

Strawson will also reject Kant's claim that transcendental idealism supports the claim of a non-empirical knowledge of appearances, that is, the forms of geometry and conceptualized time when they are considered independently of the particular contribution of the matter-producing element of our experience. The knowledge that Kant claims here is one that is based on the premise that the judgement or recognition that experience provides is rooted in the connectedness of that experience, which requires a unity and objectivity of reference.[3] That premise of Kant's argument is not one that transcendental idealism alone can support. Our alternative and common view that connected-ness is founded on the reality of objects existing independent of our experience of them is not necessarily wrong. Moreover, the doctrine that Kant is actually appealing to here is simply that of phenomenologi-cal idealism, a view incorporated within transcendental idealism, but one fully capable of having its own independent existence.

> Behind all the argument and analysis concerned with our sup-posed non-empirical knowledge of objects in space and of the natural world in general there lies ... a crude and incoherent model of the mind as it timelessly is in itself, and of things as they timelessly are in themselves, the former, affected by the latter and self-affecting, being responsible for certain features of experi-ence of which the mathematician and the critical philosopher ... can obtain knowledge, without reference to the actual course of sensible experience. (BS: 245–6)

In the fourth Paralogism of the first edition, Kant claims that his transcendental idealism enables us to escape the view that bodies in space are merely inferences drawn from our inner perceptions, and also to dissolve the supposed problem associated with the action of body on mind. Both difficulties rest on the common and false assumption that bodies exist independently of our perceptions of them. They fail to grasp the actual conditions of the very possibility of experience in general. For Strawson, this unjustified claim rests solely on the doctrine of phe-nomenological idealism taken together with Kant's further unjustified claim that this idealism is tenable only within the larger scope of his transcendental idealism. That is precisely the difficulty that Strawson finds at the root of all of the claims he has attributed to Kant.

In the "Paralogisms of Pure Reason", Kant is concerned with the "I think", which accompanies all of our representations. This is the "I think" that expresses the "transcendental unity of apperception", and that for Strawson brings the temptation to the illusion of the Carte-sian Ego. Strawson's interpretation of Kant in this context has been subjected to criticism by John McDowell in his article "On Referring to Oneself" (1998).[4] McDowell begins with a quotation from Wittgen-stein's Blue Book (1958: 66–7), in which a distinction is made between the use of "I" as object and the use of "I" as subject:

> One can point to the difference between these two categories by saying: The cases of the first category involve the recognition of

a particular person, and ... the possibility of an error has been provided for .... It is possible that, say in an accident I should feel a pain in my arm, see a broken arm at my side, and think it is mine, when really it is my neighbour's .... On the other hand, there is no question of recognizing a person when I say I have a toothache. To say "are you sure that it's *you* who have pains?" would be nonsensical... (Quoted in McDowell 1998: 129)

Wittgenstein suggests the conclusion that "I" used as subject is not referential. Since I cannot make a mistake in this use, and since there is no question of my getting the reference right, there is then no question of getting it wrong, so there is no reference at all. Wittgenstein does appear, however, at least to leave it open that the use of "I" as object is possible, and hence referential.

G. E. M. Anscombe (1975) goes further in arguing that "I" does not refer, no matter what the context:

Getting hold of the wrong object *is* excluded, and that makes us think that getting hold of the right object is guaranteed. But the reason is that there is no getting hold of an object at all. With names, or denoting expressions (in Russell's sense) there are two things to grasp: the kind of use, and what to apply them to from time to time. With "I" there is only the use.

(Quoted in McDowell 1998: 128)[5]

For McDowell, while accepting Anscombe's fundamental insight that the central use of "I" is unmediated, that is, in its subject use, we need not accept her conclusion that "I" is never a referring expression. In this regard, McDowell finds the beginning of wisdom in Strawson's *The Bounds of Sense*: "'I' can be used without the criteria of subject identity and yet refer to a subject because, even in such a use, the links with those criteria are not completely severed" (BS: 165). Thus, for Strawson, that "I" is centrally used without reference is no reason not to suppose that by "I" I do refer to the person who, for example, has a broken arm. Against Strawson's position, Anscombe thinks that if we take any or all of our utterances using "I" to be cases of referring, then the only thing that "I" can ultimately refer to is the Cartesian Ego. But, in that case, if the Cartesian Ego is an unacceptable illusion to which we are tempted, then the use of "I" as a referring expression is also unacceptable.

McDowell thinks that Strawson rejects the Cartesian Ego, but that he also rejects Anscombe's claim that the "I" is never a referring expression. Strawson reads Kant's diagnosis in "The Paralogisms of Pure

Reason" as effectively rejecting the Cartesian illusion, but McDowell thinks that Strawson also attributes to Kant the insight, counter to Anscombe's position, that there are cases in which the links to criteria of subject-identity are not completely severed, notably in those cases in which understanding "I" requires understanding that the first person is also a third person, one element among others in an objective world.

This is the point at which McDowell's disagreements with Strawson appear. McDowell thinks that Strawson is too generous in attributing to Kant the insight that counters Anscombe. We should not underestimate Strawson's own creativity in what he mistakenly offers in his reading of Kant. There is only one support that Strawson provides from the *Critique* for his giving the credit to Kant himself: "Its [the soul's] persistence during life is, of course, evident *per se*, since the thinking being (as man) is itself likewise an object of the outer senses" (B 415, cited in BS: 164). And while Kant does indeed here show himself to be immune to the Cartesian temptation, McDowell (1998: 136) thinks he needs for that purpose only to say that the "I think" that accompanies all of my representations gives no expression to "an intuition of the subject as object", and hence that the "I" that accompanies the unity of consciousness does not refer. Thus Strawson brings his own insight, quite independent of what Kant has provided, namely, that there are cases in which the links to criteria of subject-identity are not completely severed, notably in those cases in which understanding "I" requires understanding that the first person is also a third person, one element among other elements in an objective world.

Strawson's insight takes place, of course, in the context of his interpretation of Kant in *The Bounds of Sense*, and McDowell thinks that this context raises a very substantial difficulty in the light of an indispensable thought that occurs in Strawson's earlier *Individuals*: "a necessary condition of states of consciousness being ascribed at all is that they should be ascribed to the very same things as certain corporeal characteristics, a certain physical situation &c." (IE: 102). McDowell thinks that in *The Bounds of Sense*, Strawson's account of Kant's treatment of self-reference focuses on the notion of "a temporally extended *point of view* on the world" (BS: 104), a notion that does not make explicit the necessary condition for the possibility of self-consciousness, namely, seeing that this point of view is an aspect of the career of an embodied subject of experience. Strawson claims on Kant's behalf that this necessary condition is met by maintaining that the conception of "a temporally extended *point of view* on the world", taken apart from an explicit mention of embodiment, does itself provide for the distinction between phenomena and noumena, and thereby for the basic conditions for the possibility of self-consciousness (BS: 108).

McDowell thinks that here Strawson's claim is seriously wrong. Following Anscombe (1975: 49), McDowell wants to make the point that since most reports on one's own actions are made on the basis of observation, in one important sense Strawson in *Individuals* is a better guide than Strawson in *The Bounds of Sense*:

> Strawson's reading of Kant is revelatory when the question is how self-reference can be reference at all, but it is less helpful towards understanding how self-reference works, what the mode of presentation expressed by someone's use of "I" is. ... When it comes to understanding how self-reference works, we are better served by the division in P-predicates and M-predicates, as in *Individuals,* than by the Kantian abstraction of a temporally extended point of view on the world from the career of an embodied subject. P-predications include, from the start, ascriptions of undertaken bodily movements. [McDowell's note here refers to *Individuals,* pp. 111–12.] In that context, one's being a bodily agent cannot take on the look of an afterthought, a mere frame for something that could sensibly be supposed to be more fundamental to self-consciousness. (McDowell 1998: 143)

Strawson's reply begins by noting that in the text that McDowell cites, Wittgenstein apparently holds that when a subject reports on his present state of mind there is no possibility of his getting his use of "I" wrong, hence that there can be no question of his getting it right either, and hence that in cases of what Anscombe calls "unmediated" self-consciousness there is no reference to a subject at all. Anscombe herself, of course, goes further. For Strawson:

> there seems no more need to make sure of getting the subject right in such judgments as "I have fallen over" ... than there is in the type of case cited by Wittgenstein. Appeal to the ordinary criteria of personal identity seems equally irrelevant in all these cases. But, she goes on, if these criteria are irrelevant to the use of "I," and if we are still determined to find a subject, then, as she puts it, "nothing less than a Cartesian Ego will serve"; and thence she argues by *modus tollens* to the conclusion that "I" is not used to refer at all. (Strawson 1998b: 146)

Strawson thinks that Kant in the Paralogisms is solely concerned with the "I think" that accompanies all my representations, the "I think" that expresses "the transcendental unity of apperception". But McDowell has noted that while Kant did not draw Anscombe's blanket judgement on all uses of "I", there is nothing in Kant that precludes that judgement. However, while McDowell praises Strawson for having remedied Kant's omission by insisting that the central unmediated use of "I" does not sever the links with the criteria of personal subject-identity, a major difficulty remains: Strawson agrees that what he says in *The Bounds of Sense* does fall short of the notion of a *corporeal* subject, but that for McDowell the significant difficulty remains:

> I ... leave the impression, McDowell says, "that the conception of a temporally extended point of view on the objective world," by providing for "the distinction between how things are and how they are experienced as being," does nearly all the work and only needs *supplementing* with the conception of the subject as a bodily thing. And this, says McDowell, is seriously wrong.
>
> (*Ibid.*: 147–8)

McDowell thinks that it is in intentional action – speech behaviour, intentionally undertaken bodily movements – that self-awareness is most intelligible. Strawson's reply is that this is not the whole story. He asks whether we could have an "I" without a "you" and a "they": could we have self-consciousness without a consciousness of other persons? He notes that he has written extensively in *Individuals* on the point that understanding "I" requires understanding it as a subject that is a corporeal being among other corporeal beings in an objective world.

If the central question in McDowell's article is whether the user of "I" makes a reference to himself then, while the article is engaging, it is also beside the point. It is a truism that "I" in speech or thought must refer to that very same person. It is irrelevant that in the central unmediated use of "I" there is no need to invoke criteria for personal identity. That point is one that McDowell himself thinks is the beginning of wisdom on these questions, for which credit Strawson issues a disclaimer:

> What McDowell generously describes as the "beginning of wisdom" on this question is also its end; though it would be better to replace the lofty word "wisdom" with something more modest like "plain sense" (except that they often come in philosophy to much the same thing). Seriously to question whether, in any standard use of "I" a person is referring to himself or herself is as futile as

seriously to question whether in any standard use of "now" as a temporal adverb a person is referring to a (more or less extended) present. *(Ibid.*: 149)

For Strawson, the fact that McDowell's article is beside the point that it would raise does not mean that the article is without merit. It is a valuable exploration of the whole question of self-consciousness. It makes clear that in the central unmediated use of "I" there is no thought of criteria, and that it is in reporting the state of the user's consciousness that we find the "deep and deceptive" source of the Cartesian illusion with its support for the thought that the reference must be to some immaterial thing:

> My final point has been simply to emphasize the simple, indeed platitudinous, point underlying the truth, on which McDowell and I agree, that the case concerning reference to oneself is no different when one says, truly or falsely, "I am in pain" or "I see such-and-such" or "I am NN." To think otherwise is simply confusion.
>
> *(Ibid.)*

A point of connection is needed between man as a phenomenal natural being with a history in time, and man as he is in himself with no such history at all. That is a need that, for Strawson, can be met neither by Kant nor by anyone else.

This incoherence with regard to the relation between the thing-in-itself and appearances in the inner sense is matched by an incoherence in the relation between the thing-in-itself and appearances in the outer sense. Here Strawson's argument against Kant turns on two different uses of "to appear". On the first use, there is the commonplace distinction between how things initially appear to be and how, on a corrected view, they really are. But it is also the fact that our sense experience is the joint product of things-in-themselves and our human psychological makeup, and so, on the second use of "to appear", we are not bound to say that things *in general* are as they appear to us, and any necessary connection between phenomenal appearances and things as they are is effectively severed. But, Strawson observes, while there is indeed a distinction between things as they initially appear to us and the corrected view that science provides, we are not debarred from holding that these two views are of the same things in themselves, things that do not differ in their real constitution. A connection between appearance and reality is thereby maintained. That is a stance that Kant systematically rejects:

> We commonly distinguish in appearances that which is essentially inherent in their intuition and holds for sense in all human beings, from that which belongs to their intuition accidentally only, and is not valid for sensibility in general but only in relation to a particular standpoint .... The former kind of knowledge is then declared to represent the object in itself, the latter its appearance only .... We then believe that we know things in themselves, and this in spite of the fact that in the world of sense, however deeply we inquire into its objects, we have to do with nothing but appearances. (A 45)

The connection that Kant here rejects, he apparently affirms in B 45, where we are told that our intuitions are dependent on the existence of the object, and that our faculties of representation are affected by that object. But, on Kant's own principle of significance, if we are to hold that distinction between the object and its appearance, we must be prepared to supply empirical criteria for the concepts we have of the objective. Those empirical criteria are precisely the ones in play when we move from how things initially appear to us to the corrected scientific view, two views of the same object. Strawson finds Kant's treatment of the relation between appearance and reality brilliant but perverse.

In holding to the distinction between things in themselves and their appearances, Kant may seem to hold a dualistic realism of a sort, since while the distinction between the two is absolute, Kant also affirms that our sensible experience is affected by things existing apart from this experience. Kant says both that bodies are nothing apart from our perceptions, and that we are aware of the existence of objects in space, distinct from our perceptions. We may be tempted to reconcile these apparently conflicting claims by recognizing a difference in context. If the question of the reality of bodies independent of our perceptions is raised in the context of the conceptual schema of our empirical experience, then that reality is affirmed, and we have an empirical realism. But if the question is raised in the context of the entire critical philosophy, then the reality is denied, and we have a transcendental idealism. For Strawson, that reconciliation is possible only within the context of transcendental idealism itself, and it does not give that idealism a coherence and intelligibility that it has already been shown to lack.

Strawson thus finds that none of the identified doctrines of transcendental idealism are worth keeping, but he maintains that there are nevertheless some truths that do have faint analogies with those doctrines. In the chapter "The Ground of the Distinction of all

Objects in general into Phenomena and Noumena", Kant is strongly committed to the principle of significance, that the categories of the understanding may be used only where their empirical employment is possible, within the bounds of the forms of space and time. The employment of the categories does give to experience the unity that makes possible an objective reference, without which experience itself would be impossible, yet we must resist the temptation to apply those same categories to things as they are in themselves.

Such an application would require an intellectual intuition, and while we lack that intuition, the *idea* of such an intuition is itself free of contradiction. Thus while we can have no *knowledge* of things in themselves, Kant thinks that we may *think* of such objects in terms of the categories, and that we may do so in terms of the interests of morality and religion. The objects of an intellectual intuition may be called noumena.

Kant's appeal to the idea of an intellectual intuition is one that Strawson finds without merit. But Strawson does find acceptable the concept of an objective reality set as a limit to any claim that our sensible experience and our consequent theories of explanation are coextensive with the real. We have five senses, but we may well recognize the possibility of an additional physical sense that would inform us of things we presently do not recognize. Moreover, the advances of science may continuously provide us with knowledge of some properties of things of which we are presently unaware. Thus there may indeed be aspects of reality of which, at present, we have no conception. Strawson's notion of such bounds of sense differs from Kant's. For Kant, the categories *may* be applicable to the noumenal. Strawson finds it more realistic and less perilous simply to say that the categories may have an employment beyond our present use. Such an extension of the categories must have consequences or implications that must be both testable and beyond what earlier unproblematic concepts already provide. Strawson's substitution has at most some of the negative aspects of Kant's noumena. There is some analogy between these two accounts of the bounds of sense, but if the analogy is pressed, it becomes ever weaker.

Looking back over the whole of the *Critique*, Strawson thinks that we might well ask how it is possible for anyone to maintain that our experience must have certain general features. If that claim for generality cannot be maintained, why not? If it can be maintained, then what are the conditions that make certain features indispensable? To ask why there are *any* limits to experience is absurd, since that is like saying that experience might be *this* way, and then going on in an incoherent manner to provide the details. The real question is properly put in terms of the arguments and tests used to support the claim of indispensability.

> Here ... to begin with ... we are concerned with the temporally extended experience of conceptualizing or thinking beings. This conception is given content ... by reference to general features of our actual experience which are exhibited in relations of progressively or mutual dependence. Thus we proceed from the necessity of conceptualization to the self-reflexiveness of experience – to objectivity and the potentiality of self-consciousness – to the distinction between objective time-relations and time-relations between subjective experiences – to the idea of a persisting framework within which objective time-relations hold – to the idea of re-identifiable particular objects – to the idea of regular law or causality – to that of law-governed objects in space. (BS: 271–2)

Any of these claimed necessities may be challenged by providing a counter-example drawn from our experience. We may lessen the likelihood of there being a counter-example by making the principles of necessity general in statement and loose in application. Even so, we may indeed wonder whether such necessities are indeed characteristic of the experience of infants and non-human animals. We may suppose on analogy that their experience is one in which the words of human discourse play no part, an experience that is simply a diminished or confused version of our own. There is, however, no empirical experience to show that those animals are confused. We have no words to say what it is to be without words. We must be "content with know ing ourselves" (BS: 275).

In *Individuals*, Strawson seeks a descriptive metaphysics that would be content to describe the actual and ordinary structure of our thought about the world, in contrast to the revisionary metaphysics of the past, which had attempted to provide a better structure. In *The Bounds of Sense*, Strawson attempts to make manifest much of the foundation of this descriptive metaphysics. The Analytic provides a positive and constructive account, while the Dialectic in turn helps to clear the way by negating the metaphysical illusions of the revisionists Descartes, Leibniz and Berkeley.

Strawson is rightly recognized as an established participant in the analytic tradition that dominates contemporary Anglophone philosophy, a tradition that has generally been seen as severely set apart from the metaphysical pursuits that have been a dominant feature of philosophy's past. Thus the publication of *Individuals* in 1959 with its "descriptive metaphysics" had all the appearance of an innovative marriage, a new bend in the road, and *The Bounds of Sense* may rightfully be seen as furthering and strengthening this attempt. In his essay "On Strawson's Rehabilitation of Metaphysics" P. M. S. Hacker places Strawson's initiative in some kind of historical perspective and provides an assessment of its viability. Hacker begins by noting a historical ebb and flow between times of great metaphysical system-building and times of anti-metaphysical reaction. The systems of the Continental Rationalists and the British Empiricists in the seventeenth and eighteenth centuries were followed by the attacks of Hume and Kant, each done in his own way. The German Idealists of the nineteenth century brought a new wave of metaphysics in the grand manner, soon met by the counter-current of positivism. This was in turn followed by such system-builders as Henri Bergson, F. H. Bradley and Heidegger. The reaction came soon enough with the manifesto of the Vienna Circle in 1920: the pamphlet titled "The Scientific World Conception".

For Hacker, the Vienna Circle's attack on metaphysics had much in common with Hume's earlier attack on his predecessors, but this new attack was harnessed to the logical analysis of Russell and the early Wittgenstein. Rudolf Carnap was particularly fervent in the cause, and the doctrines of the Circle as logical positivism were transmitted to the Anglophone world by Ayer's "pugnacious" *Language, Truth and Logic* in 1936. As we have seen, this was the philosophical environment that Strawson entered as a student in Oxford, where he read Ayer's work with an early enthusiasm that was in due time replaced by a dissatisfaction with its "undiluted classical empiricism" (Strawson 1998a: 8). Ayer and Strawson are thus both well within the analytic tradition, but they are clearly at odds on the legitimacy of the philosophical enterprise. Hacker's essay considers the question of the compatibility of Strawson's simultaneous commitments to analysis and to the construction of a descriptive metaphysics.

On Hacker's interpretation, Strawson's descriptive metaphysics does not differ widely from the analytic tradition in general in its common intent to clarify the concepts we use in our discourse about the world. One difference is that with Strawson, the concepts under scrutiny in descriptive metaphysics are "characteristically highly general, irreducible, basic. And, in a special sense, non-contingent" (Hacker 2003: 49). Another difference, and a difficulty for Hacker, is that while decriptive metaphysics is centrally concerned to make manifest the structure that natural language assumes in its ordinary use of words, this effort must by its very nature depart from that use of words, a use that in the end is its only sure guide.

The fact that the concepts that descriptive metaphysics investigates are highly general gives it a likely tie with the concerns of traditional metaphysics, which attempted to make manifest necessary features of reality, for example, that every event has a cause, and that every attribute inheres in some substance. In parallel, descriptive metaphysics fastens on those concepts that are essential to any account we could give of our experience. Thus where traditional metaphysics aimed for the necessary superphysical structure of reality as it is in itself, descriptive metaphysics seeks only to make manifest the connections that obtain among the major structural elements of our human conceptual scheme. Traditional metaphysics is then rightly dismissed as a fiction.

For Hacker, so far so good, but now a difficulty in Strawson's account presents itself. For his proposed descriptive metaphysics, there are certain necessary truths that unchangingly constitute our conceptual scheme, for example, "that places are defined by the relations of material bodies, that material bodies provide the framework for spatial location in general, that they are basic from the point of view of referential identification and re-identification ..., that persons have bodies ... and so on" (Hacker 2003: 55). These propositions make up the fundamental features of our conceptual scheme, but Hacker thinks that Strawson's account falters at this point in its failure to make clear the status of those propositions. Since they are held to be necessary, they cannot be empirical, but neither are they merely analytic, and they cannot be synthetic *a priori*, since in *The Bounds of Sense* Strawson has concluded that Kant has no clear and general conception of that notion (BS: 43). Moreover, Hacker cannot see why something that conditions our whole way of talking should be called necessary; the whole of our social existence is conditioned by our sexuality, but we can certainly imagine the very different lives of asexual beings.

Hacker thinks that the later Wittgenstein's way out of this apparent quandary is to give the name "norms of representation" to those propositions that describe the conceptual connections among the major structural features of our conceptual scheme. Thus when we rule out the intelligibility of "uncaused events" we are not placing limits on nature, we are just reminding ourselves about propositions to which we cannot assign any significance. Traditional metaphysics erred in its attempt to transfer our norms of representation with its necessities and connections to the structure of the objective world. The proper refutation of scepticism does not come from "proving" the existence of material bodies or other minds, but rather by showing that such scepticism has no sense, no significance.

In that light, what remains of the perceived difficulty that Strawson's description of the fundamental structure of our ordinary language is too far reaching to be done in terms of our ordinary use of words, our "only true guide"? It seems to Hacker that what Strawson seeks and finds are not patterns *submerged* beneath the surface of our ordinary language, but patterns in full view, although "it takes uncommon skill to discern them" (Hacker 2003: 62). The perceived difficulty may not be insuperable.

Hacker concludes that Strawson has preserved the letter of traditional metaphysics, while abandoning its spirit. Traditional metaphysics sought the structure of a supersensible reality through the creation of new concepts, but the proper task of philosophy is instead the description of a conceptual structure already in place. For Hacker, Strawson has pursued that task with "characteristic elegance, economy, and profundity" (*ibid*.: 65).

Whatever we may make of the cogency of Hacker's evaluation of Strawson's philosophy, I think his essay is most helpful in marking Strawson's place in the ebb and flow of metaphysical and anti-metaphysical philosophy. Strawson did much to establish that place through his reconstruction of Kant's Analytic and his simultaneous rejection of Kant's transcendental metaphysics. This served both to distance himself from the traditional metaphysical traditions of Descartes, Leibniz and Berkeley, and to provide explicit detail for the programme of descriptive metaphysics set forth in *Individuals*.

Strawson clearly identifies descriptive metaphysics as an empiricism, but he also rejects both the older classical empiricism of Hume and its contemporary form in Ayer's *Language, Truth and Logic*. A consideration of Strawson's view of his rival empiricists provides us with a more comprehensive view of his place in contemporary philosophy. For Strawson, Hume is both the arch-sceptic and at the same time the best warrant *against* the particular scepticisms with which philosophy has been concerned since the time of Descartes. All that gets worked out when he revisits Hume in *Skepticism and Naturalism*, the work we consider next.

Chapter 4

Skepticism and Naturalism: Hume revisited

Chapter 1: Skepticism, Naturalism and Transcendental Arguments

Strawson's interest in Kant did not end with the publication of *The Bounds of Sense* in 1966. He continued to give regular graduate seminars on Kant for the following twenty years, and, in a series of articles, he both amended and developed the views he had established in that book.

Kant had said that it was Hume who had awakened him from his "dogmatic slumber" and set him on the path to his critical philosophy. While Strawson continued to see Kant as the greatest of the moderns, he has also been prepared to see Hume as his hero on particular issues of continuing interest. He can view Hume as both a naturalist and a sceptic, with a tension between those two outlooks that in some ways is reminiscent of the tension he finds between Kant's empirical realism and his transcendental idealism. Strawson gave form to his reflections on Hume in the Woodbridge Lectures at Columbia University, subsequently published under the title *Skepticism and Naturalism: Some Varieties* (1985). As the theme of this work, Strawson appropriately takes a quotation from Gibbon: "The satirist may laugh, the philosopher may preach; but reason herself will respect the prejudices and habits, which have been consecrated by the experience of mankind".[1]

Strawson terms David Hume simultaneously the arch-naturalist and the arch-sceptic, but he suggests that the issue of this identification becomes more complex when we recognize varieties and shades of difference within both naturalism and scepticism. We may distinguish between a strict or reductive or hard naturalism and a catholic or liberal or soft naturalism,[2] and we all may be sceptical about some things and not about others. Scepticism is doubt rather than denial, since we may recognize the truth of some claims about our human situation, and at the same time find unacceptable some of the justifications offered in their support. Descartes used doubt as a methodology in support of his claims about the substantial self, God and the existence of a material world. Hume also used doubt, but with notably different results. There are indeed varieties of both naturalism and scepticism, but, under certain rubrics, Hume may properly be seen as a member of both camps.

Strawson begins his account of these varieties with a consideration of traditional scepticism as it was attacked by Moore in his well-known "A Defense of Common Sense" (1925). In "Proof of an External World" (1939), Moore claimed to dispel the sceptic's doubts about such things as the existence of a material world external to consciousness by the simple means of holding up first one hand and then the other, saying that two hands exist and hence that external things exist. The premise is true, and it is certain that the conclusion follows.

Barry Stroud (1979) thought that Moore had missed the point of the sceptic's doubt. The sceptic does not deny our experience, he simply claims that it could be just the way it is in the absence of an external material world, a sceptical point common to Berkeley, Descartes and the phenomenologist. Stroud's own approach was not to follow Moore in offering a counter-argument, but instead to defuse scepticism by neutralizing it, by making it impotent. On Stroud's view, an unsuccessful attempt in this direction was made by Carnap (1950). Stroud agrees with Carnap up to a point. Moore's approach is powerless to answer the sceptic's *philosophical* question about an external world, since while within the internal framework of a practical and conventional way of organizing our experience we may accept the existence of material bodies, external to that framework the sceptic's question remains intact. Carnap would now smother the question out of existence by making it meaningless on the basis of his own dogmatic verificationism but, for Stroud, the sceptic's question at least seems intelligible, so that its challenge remains in play.

Stroud finds in what he calls "transcendental arguments" a further attempt to provide a meaningful answer to the sceptic's challenge. In its more popular modern form, these arguments take the view that the existence of bodies external to the mind offers the best *explanation* of the nature of our sensory experience. In one form, the line starts with what the sceptic himself does not deny, namely, the presence of self-conscious thought and experience, and then proceeds to argue that this assumption in turn presupposes both external objects and other minds. In a second form, the transcendental line argues that the sceptic cannot so much as raise his questioning doubt without assuming some of the positions that his doubt would deny.

Strawson (SN: 9) notes that Stroud himself found those transcendental arguments unconvincing, since they are faced with an unanswerable dilemma. *Either* the argument rests on an undeclared dependence on a simple form of verificationism, *or* we are committed to believing that we have a knowledge that the sceptic precisely questions, namely, the existence of external objects and other minds. The sceptic does not deny that we hold such beliefs, he only challenges the claim that we have a knowledge that supports them. Such "transcendental arguments" leave the sceptic untroubled in his conviction.

Some philosophers have claimed that the sceptic's challenge is not only meaningful, but also that it can be met directly and successfully. Descartes's argued rejection of a *deus deceptor* is replaced in our times by the contention that having an external world is the best explanation we have of the nature of our sense experience. Others have indirectly confronted the challenge either by claiming in the manner of Carnap that it is unintelligible, or, as the transcendental arguments would have it, that it is self-defeating. Strawson finds another and better way in Hume, a way that has in our day a close and powerful exponent in Wittgenstein, a way that Strawson will call naturalism.

Strawson cites a famous sentence in Hume's *Treatise of Human Nature*: "Reason is and ought to be the slave of the passions and can never pretend to any other office than to serve and obey them" (II III iii, 415). The same thought is expressed towards the end of the first book of the *Treatise*, where Hume maintains that all of the *arguments* either for or against the sceptic's doubts concerning objects external to the mind are useless. We cannot help believing in the existence of such bodies, nor can we help forming the expectations and beliefs that are consequent on that conviction. Strawson notes that what Hume says here about bodies he might also have said about minds other than our own, although that parallel is not drawn. The basis of Hume's opposition to a total scepticism that would undermine all of our common practices is plain: "Whoever has taken the pains to refute the cavils of this total skepticism has really disputed without an antagonist and endeavored by arguments to establish a faculty which Nature has antecedently planted in the mind and rendered unavoidable" (SN: 183). For Strawson, Hume would thus respond to the challenge of a total scepticism not by a counter-argument in the manner of Descartes, nor by some form of a transcendental argument, but rather by simply passing it by.

Strawson would at least initially cast Hume as the hero of the story, with the dual roles of arch-sceptic and arch-naturalist. He does so while noticing an apparent tension between these two roles. Hume contrasts the question of whether there are external bodies with the question of what causes us to believe that they exist. For the first question, Hume takes for granted and beyond challenge in all our reasoning the natural belief in the existence of bodies, while he does not similarly take for granted our equally natural belief with regard to the causal question. It is thus that Hume may be seen as both arch-naturalist and arch-sceptic. Strawson sees this tension within Hume's thought as not unlike the tension between Kant's empirical realism and his transcendental idealism. The difference is that while Kant leaves us with his own kind of idealism, Hume on the causal question leaves us with an unrefuted scepticism.

Hume, as the arch-naturalist, makes Nature and its attendant beliefs dominant over the pretension of Reason, but Reason does have a legitimate role as slave of the passions. Within the framework of the belief that Nature provides, Reason rightly requires the construction of a system that is consistent and coherent. A justification for induction is neither necessary nor possible, but here we may nonetheless form rules for judging "cause and effect". Reason refines and elaborates what we are committed to by Nature.

In comparing Hume and Wittgenstein, Strawson primarily has in mind the latter's *"On Certainty"* (1969).[3] Like Hume, Wittgenstein also draws a distinction between those propositions that are open to question and those that are not. Unlike Hume, we find in Wittgenstein no explicit appeal of the sort we find in Hume to "Nature" as the foundation for that distinction, but, for Strawson, the points they hold in common are more numerous and more telling than their differences. Above all, they agree in their distinction between those things we must simply take for granted and those things that are appropriately matters of enquiry. Thus Wittgenstein's talk of belief as *"beyond being justified or unjustified*; as it were, as something *animal"* (*ibid.*: §359) echoes Hume's appeal to Nature.

Again, Wittgenstein says that "certain propositions seem to *under-lie* all questions and all thinking" (415; that some propositions *"are exempt from doubt"* (341); that "certain things are *in deed* [in *der Tat*, in practice] not doubted" (253) ... Again, he speaks of "propositions which have *a peculiar logical role* in the system [of our empirical propositions]" (136); which belong to our *"frame of reference"* (83); which ... is the *substratum* of all my enquiring and asserting" (162) or "the *scaffolding* of our thoughts" (211) ...

(SN: 15)

Strawson thinks that, while it is not easy to draw out from all of this one clear statement of Wittgenstein's position, it is clear that his general tendency and intention is to provide a realistic account of how it is with us in practice. While this is broadly in concert with Hume, the contrast that Hume draws between the contributions of Nature and those of Reason is not so sharply drawn by Wittgenstein. In an extended metaphor (Wittgenstein 1969: §96–9), he likens those propositions that are subject to empirical review to the water moving in a river, while those propositions that are relatively stable, and not subject to the same kind of review, are like the river's banks and bed, consisting partly of hard rock and thus subject to little or barely perceptible change.

It might be suggested that Wittgenstein is closer to Carnap than he is to Hume, but Strawson finds a critical difference. Carnap speaks of our *choosing* the framework that is the foundation of our thought, while, for Wittgenstein, it is not as if "we chose the game" (*ibid.*: §317). For Strawson, that is confirmed in this passage: "I want to say: propositions of the form of empirical propositions, and not only propositions of logic, form the foundation of all operating with thoughts (with language)" (*ibid.*: §401). Strawson finds here an allusion to the *Tractatus*.

Hume is indeed simpler than Wittgenstein. Hume includes within his framework of Nature only our beliefs in the existence of body and the general reliability of induction. Wittgenstein is more complex. The foundational framework of our thought is both more various and more dynamic than what we find in Hume's Nature, since what is at one time regarded as a part of this framework may later come to be seen as a hypothesis subject to empirical review.

With the important differences between Hume and Wittgenstein acknowledged, Strawson still finds them in fundamental agreement on the thesis that foundations of our practice are neither grounded beliefs nor open to serious doubt. Thus the way to rebut the arguments of the total sceptic is not by way of counter-arguments, but rather to recognize that they are equally idle, since there are no *reasons* for our foundational beliefs, we simply cannot help holding them. Strawson clearly distinguishes these beliefs from the argued theses supporting scientific theories.

> We accept the scientific theories ... just because we believe they supply the best available explanations of the phenomena they deal with. That is our reason for accepting them. But no one accepts the existence of the physical world *because* it supplies the best available explanation etc. That is no one's reason for accepting it. Anyone who claimed it was his reason would be pretending. It is, as Hume declared, a point we are naturally bound to take for granted in all our reasonings... (SN: 20)

For Strawson's naturalist, our foundational beliefs in the existence of bodies and other minds neither require, nor have the possibility of, rational justification of the sort that both counter-arguments and transcendental arguments would attempt to provide. Transcendental arguments take the view that the existence of bodies external to the mind offers the best *explanation* of our sensory experience. We have already seen Stroud's claim that such arguments are faced with a disabling dilemma: either they tacitly assume a simple form of verificationism, or they assume, as established, claims that the sceptic is happy to continue doubting.

Having his own way with scepticism, the naturalist is obviously going to be undisturbed by a failure of the transcendental argument. But in so far as such arguments rely on the notion of a connectedness among concepts, for example, the connection between our experience and external bodies, the naturalist may happily find it appropriate to investigate the connections that may exist among major elements in the framework of our conceptual scheme, and that is a task that Strawson is quite willing to share.

> But whether or not they are strictly valid, these arguments, or weakened versions of them, will continue to be of interest to our naturalist philosopher. For even if they do not succeed in establishing such tight or rigid connections as they initially promise, they do at least indicate ... conceptual connections, even if only of a looser kind; and ... exhibit [our conceptual scheme] not as a rigorous deductive system, but as a coherent whole whose parts are ... interlocking in an intelligible way – to do this may well seem to our naturalist philosopher the proper, or at least major, task of analytic philosophy. As indeed it does to me. (Whence the phrase, "descriptive" [as opposed to valedictory or revisionary] metaphysics.) (SN: 23)

This is plainly a reference to the distinction drawn in Strawson's earlier *Individuals*. Strawson evidently found in Kant's first *Critique* and in his *Prolegomena to Any Future Metaphysics* not only a model for the demolition of an obsolescent past, but also the opportunity and the challenge to continue the metaphysical enterprise in an analytical vein. This tie between *Skepticism and Naturalism* and *Individuals* is but one manifestation of the unity that marks Strawson's entire career in philosophy.

While Hume speaks of Nature as the source of our conceptual framework, and Wittgenstein speaks instead of the language games we learn from childhood onwards, Strawson finds that they have in common a naturalist position that sets both of them in contrast with the attitudes of other philosophers. Kant found it a scandal that the existence of bodies outside us must rest simply on faith devoid of any satisfactory proof (1929: B xi), while in *Being and Time* (1962: I.6), Heidegger finds the scandal to rest, not on the failed attempts to provide proof, but rather on the repeated expectation and attempts to provide such proofs. Wittgenstein can identify the source of their scandal: "It is so difficult to find the *beginning*. Or better: it is difficult to begin at the beginning. And not to try to go further back" (1969: §471). The naturalist will avoid the scandal simply by refusing to go back, by finding either in Nature or in our language games the structural framework that is the unreasoned and unavoidable beginning of our whole conceptual scheme.

The naturalist will properly be asked to identify the elements contained in that beginning. Hume identifies just two: the existence of external bodies and the habit of induction. Wittgenstein was more various and prepared to agree that today's foundation may tomorrow become a hypothesis subject to analytical challenge, the fate of the geocentric theory being a ready example. From this standpoint, however, the whole naturalist approach is apparently put into question, and the challenge of the sceptic returns. A notable example of that challenge is the historicism of R. G. Collingwood, who held that metaphysics is an essentially historical study, an attempt to establish the "absolute presuppositions" of the science of the day. There is nothing in metaphysics that is "fixed and unalterable".

Strawson finds no need to submit to a historical relativism of that sort. The human condition is indeed subject to change, but there is also much that is stable. We have an enduring *world-picture* or framework, which, in Witttgenstein's words, is "not subject to alteration or only to an imperceptible one" (quoted in SN: 27). Strawson does not in the present work compile a list of the elements specific to that framework, nor is he engaged in the connective metaphysics task of showing their interrelatedness, but he identifies four such elements: the existence of body, knowledge of other minds, the practice of induction, and the reality and determinateness of the past. Strawson will refuse to offer any arguments in support of those elements, since, from his naturalist point of view, all arguments and counter-arguments in that regard are idle. Those elements are included in the framework to which we are simply and inescapably committed, the bed and the bank for the currents of our river.

Chapter 2: Morality and Perception

Having considered these natural commitments of a properly descriptive metaphysics, Strawson now extends the scope of his enquiry to a consideration of the kind of natural commitments we might find in the area of morality, the attitudes and feelings we have in regard to the actions of ourselves and others, and the attendant questions of human freedom and responsibility.[4] As in the area of metaphysics Strawson was primarily concerned with the challenge of the sceptic and the counter-arguments it has evoked, so now in questions of morality he will find a parallel concern. We have attitudes and feelings about the actions of ourselves and others, we praise and we blame, and we are brought quickly to the free will controversy. Strawson thinks that the challenge to our disposition to assign freedom and responsibility has been characterized well by Thomas Nagel (1979). Once we see persons and events in the objective light of occurrences in nature, whether by cause or by chance, then the illusion of moral value freely chosen is stripped away.

Strawson finds the arguments in support of free will intended as counter-arguments to Nagel's not notably successful. However, such counter-arguments are also idle, since they are directed against an argument that is itself not efficacious. We are no more to be argued out of our idea of moral desert than we are to be argued out of our belief in physical bodies. These beliefs are simply a natural and inescapable aspect of our human existence as social beings. Naturalism is once again our appropriate response to the sceptic and his adversary alike, and Strawson finds this parallel between our beliefs in external bodies and in moral response already drawn in Hume's contemporary opponent, Thomas Reid (SN: 33).[5]

Sometimes we do indeed detach ourselves from making moral judgement, confining ourselves to putting things in an objective light. We may do this not simply as an intellectual effort to see the actions of persons in the same way we see non-personal objects, but also as an effort to dampen down a too strongly reactive attitude towards actions we find unacceptable. That effort may be made and sustained for a time, particularly in cases of extremely abnormal behaviour, but Strawson thinks that such detachment cannot last very long, since in the end it would entail the loss of all personal relationships, a price too great to pay, since as human beings we are committed to participant relationships and to a sense of freedom and responsibility.

Between these two attitudes, there is a tension that tends towards mutual exclusion. From one point of view, by our very nature as social beings, we are apparently committed to the belief that actions may rightly be judged in terms of moral desert: that there is an objective morality. From the other point of view, evaluative statements about human actions are neither true nor false, since there is no moral reality to serve as a criterion. Spinoza held that the notion of a moral right or wrong is an illusion, or, in John Mackie's (1977) terms, a human invention.[6] Strawson observes that the latter view is sometimes mistakenly embodied in the slogan, "To understand all is to forgive all". He drily adds that the best comment on that slogan was made by Austin: "That's quite wrong; understanding might just add contempt to hatred".

If these two standpoints tend towards being or are actually mutually exclusive, we might rightly ask which one corresponds to things as they really are. Strawson's approach to this dilemma is by now a familiar one. He argues that to ask which standpoint is right is to presuppose that there is a point of view external to both standpoints from which they may be appraised. The true illusion here is to suppose that for us there is indeed a point of view of that kind. Each of the two frameworks has its own internal and appropriate criteria, but there is nothing external to those frameworks by which they may be judged.

We may recall that at the outset, Strawson warned us that the terms "scepticism" and "naturalism" have diverse uses, and he now provides distinctions that serve his present purpose. A first sense of "naturalism" is the one employed by Hume in support of our beliefs in external bodies and the general principles of induction, beliefs that neither have nor need rational justification. That naturalism may also be seen as an effective response to the challenge of the sceptic on the issue of our unavoidable belief in moral desert. There is, however, a twist for the issues of morality that is absent in the case of bodies and induction. Sometimes, from within the context of morality itself, we recognize an obligation to take on the role of a detached observer rather than as a participant in interpersonal dialogue. But to the role of a detached observer we may quite properly assign a second sense of "naturalism": the sense that the same criteria may be applied across the board, applying to persons and things alike as the natural objects of our observation and predictions. This second naturalism is hard or reductive. It is set in contrast to the first naturalism, which makes moral praise and blame a function of beliefs imposed on us by our nature. This naturalism is soft or liberal or catholic.

Strawson sees in Kant's theory of noumenal freedom and in the non-natural qualities advocated by contemporary intuitionists an attempt to mount counter-arguments to hard or reductive naturalism. The soft or non-reductive naturalist makes no such attempt; he simply says that to surrender moral principle is counter to our nature. The hard naturalist would make "morality" to manifest a lack of reason, but the soft naturalist can reply that there is only a lack where there is a need, and, in this case, there is no need. Adherence to moral principle does not need nor does it allow an argumentative support; it is the natural framework of our human condition and not the result of a choice that needs justification. The soft naturalist is catholic or liberal in the sense that he will recognize circumstances in which the "objective" view of the hard naturalist is our obligation, a tolerance for which the hard naturalist has no place.

Strawson thinks that while there is a tension between hard and soft naturalisms, they may rightly be seen as consistent with each other. Both points of view are viable within their own frameworks. For those who may find his stance suspicious or evasive, Strawson offers as a parallel case the attitudes we adopt in regard to our perceptions of the physical world. Here we may distinguish between a common-sense realism, which holds that objects do in reality have the properties we ascribe to them, and a scientific realism, which holds that objects have only those properties that science ascribes to them. Scientific realism stresses the peculiar role that our human sense faculties play in our account of the physical world. We see that world from one particular perspective, and we may well wonder how that same world appears to, for example, a bat. For the scientific realist, the real properties of physical objects are not dependent on the various kinds of sense faculties that range across species, they are instead the constants that are in place whatever the nature of the perceiver. All else is an illusion.

There may now appear to be an irreconcilable opposition between the two realisms. The defender of common-sense realism will hold that his point of view is one that is our natural belief. He will point out that all of the primary qualities that the scientist accords to objects presuppose the very qualities that he would deny them. In the rising tensions of debate, he may accuse the scientist of replacing "the rich reality of the world by a bloodless abstraction" (SN: 44).

The point of Strawson's comparison of the tensions between common-sense and scientific realisms and those between hard and soft naturalisms is now plain. In both cases, the apparent contradiction is resolved by the relativization of the concepts. In both cases, the points of view are fully human and fully natural. We are capable of looking at things in more than one way.

This relativization of concepts, this making it all depend on which one of two naturally acceptable points of view is put in play, may well appear to both sides to be surrender rather than accommodation. Each contender may continue to insist that his way is the only way. Strawson acknowledges that there are features that fail to support the relativization move as well as those that support it. On the question of perception, where the division is between two forms of realism, the common-sense and the scientific, any claimed contradiction between the two is plainly more seeming than real. Blood manifests itself to the naked eye as red, and manifests itself under the microscope as mostly colourless. The two manifestations are equally real, and there is no conflict. Accommodation is not a problem.

The question of morality is more complex. Here the division is between hard and soft naturalisms, and any parallel to the accommodation possible within the two realisms is far from exact. There are dissimilarities, and we do not find it so easy to shift back and forth between alternative points of view. Nonetheless, we can attempt to understand moral criteria that are not our own, to put ourselves in another person's shoes. Moreover, we often find within ourselves contending moralities, even where one of them may be dominant. There are also historical shifts in moral criteria, Strawson's example being our common attitude towards the institution of slavery. Strawson does not think that this results in the historicism of Collingwood, since admitting a range of diversity in moral outlook does not deny that certain norms are universal. Such characteristics as generosity, justice and honesty are commonly seen as admirable moral characteristics. We may also respect another person's acting in accordance with the dictates of his conscience, even when we think that conscience mistaken.

There is indeed no exact parallel between the two realisms, common-sense and scientific, and the two naturalisms, hard and soft. Nonetheless, to see the plausibility of accommodation between the two realisms should lead us to see at least the possibility of a degree of similarity in the case of the two naturalisms. To this the "hard-liner" may reply that all that has been said so far supports rather than denies his point of view. All of these relativities, which the accommodationist himself recognizes as internal to our moral attitudes, simply underline the subjectivity of those responses, and the consequent impossibility of objectivity. This is not the case from the scientific point of view, where the verificationist tests of success in prediction and control provide objective standards. Science acknowledges the presence of subjective experiences, but the varying reactions that they entail are all produced by causal factors, which the scientist alone is well equipped to make plain.

Strawson thinks there is a patient reply to that hard-line insistence. The hard-liner is not wrong in viewing the world in terms of science's abstract terms, which give no place to the conditions of our varying modes of perception; nor is he wrong in holding that all of our human actions may be viewed in those same abstract terms. But he does go wrong if he thinks that those views are incompatible with the views that blood is red or that some actions are either good or evil.

> Though we can, by an intellectual effort, occupy at times, and for a time, the former pair of standpoints, we cannot give up the latter pair of standpoints .... What the relativizing move does is to remove the appearance of incompatibility between members of the two pairs of views. Without the relativizing move, the scientific hard-liner ... could stick to his line; admitting that we are naturally committed to the human perceptual and morally reactive viewpoints, he could simply conclude that we live most of our lives in a state of unavoidable illusion. The relativizing move averts this (to most) unpalatable conclusion. It would surely be an extreme of self-mortifying intellectual Puritanism which would see in this very fact a reason for rejecting that view.   (SN: 50)

Chapter 3: The Mental and the Physical

Up to this point in his overall argument, Strawson has had two very different uses for "naturalism". In one use, naturalism provides a way of dealing with certain traditional scepticisms. The sceptic would argue us out of our natural beliefs, and the effective response is the realization that both his reasoned arguments and the reasoned counter-arguments of his opponent are equally pointless. There are certain natural and humanly unavoidable beliefs that provide the frameworks within which all of our reasonings take place. As Hume would have it, reason is indeed the slave of the passions. From this perspective, the question of the relativizing of concepts has yet to be considered.

In a second use, we come to a particular consideration of some of those beliefs. We come to see that while we cannot be argued out of our natural beliefs that the ordinary bodies we experience are phenomenally propertied, and that human beings are the proper objects of moral attitudes, we can nevertheless understand a point of view that would leave no room for either phenomenal or moral properties. At this point, there arises the temptation to make that viewpoint exclusively correct, to adopt a reductive naturalism that would provide us with a world that is both morally and literally colourless. This reductionism is accomplished by first stripping that objective world of any moral dimensions while leaving it still perceptible, and then stripping it of all phenomenal characteristics, thus leaving it imperceptible as it really is. It is as a corrective for this reductive form of naturalism that the relativizing move is now made. This move enables us to recognize once again that there are two independent and internal frames of reference within which our reasonings take place, and that there is no point of view external to those frames that would provide a criterion for their ranking or validity. Neither frame can claim to be exclusively correct.

These ways of dealing with the varied forms of naturalism may seem to have yet another use in the case of the much controverted identity thesis, namely, the claim that all of the events of a person's mental history are identical with events in his physical history. On this thesis, mental events are no more than a subclass of the events of neurophysiology. This might appear to be just a particular instance of the apparent conflict between a reductive materialism and an affirmation of the proper reality of consciousness, and that conflict would indeed arise if we accept the Cartesian two-substance thesis of an essential distinction between mind and body. On that view, the identity thesis is simply false. The issue is more complex if we hold instead that a person is a type of unitary being having both mental and physical predicates. Readers of Strawson's earlier *Individuals* will recognize here a familiar theme.

On this unitary view, one particular *state* of an individual of this type may have both a mental and a physical description, and one particular *event* may also have both aspects. On this view, the identity thesis will hold not that every state that has a physical description also has a mental description, but rather the converse, namely, that every mental description also has a physical description. In sum, mental events are a subclass of physical events.

There is much contemporary controversy on the identity thesis. Strawson's way with it is one that we can surely anticipate: he is not concerned to refute the arguments and counter-arguments that have been made; he will instead circumvent them. One point is plain at the outset. We might readily concede to the identity theorist that the total state of a person at a given moment may allow a physical and usually both a physical and mental description. However, such a concession would in principle allow in a person's total state the presence of distinct components with none of the mental being identical with the physical, and that will not be enough to satisfy the identity theorist. He wants identity, not distinction.

Again, we might assume the presence of physical laws such that every movement of a person's body is seen as the causal outcome of the stimulation of some sensory surface taken together with that person's internal constitution. From this perspective, all history may be told in electrochemical terms. But from another and more familiar perspective, an account of why Socrates is in prison awaiting his death cannot be told simply in terms of the passage of blood and air and bones; it must include desires, intentions, memories and beliefs.[7] So for Strawson there are apparently two stories, one told in terms of neurophysiology, the other in terms of "'folk psychology' ... the terms employed by such simple folk as Shakespeare, Tolstoy, Proust, and Henry James" (SN: 56).

No one thinks that you can completely correlate or map the personal history on the physical history, yet neither is it commonly thought that these two histories have no relation to each other. In an attempt to avoid the arguments for and against the identity theory, it may seem reasonable to think that each *particular* mental event has a basis in some *particular* physical event, but that would still leave open the question of the exact nature of the relation between those two events. Apparently we are reduced to the alternatives of holding that the two events are simply identical, or that there are indeed two events and that they have a causal relationship.

To consider the alternative that there are indeed two events and that they are causally related leads directly to further questions. Imagine with Strawson the instance of John's recognizing the face of a friend in a crowd. There is more in play here than just a mental event and physical event, since there *is* the event outside John's life that is happening *in* John's life. Both the biographer and the scientist can offer descriptions of that happening in the predicative terms appropriate to their points of view. Nothing need be left out of either account, but neither account, even in its own terms, can be exhaustive. We have now the question of the interface between the two accounts. We *can* say that every mental event has a physical basis, but Strawson suggests that it is well to leave things where they are, with the two different stories told from two different points of view left in place, and not to press for a resolution of their differences. The identity theory could be secured only by bracketing out the personal story in favour of the physical one, a step for which we have neither need nor practical use.

If our choice with regard to the relation between the mental and the physical is limited to the identity account and a causal account then, with the failure of the former, the latter would apparently have to be accepted by default. The causal account apparently has, however, its own difficulties. We have a *use* for the notion of cause when it is associated with the notions of prediction or control. But even if, contrary to fact, we could obtain an exhaustive specific account of the physical realization of a mental event, that would still fail to provide an account of human behaviour. That behaviour is part of the biographer's story, told in terms of such events as intentions and desires having their own internal connections, events that have no causal efficacy of their own only if we think that the physical explanation is the only one available. Strawson cites with approval Donald Davidson's (1980) stress on the discrepancy between the personal story told by the biographer and the story given in a complete causal account of a purely physical organism. We have a use for causal explanation within both of those accounts, but we have no use for that concept if we attempt to reduce the two accounts to one, since it is useless to look for unity where none is possible.

Strawson concludes that if we feel that in our need to "keep our metaphysics warm" we have to choose between the identity and causal accounts of the relationship between the mental and the physical, he would without enthusiasm but with some conviction opt for the causal. He thinks that the advances of science may produce ever greater evidence of the *general* dependence of the mental on the physical. It is also plain that he does not think the gap will ever be completely closed.

The question of the relationship between morality and perception apparently has some parallel to similar questions about morality and about sense perception. In the latter two cases, the conflict is between common beliefs about human behaviour and about physical things, and the opposing sceptical view that those beliefs rest on an illusion. In both cases, Strawson suggests resolving the conflict by the relativizing move, which provides for the coexistence of opposing but not contradictory points of view. That relativizing move does not at first glance seem to be available in the case of the relationship between the mental and the physical, since in this case the conflict appears to be between two aspects of a single reality that is assumed by both sides, with neither side regarding the other as an illusion. Neither side can claim to give an exhaustive account of reality. Rather than conflict, there is the search for the way in which the two aspects are related to each other.

Conflict does arise, however, if we embrace the view of one side as giving an exhaustive account of what is ultimately real, notably the exclusionary view of the identity theory. We might say that on this theory there is indeed just one and the same happening or event, and that while there are two descriptions of that event, the correct one is done from an exclusively physiological standpoint. On Strawson's view, even that account will not be enough to satisfy an identity theorist. What that theorist really seeks is a reductive naturalism that would dismiss everything that is unexplainable in terms of physical science, a view that Mackie (1976: 169) attributes to both J. J. C. Smart and D. M. Armstrong. Seen in that light, the identity theory is seen as a kind of scepticism, and once again Strawson invokes his own non-reductive naturalism:

> I want simply to say that against all these reductivist (or skeptical) stances, as also against skepticism more traditionally and properly so-called, I have tried to set up another kind of Naturalism – a non-reductive variety – which recognizes the human inescapability and metaphysically acceptability of those various types of conception of reality which are challenged or put in doubt by reductive or traditionally skeptical arguments.   (SN: 68)

Chapter 4: The Matter of Meaning

Strawson has yet one more possible use for the relativizing concept: its employment in the debate between nominalism and realism, in both its traditional and its contemporary forms. Here the debate is on the question of the *meaning* of the universal and particular terms of our discourse.

We think of attributes, properties, kinds and types as *universals*, in contrast to their *particular* exemplifications or instances or tokens. With Frege, we may distinguish among the *thought* expressed in an utterance or inscription; the *proposition* asserted or denied; and the *statement* asserted or denied. Universals are not natural objects, since in themselves they have no location in space or date in time. If universals are objects at all, they are objects of thought alone. These non-natural entities are sometimes called "*intensions*". These intensions are subject to suspicion and indeed hostility by the reductive naturalist. He has no room for such "objects", since they are no more situated in space and time than are fictional entities. Strawson observes that such pruning does raise some critical questions, since intensions *do* play a significant role in our ordinary discourse, indeed intensions may be used to make statements that are true or false. The reductive naturalist may thus rightly be challenged to explain and defend his position.

What meaning, if any, do intensions have? The reductionist may seek support for his contention that they are devoid of meaning by adverting to the traditional distinction between necessary and contingent truths, between truths of reason and truths of fact. Necessary truths are not so by any kind of natural or physical necessity, but rather by "logical" necessity. Such laws as those of contradiction and the excluded middle are not informative about the world; they tell us nothing about how things are. To say that either it is or is not raining in Singapore is not to give a weather report. Thus for the reductive naturalist, all necessary truths say the same thing about the world, namely nothing.

Strawson finds a ready instance of this sort of rejectionism by the reductive naturalist in Quine (1953). There still remains the fact that we do commonly suppose that there are necessary relations between abstract objects, even if there are no such objects, and the rejectionist remains under a complex obligation to account for our belief that we have these intuitions of conceptual or logical necessity. Without difficulty, the rejectionist can allow that we do demonstrate the mastery of a concept when we use it correctly in discourse, that we do use certain words to signify certain properties, that we say that certain properties necessarily involve the possession of other properties. All that the rejectionist will allow, but he objects to the further claim that we have some theoretical *picture* that explains how it is that we do such things. The later Wittgenstein of the *Philosophical Investigations* offers, of course, the most powerful and influential attempt to rid us of the fantasy that there are such pictures.

That attempt is often summed up in the maxim that the meaning of the word is the same as its use. When across time I come to know the meaning of a word, then I find it "utterly natural" and "a matter of course" (Wittgenstein's own phrases) to use that word in a certain way. That undermines the picture of the learner being acquainted with some abstract thing or universal that he uses as the criterion of correct use. That explanatory *picture* is the fantasy we must reject. Learning the meaning of a word is simply utterly natural and a matter of course in practice.

It might be objected that it is not enough to tie meaning to use: that what is needed is a criterion for *correct* use. Wittgenstein's reply is that there is indeed a criterion for correctness. It is found in the fact that language is a social phenomenon; it is the product of communities of language users. Correct use means conformity with the common practice within the community based on what is publicly observable. Coming to know the meaning or use of a word is an inner process that is always subject to outward criteria, and even for the logical truths there must be a common public recognition of what constitutes a demonstration of necessity. From a philosophical standpoint, there is nothing more to be said. There may be cultural, historical or biological explanations of how we have come to present practice, but there is no need for philosophy to use abstract objects or intensional relations as the criteria for correct use. Such entities have no place in that natural world, which is the only one there is.

Strawson thinks that this Wittgensteinian reductionist or nominalist picture rests on two key notions: (a) the speaker who has learned to use an expression finds it "utterly natural" to apply it to a particular case, and this replaces "knowledge of the universal"; (b) correct usage is simply common agreement of usage in a shared form of life. Objections may be made to each of those two claims.

In the first case, we may indeed find it natural to see a particular thing as a car, but the question remains of why it is that we have this experience of recognizing, of *seeing as*. Wittgenstein himself says "What I perceive in the dawning of an aspect [i.e. in coming to see something as something] ... is an internal relation between it [the object] and other objects" (1973: 212). Strawson's reply is that this cannot in the end mean anything other than "falling under the same universal as ...": "the mere acknowledgement of something implicit in our commonest and most evident experience (Platonism demystified)" (SN: 83).

In the second case, the reductionist claims that the criterion for the correct use of a word or expression is simply observable agreement in linguistic practice. Strawson's reply is that this claim commits the reductionist to the recognition of an identity of type across different instances or tokens, a recognition that holds for both situation-types and sentence-types. "Type" in this case is not a mysterious something in the world, because for Strawson it is not in the world at all. It cannot be perceived, only its instances or tokens can. It is indeed an object of thought alone, and thus it is an intensional entity, but it is also an indispensable aspect of our common linguistic practice. The nominalist or revisionist will say that "being an object of thought" is on reductionist terms identical with "being a neural constituent of thinking", but the intensionalist will reply that to say that Socrates is the object of my thought is *not* to say that Socrates is located in my brain. What is true of particular natural objects is also true for abstract objects.

The ultimate issue in the debate between the realist and the nominalist will apparently come down to the question of whether the occurrence of that abstract thinking that both camps acknowledge will also involve our further recognition of abstract entities as objects of such thinking.

For the nominalist or reductionist, when a claim of conceptual truth is made with a recognition of such abstract entities, that claim is subject to debate, and the terms of that debate are no more than those dictated by our natural communal disposition to share in a linguistic "form of life". The reply of the believer in the reality of universals is that while we do indeed by nature share this disposition, truths about the abstract objects of thought are themselves no more completely dependent on our nature than are the factual truths about empirically encounterable objects. Abstract entities stand in relationships with each other that are discoverable by the human power of rational intuition.

In opposition, Quine famously holds that all propositions are empirical, concerned only with the natural world, and that they are therefore subject to continuing review and refutation. No proposition is guaranteed. All that he would require is that our systems of belief should maintain consistency. Against Quine, Strawson notes that this point of view does apparently call for consistency to be an unconditioned and necessary need. A Wittgensteinian might reply that this need is itself no more than a fact about the practice of a particular community of language users. Against that, Strawson notes that we are not only *observers* of language games, we ourselves are also *users*, and it is this role alone that enables us to understand language games other than our own.

> To put the point in old-fashioned language, we do naturally claim the power to discern "relations of ideas", as Hume would put it (i.e. relations of incompatibility, entailment, or equivalence); or, as Descartes would say, the power of "clear and distinct perception" of necessary truths; or, as both he and Spinoza would say, the power of "rational intuition" of such truths.   (SN: 91)

If those claims are justified, then the whole apparatus of meanings, universals, intensional objects generally, and necessary truths, all of this is in order as it stands and neither admits nor allows any further reduction.

The debate between the nominalist and the realist might seem to be resolvable by the "relativizing concept" that Strawson has proposed for the other dualities he has been considering. We might here once again say that there are two points of view, one being that of the external observer or nominalist, the other being that of the internal participant or realist. Each point of view is one that I may rightfully occupy on an occasion, and in so doing I am not debarred from rightfully occupying the other on another occasion. Strawson thinks that such a relativizing move, while acceptable and fruitful for the earlier dualities, is one that has little prospect for acceptance in the debate between nominalist and realist. The two camps are too deeply entrenched, and their quarrel is now set in antagonistic tones, so that the nominalist will find the realist the prisoner of a picture that holds him captive, while the realist will find the nominalist held in the grip of a reductive rage. If the conflict is irreconcilable, then Strawson's own sympathies lie with the liberal or catholic or soft naturalist rather than with those of the hard or reductive naturalist, an allegiance that will come to the reader as no surprise.

Strawson began this study of the varieties of scepticism and naturalism with an epigram from Gibbon. He concludes on the same note: "Philosophy alone can boast (and perhaps it is no more than the boast of philosophy) that her gentle hand is able to eradicate from the human mind the latent and deadly principle of fanaticism".

Hilary Putnam has written an engaging essay (Putnam 1998) on what he sees as a tension between the Strawson of *The Bounds of Sense* and the Strawson of *Skepticism and Naturalism*, between Strawson's

Kantian and Humean tendencies.[8] In *Skepticism and Naturalism*, Putnam finds Strawson taking a hard Humean line in which both the sceptic's doubts and the various attempts to rebut those doubts are all seen as pointless; we commonly believe in the external world and the uniformity of nature, and this is a matter of natural inclination and not one of reasoned conviction. Putnam sees this as a later expression of Strawson's earlier claim in *An Introduction to Logical Theory* that the practice of inductive reasoning cannot be given a general justification.[9]

Wesley Salmon (1957) had objected that if induction cannot be given a general justification, then our empirical knowledge is merely a matter of convention. Strawson's counter[10] was that Hume did not make induction a convention; instead Hume thought that induction was a natural inclination. Conventions are a matter of choice, not so our natural inclinations. It is at this point that Putnam thinks that a tension in Strawson's thought becomes manifest. In *Individuals*, Strawson says that Kant's insights are an effectively argued case against sceptical confusions, since they show that the doubts of the sceptic are unreal because they reject the very concept scheme that would make those doubts possible. In contrast, in *Skepticism and Naturalism* Strawson adopts the Humean line that our basic concept scheme is not one we choose, and that to ask for any reasoned justification is simply a mistake.

In an effort to make the tension between Strawson's two tendencies even more apparent, Putnam notes that Strawson, in his reply to Salmon, claims that "If it is said that there is a problem of induction, and that Hume posed it, then it must be added that he solved it". For Putnam, Strawson is assuming both that the sceptic's demand for justification *does* represent a problem, and that it is altogether clear that we are unable *by reasoning* to provide a "canon of induction" that would satisfy that demand. Putnam holds, *contra* Strawson's two assumptions, that it is not at all clear that there are canons of induction. The fact that we distinguish between correct and incorrect practices does not mean that there is an accompanying set of "rules". There are right and wrong ways of using a screwdriver, but that does not mean that there are explicit rules governing that use. But if there are no canons, then the "problem" of whether such a canon represents our natural beliefs simply does not arise.

Putnam's point here is that when Hume addresses the question of whether reason can tell us anything about what will happen in the future, he depends on a number of premises that must certainly be unacceptable to Strawson. Three examples will serve: (a) for Hume, an event occurring at one time has no logical or conceptual connection with what happens at another time, since those events are "loose and separate" existences; (b) the idea of a physical object enduring unobserved is incoherent; (c) only impressions and ideas exist, so that the idea of "material bodies" is incoherent. For Putnam, when Strawson wears his Kantian hat, he is surely aware that in these cases the sceptic's doubts reject the very conceptual schema that makes those doubts possible, but it is not evident how all that will be when Strawson wears his Humean hat. Putnam thinks that Strawson attempts to resolve the tension by saying that while Kant does show us how all of the elements of our conceptual schema hang together in their connectedness, he does not speak to the sceptic's challenge to that whole schema, and that Hume does speak to the challenge by contending that the question of a justification *cannot* even arise.

For Putnam, it is precisely that Humean *cannot* that is critical. On the issue of justification, we may either say with Hume that it cannot be raised because we are "hard-wired" to a set of natural inclinations, or we may say with Kant that it cannot be raised because it is not so much as intelligible. The tension, or indeed the conflict, remains, and it is evident that Putnam's own preference is Kantian.

In reply, Strawson notes that not only does he share with Putnam a general preference for Kant, but that they share as well a number of enumerated specific points, so that in the end, while there is not total agreement, the differences are small.

1. Inductive reasoning as a practice neither needs nor admits a justification.
2. There is no question of justifying by argument our belief in the reality of an external world.
3. For Putnam, those two points taken together rest on the fact that this sceptical doubt is "meaningless, or incoherent, or unintelligible". To raise the doubt can only be done from within the challenged schema. It is at this point that a difference between Putnam and Strawson becomes evident. Putnam thinks that invoking Hume on "natural belief" is gratuitous, and that Strawson's Humean tendency comes from his thinking that there *is* a problem of justification, and that Hume has solved it. Strawson's reply is that close attention to his text and its context shows that he does not think that at all. He takes Hume to have rightly dismissed the "problem" altogether.

4. Strawson shares with Putnam an appreciation of Wittgenstein's *On Certainty*. However, Wittgenstein does not speak of our "conceptual schema", but rather of that world picture that is the scaffolding of all of our thoughts, exempt from doubt, "as it were something *animal*" (Strawson 2003b: 289). For his own part, Hume says only that our natural beliefs are things we *must* take for granted, that they are not subject to rational doubt. Nonetheless, while nature may allow us no option, this on Strawson's view may simply be the outcome of a natural evolutionary process, so that the incoherence of the sceptic's doubts is not clearly incompatible with Hume's naturalism.

5. Strawson agrees with Putnam in rejecting "the whole Humean caboodle" that impressions and ideas are the only things that can be thought to exist.

6. Strawson agrees with Putnam in rejecting Hume's doctrine of "loose and separate" existences: the idea that an event occurring at one time has no conceptual or logical connection with an event occurring at another time. It is essential for Strawson, however, to remember that while the occurrences themselves have no logical connections, there may be connections among concepts, descriptions or propositions recording their existence.

7. Strawson agrees with Putnam in rejecting a sense-datum account of perception, that is, the view that in some mysterious way the perceiving subject is directly aware of a mysterious entity called the sense-datum, an entity that is *not* a state of the perceiver. Strawson and Putnam hold instead what Putnam calls an adverbial view and what Strawson calls an adjectival view, that is, that experiencing something means having a certain sort of predicate apply to a perceiver. This is without prejudice to the claim in point 6 that the perceiver's experience is an existence distinct from but causally dependent on the existence of the object.

8. Strawson agrees with Putnam that there is no essential conflict between the psychological and physical descriptions of our behaviour. A minor difference is that for Putnam "because" operates in two different ways in the two kinds of explanation, while Strawson finds no difference.

In support of his contention that there is no tension or conflict between the best of Kant and the best of Hume, Strawson comes finally to a consideration of "that old chestnut, 'the existence of the external world'" (ibid.: 291). For Putnam, the sceptical challenge in this case is rejected as simply unintelligible, a rejection that Strawson finds strong. He finds much stronger, but perhaps too strong, Wittgenstein's claim that the existence of the external world is not just one belief among others: that it is instead the framework of all coherent thought. Nonetheless, on this issue, Strawson is prepared to play the role of defending counsel for Hume. We may successfully maintain in a chastened way that while the sceptic's challenge does indeed have no practical consequence, it does remain a logical possibility. Those who rail against that possibility are, sometimes vehemently, the victims of a disorder: the tendency to reject our inner or subjective experience. This is a disorder not shared by Descartes, Locke, Hume, Kant and, Strawson is sure, Putnam.

Chapter 5

Analysis and Metaphysics:
Summing up

Beginning in 1968 and continuing until 1987, Strawson gave almost yearly at Oxford a series of introductory lectures in philosophy. In the course of those years, his account of the foundations of logical theory, his effort to provide a metaphysics that would be descriptive rather than revisionary, and his critical accounts of the philosophies of Hume and Kant were all in hand. We have seen how these works are closely and progressively related in their pursuit of certain common themes. Those lectures were gathered together and form the content of *Analysis and Metaphysics*, published towards the end of his career in philosophy. They are both introductory and comprehensive in two senses: (a) they do not presuppose any earlier familiarity with the subject; and (b) they are concerned for the most part with the general nature of philosophy rather than with a close analysis of particular problems. The book is introductory, but it is not elementary since, as Strawson puts it, there is no shallow end to the philosophical pool. It is comprehensive not in the sense that it is a summation in detail of his points of view, but in the sense that it shows the ways in which Strawson, in common with other writers in the analytic tradition, attempts to practise philosophy in its approach to resolving certain major issues arising in the connected fields of metaphysics, epistemology and the philosophy of language. The first seven chapters are based on the original set of lectures. The eighth chapter stems from a consideration of Tarski-based structural semantics in relation to meaning and understanding. The last two chapters are drawn from *Essays on Davidson: Actions and Events* (Vermazen & Hintikka 1985) and *Spinoza: His Thought and Work* (Rotenstreich & Schneider 1983).

Chapter 1: Analytical Philosophy: Two Analogies

Strawson begins with the evident fact that across time, and in the general cultural context, the term "philosophy" has had diverse and sometimes opposing meanings. One of Milton's characters says: "How charming is divine philosophy".[1] In apparent opposition is the line from Keats's *Lamia*: "Do not all charms fly at the mere touch of cold philosophy?" Strawson finds the opposition to be apparent only, since the authors are using the same word to refer to different things. Keats's "philosophy" is applied to natural science, while for Milton the word is applied to "eloquent reasoned reflection upon the moral nature of man". Keats's "philosophy" is thus dated in the sense that it is tied always to a particular moment in the ongoing advance of science, while for Milton the term refers to a systematic reflection on perennial questions about the human situation. That sort of reflection is instanced in our time in the work of such philosophers as Heidegger, Sartre and Nietzsche, where the result may be a new perspective on the place of human beings in the broad sweep of history.

For Strawson, analytic philosophers offer in contrast no such new and revealing visions of human destiny. They are instead concerned with "conceptual analysis". Analysis in this sense means a sort of breaking down, a consideration of the "pieces" of a concept and their interrelationships. This may serve as a definition, but it still leaves a great deal of room for a description of the activity involved.

One such description draws a strong and surprising similarity between the analytic philosopher and the therapist. This sort of philosopher has no doctrine; he has instead a technique, a therapeutic cure for certain kinds of intellectual disorder that results when language goes on holiday from its ordinary uses:

> When we try to think at a philosophical level, we are apt, according to this view, to fall into certain obsessive muddles or confusions; to see ourselves as led by reason to conclusions which we can neither accept nor escape from; to ask questions which seem to have no answers or only absurd answers; to become unable to see how what we know very well to be the case can possibly be the case; and so on. (AM: 3)

It is Wittgenstein (1973: §255) who suggests that the proper role of analytic philosophy in the face of such confusions is like the treatment of an illness. The analysis enables us to realize that we have been held captive by an inappropriate model, that our obsessions are much like those of the neurotic. Language leads us into these obsessive disorders when it is idle, when its engine is idling rather than engaged in use, when it goes on holiday and is detached from its ordinary and rightful use in practice. That description of the role of the philosopher has been met with bitter rejection by philosophers such as Russell and Karl Popper. Strawson himself thinks that in their zealous forms both rejection and advocacy of the therapist model are extreme, and that extreme positions are rarely right.

Strawson finds another and potentially more promising model for the analytic philosopher in an analogy drawn between the work of the philosopher and the work of the grammarian. We are able effectively to use a language long before we are introduced to the complex structures of that language's formal grammar. In a very real sense, formal grammar is of no practical use to someone already fluent in a given language, since a speaker may be perfectly able to follow the rules of a grammar without being able to state what those rules are. As individuals and as a race, we master a language long before an account of its grammar is written down.[2]

But mastery in the use of any language that goes beyond the most rudimentary thinking will require more than just an implicit knowledge of grammatical forms, since grammar itself is intertwined with a mastery of all the rich and subtly refined complex of concepts and general ideas used in our thought about the world. We have a mastery, a practising use of that complex long before we are able to attempt a theoretical account of its foundations. We use "same", "real" and "exists" long before we encounter philosophical questions about identity, reality and existence. We also speak about right and wrong, punishment, being the same person, remorse and joy, knowing and believing, classifications of kinds of things, political states and economic corporations, and we do all of that without any general theory of our practice.

Grammar's forms are thus distinguishable from but also intertwined with a complex conceptual apparatus. For the grammar that is already established in the practice of language, the grammarian attempts to provide a systematic account of the rules we so effortlessly follow. In a similar manner, the philosopher attempts to provide a systematic account of our complex conceptual apparatus. The attempt to provide such an account is a difficult one, as is evident in the tentative and awkward nature of our initial attempts to explain and describe what we easily enough do in practice.[3]

There are certainly objections to this model of the philosopher having a task parallel in many ways to the task of the grammarian. We are sometimes called to give and explain the use of words, and in practice we have ready and operative replies. For the unknowing, the chemist can indeed usefully provide a definition for "ion", as the lawyer can for "tort"; we can indeed be instructed in the use of a word, but the instruction we receive presupposes a whole conceptual apparatus for which we have no need of instruction. It is with that apparatus that the philosopher is concerned, with such concepts as those of identity, meaning and existence.

In his effort to be clear about the role of analytic philosophy, Strawson has thus offered two analogies: the philosopher as therapist and the philosopher as grammarian. The two seem to have much in common. They both stress the actual use of concepts in both our ordinary and our professional experience. But they are significantly different in that the grammatical model sees the role of the philosopher as a positive attempt to explain what is already well in place in our conceptual apparatus, while the therapist model sees that role as a negating attempt to cure the ills that come from allowing our practical concepts to idle in the mind, a cure that is effected when the puzzles are "solved" by simply disappearing.[4]

Strawson himself prefers the grammatical model, although he agrees that the history of philosophy abounds with needless puzzles for which a therapeutic approach is appropriate, and he acknowledges that the grammatical model provides the sceptic with an abundance of challenges. Ordinary language has a grammar whose structure may indeed be mastered in use long before being given a formal structure, but we may well wonder about the claim that there is a parallel conceptual framework that the philosopher fruitfully investigates. A sceptical position of that sort would surely be unacceptable to Aristotle, Descartes, Locke, Hume and Kant alike, and Strawson notes that the analytic philosopher has a ready reply to such a challenge. He can agree that there are differences between ordinary and specialized scientific languages, but then point out that the specialist himself uses at least some ordinary terms in his explanations. Moreover, while instruction in the use of terms is necessary *within* the framework of any particular science, those terms do not enable us to fit that science into our general conceptual framework. A mathematician may provide a brilliant new proof and yet be unable to say what "proof" means. Besides mathematics, there is the philosophy of mathematics, and here once again the conceptual structure of ordinary language will come into play.

The analytic philosopher who favours the *therapeutic* model has his own response to the challenge, which comes from the distinction between ordinary and specialized language. As long as we use ordinary concepts in their ordinary roles, and technical concepts in their specialized roles, all goes well enough. Problems arise only when we seek commonality between terms used both ordinarily and technically, when we drift away from the actual use of those terms in their appropriate contexts. It is in this way that we create those bizarre and senseless theories that Wittgenstein calls "houses of cards". The cure for this illness is not some new theory, but rather the therapy of being reminded of the actual and proper use of terms.

Strawson agrees that there is considerable merit in this therapeutic approach. There are numerous examples in the history of philosophy of a kind of intellectual imperialism: the way in which a philosopher will make the terms appropriate to one particular scientific discipline the master key to all general understanding. A prime example is Descartes, for whom the fully certain truths of mathematics are the consequence of its rigorous deductive methodology. Mathematics becomes the model for all of our enquiries, and there then emerges the picture of a dualistic world comprising (a) matter, whose only real properties are those of spatial extension, and (b) thinking substances, whose essence is thought. That picture has fairly drastic consequences: the existence of a material world needs to be proved, and proof comes only by the absence of a "*deus deceptor*", and all our false beliefs arise only by our willing them so. The therapist's way of showing that Descartes's "house of cards" is a needless illusion may well encourage the general conviction that *any* attempt at a positive systematic theory will fail, but Strawson is not yet ready to regard this issue as a closed case, and so he turns to a further consideration of what forms such a positive theory might take.

Chapter 2: Reduction or Connection?

Strawson has been concerned from the outset to be clear about the notion that the philosopher's enterprise is properly one of analysis. He observes now that "analysis" taken in the positive sense of the grammarian has more than one employment.

Analysis is sometimes taken to mean taking something complex and reducing it to its various elements. What counts as an element will be a function of what kind of thing we are analysing. Chemical analysis stops with chemical elements taken as simple, while physical analysis goes further. If we apply this reduction model to the

philosopher's conceptual analysis of ideas, then we shall be search-
ing for those simple ideas that are the elements out of which all our
complex ideas are constructed. Strawson finds this an implausible
project, since there is the recurring difficulty that what is presented
in reduction as a simple element may tacitly contain precisely the
complex idea that is being analysed. He suggests that instead of using
the reduction model of what "analysis" means, we consider what he
terms the connection model. Instead of attempting to reduce complex
ideas into their irreducible elements, think of a large network of ideas
that are interrelated in such a way that we can understand each only
in the context of all the others.

> If this becomes our model, then there will be no reason to be
> worried if, in the process of tracing connections from one point
> to another of the network, we find ourselves returning to ... our
> starting point. We might find, for example, that we could not
> fully elucidate the concept of knowledge without reference to the
> concept of sense perception; and that we could not explain all
> the features of the concept of sense perception without reference
> to the concept of knowledge. But this might be an unworrying
> and unsurprising fact. So the general charge of circularity would
> lose its sting, for we might have moved in a wide, revealing, and
> illuminating circle.   (AM: 19–20)

Strawson finds instances of the reductive model in the empiricist
tradition. Hume would make simple impressions and ideas the ultimate or simple elements of analysis, and irreducible elements are also
the framework of Russell's logical atomism. Reduction of that sort
has an obvious appeal, since the notion of finding something absolutely fundamental is what may attract us to philosophy in the first
place. Strawson suggests that there is a way in which the alternative
and appropriate model of connectedness both avoids the evident and
inherent difficulties of the reductionist or atomist model, and at the
same time preserves the notion of identifying something absolutely
fundamental.

To see this advantage in the connective model, consider how we
come to master the language of one of the specialized sciences. The
acquisition of the theoretical concepts of that discipline will depend
on the prior and presupposed use of the pre-theoretical concepts of
ordinary language. Ordinary language does not depend on the theoretical terms of the special sciences. The concepts of ordinary language are many, heterogeneous, provincial and reducible, but we may

nonetheless look for the ones among them that are highly general, that resist reductive definition and that are not contingent. Such concepts are basic in the sense that they form the *framework* of the ordinary language that is presupposed by the specialist. On the connection model of analysis, the task is not to reduce the complex into its simple elements, but rather to trace the connections contained within a system.

Making such non-contingency one of the features of a basic concept may seem evidently open to challenge. Strawson attempts to meet that challenge by pointing out a distinction in the use of the term "contingent". In one sense, a proposition is contingent if its denial does not generate a contradiction; thus the proposition that there are sentient beings is contingent. There is another sense. As sentient beings, we human beings have the concepts of colour and sound, but, as the blind and the deaf make manifest, we can perfectly well and without contradiction conceive of a colourless or soundless world as a human being's world. Colour and sound are not necessary constituents of human experience. Strawson thinks it improbable that this stripping down of the necessary conditions of our human experience should go on indefinitely; at some point we will come to what is irreducible, to those basic concepts that are necessary for any intelligible notion of what we mean by human experience. Readers of *The Bounds of Sense* know that Strawson finds Kant to be the philosopher who has made the most serious and determined effort to identify both the upper and the lower bounds of the minimum conceptual structure of our experience as it exists in fact.

In sum, Strawson has now identified two additional models for the work of the analytic philosopher: reduction and connection. Connection is more modest in its expectations and it is the one that Strawson himself prefers, since it is free of the charge of circularity that overhangs the reductionist or atomist model. Connection is, however, also subject to a different kind of challenge from the sceptic. We have already seen Strawson draw a comparison between two other models for the work of analysis: the positive model of the grammarian and the negative model of the therapist. The therapist is likely to cast a cold eye on the whole effort of establishing an underlying structure of our experience. His basic message is that any effort to provide a general theory inevitably leads to those confusions that therapy alone can cure. Strawson replies that the therapeutic model is itself a general theory, and that it would be difficult to support an extreme claim that there are no connections among our various human concerns.

Chapter 3: Moore and Quine

From the outset of these investigations, Strawson has been concerned to be clear about the kind of thing that philosophy is about, particularly analytic philosophy. He has considered two analogies to the work that the philosopher does, those of the therapist and the grammarian, and, while recognizing the frequent usefulness of the negative role of the therapist, he has given reasons for preferring the positive role of the grammarian. From that perspective, he has made a further distinction between analysis taken as reductive and taken as connective. Again, while recognizing the attractive charm and the real although limited usefulness of the reductive way, he has found the connective way more promising.

To this question on the nature of philosophy's task, Moore offered an answer that Strawson finds in concert with his own, although on first hearing it may seem to differ. In *Some Main Problems in Philosophy* (1953), Moore says that the most important and interesting thing that philosophers do is giving a general description of the whole universe. He starts out by giving what he regards as the common-sense view of certain fundamental questions, then giving the descriptions and definitions that the philosopher argues for in response to those questions, sometimes adding to and sometimes subtracting from common sense. The question of what kinds of things there are and are not in the universe is the most important one, and this is the area that Moore calls metaphysics or, in today's language, ontology. The general description of the whole universe will also include epistemology and logic. Moore had already addressed the whole important question of ethics in his earlier *Principia Ethica* (1903), and it is set aside and plays no part in his or Strawson's present considerations.

We have, then, the trio of metaphysics, epistemology and logic. In metaphysics, Moore talks about the "important" kinds of things that exist. Plainly, what is said to count as "important" in life will vary most widely among individuals, but Moore thinks that, for common sense, there are two items that are certainly on the list of the most important things that are, namely, physical bodies and states of consciousness. The accounts of Moore and Strawson differ in that while Moore talks about things that are, Strawson prefers talking about the concepts we use in talking about those things. The difference is real, but not without connection. It is the same enterprise to identify our most general concepts and to identify the most general kinds of things that exist. Where Moore talks about the "important" things in our experience, Strawson talks of our basic "general" concepts. We may recall that in Strawson's *Individuals*, primacy among individuals is given to things and persons, and descriptions of persons have both physical and mental predicates. The similarity to Moore's "physical bodies" and "states of consciousness" is evident.

It might be objected that it is the proper task of the philosopher precisely to challenge the ontological assumptions of common sense. Berkeley is but one example of that challenge in practice. Strawson's mild rejoinder is that it is only appropriate that we should give some weight to our most basic concepts and the ontological implications that follow. In the light of all that has been said about the importance of tending to the actual *use* of our concepts in their native practice, we should give primary importance to being clear about how our most general concepts do actually function. The proper task of the philosopher is to be clear about the most general concepts we use in organizing our experience of the world. What is our *working* ontology? Moore made metaphysics, epistemology and logic the trio that compose our effort to give a general description of the whole universe. Strawson says that the three are actually just three aspects of one unified enquiry, an assertion that he will then attempt to demonstrate in all that follows.

Strawson's demonstration starts with the question of how logic is related to our general structuring of concepts or categories. Expanding on what Kant claimed, we can say that the *use* of concepts is in forming judgements about what is or will be. Logic studies the *forms* of our discourse completely apart from any particular *content*, but in the long tradition in Western philosophy, there is nonetheless an intimate connection between logic and ontology. For Strawson's present purpose of analysing that connection, it is both necessary and sufficient to have a knowledge of the main features of the first-order predicate logic, which has its current foundations in Frege and Russell.

In a two-valued logic, every proposition is either true or false. If the truth-value of a compound proposition is altogether determined by the truth-values of the simple propositions it connects, then those connectors are said to be truth-functional. Up to this point, logic has nothing to say about the ontological order, about what exists and what does not. Turn next to a consideration of the internal structure of simple propositions. Here there is a distinction in logic between predicate letters (capitals) and individual variable letters (small). Thus the proposition "Socrates is mortal" has the logical notation

"Ms". The grammatical distinction between subject and predicate seems naturally associated with the functional distinction between reference and predication. If those distinctions can in turn be paired with ontological distinctions, then a connection between logic and ontology will be established.

Strawson addresses that issue by noting that our thought is not limited to propositions about individual objects of reference and what may be predicated of them: we are capable of generalized thinking. Instead of saying that Socrates is mortal, we may want to say that all human beings are mortal, or that some human beings are mortal. In standard logic, that is accomplished by quantification over particulars. There are two "quantifiers": the universal quantifier x is the symbol for "every", and the existential quantifier $\exists$ is the symbol for "some". In the canonical notation of contemporary logic, the logical notions of reference and predication, truth-functional composition, quantification and identity correspond to individual variables and predicate letters, propositional connectives, quantifiers and identity. The notation also includes brackets or some other device to indicate the scope of connectives and quantifiers.

There is the question of how the framework of the canonical notation of logic is related to the ontological structure of reality. Quine finds the connection very close: "The quest of a simplest, clearest overall pattern of canonical notation is not to be distinguished from a quest of ultimate categories, a limning of the most general traits of reality" (1960: 161). The tie between logic and ontology in the framework of all of our thinking that would thus be provided for requires some actual filling out in practice, and Quine would accomplish that through the memorable epigram, "To be is to be the value of a variable". That statement's very conciseness leaves much to be understood, but Strawson thinks that an indirect approach to what it intends can be made. If we are talking seriously about the world as we take it to be, and if we use a singular substantive to refer to a particular individual person or thing and attribute some characteristic to that individual, then plainly what we say may be true only under the condition that we think that individual *exists*. In just the same way, when we talk in generality about some or about all individuals, and in logical notation make use of an existential or universal quantifier, we equally believe that there exists at least one such individual. To be is indeed to be the value of a variable.

In all of this, there are fundamental disagreements between Strawson and Quine. Quine thinks that references to individuals are always paraphrases of variables under quantification, and that clarity of thought is obtained without loss when we substitute the paraphrase and eliminate the direct reference. The connection of logic and ontology would in this way be secured. Strawson's reservations about this doctrine begin with the need to know just how our statements in ordinary language get rendered into quantifying paraphrases. That such paraphrases can be made is evident enough, but Quine has in mind only those paraphrases that meet two conditions: (a) they must be done in a vocabulary that is clear and scientifically acceptable; and (b) they must conform to the principle of economy, so that ontology is restricted to what is strictly necessary. With this strict and lean parsimony, much of ordinary language can be done away with.

The basis of Strawson's disagreement with Quine's programme is now evident. Strawson has already made his distinction between the reductive and connective models of analysis. Quine's programme is obviously an exercise in ontological reduction, a form of analysis whose appeal and utility are, for Strawson, outbalanced by both the impossiblity of its realization and its tendency to foster misleading pictures of the world.

> The ontological reductionist draws, in principle, a single sharp distinction among the kinds of things which, taking the loose and self-indulgent habits of our ordinary talk as our guide, we seem to refer to. There are those among them which we must truly regard as the indispensable objects of reference, those which resist the pressures of critical paraphrase; and there are the rest – the ones that can be pitched into the ontological dustbin. But one can easily imagine a less austere, a more tolerant and what might, in one sense, be called a more catholic, approach. Instead of just the saved and the lost, we might have an ontological hierarchy; instead of just the ins and the outs, an order of priority. (AM: 46)

Strawson's preference in analytic philosophy is clearly for the connective rather than the reductive model. In order to make real progress on the issue of the relation between logic and ontology, Strawson sees a need at this point to bring in the third member of Moore's trio: to have epistemology join logic and ontology in the mix. Strawson is still in pursuit of his claim that all three are actually just three aspects of one unified enquiry. The claim is not simply asserted, it is defended, as will now become evident.

Chapter 4: Logic, Epistemology, Ontology

Strawson's explication of the relations among logic, epistemology and ontology begins once again with Kant's dictum that our use of concepts is in making judgements, the forming or holding of beliefs about what is the case. That establishes the relevance of a study of the general forms of judgement. We evidently want our judgements to be true, that is, that what we think ought to correspond to what is the case in the world, that things are as we take them to be. Whatever we take the merits of this venerable correspondence theory of truth to be, it at least has the merit of underscoring the distinction between our judgements about the world and the way things are in reality. Judgements may be either true or false, and the criterion is reality as it is in itself. "It is raining in Paris" is true if and only if it is raining in Paris.

We may debate whether a particular judgement is true or false. That is plainly how it is in our disagreements over whether our moral judgements correspond to natural facts. In addition it may be argued that the truths of logic and mathematics have a value criterion other than that of correspondence. The challenges to an all-embracing correspondence theory of truth that may arise from issues of that sort are of no interest to Strawson in his present enterprise. He is concerned only with judgements about the natural world, that is, with the questions that result from the claimed correspondence between the natural world as it is in itself and, in distinction, our beliefs about that world.

We come to form judgements about that natural world by way of our *experience*, and we are now drawn immediately into questions of *epistemology*. The reader of Strawson's *The Bounds of Sense* will recall that he finds Kant's efforts to establish the bounds of our possible experience both brilliant and without parallel in modern philosophy. For Kant, all of our experience arises with sensation. Our intuitions or immediate experiences of the world are without exception sensuous. The forms of those intuitions, space and time, are blind without their use in concepts, but the concepts can in turn mean nothing apart from their direct or indirect relation to a possible experience of the real. For Strawson, that is the central tenet of all *empiricism*, and he thinks that Kant's version of empiricism avoids the errors inherent in other versions, both early and late.

Empiricism begins with the duality of the judging subject and objective reality. Experience bridges the gap and in so doing it gives all of our concepts their sense of content. Our concepts apart from their employment with sensation are empty. The evident danger in this approach is that objective reality may get swallowed up by the subject's experience, with various idealisms and phenomenalisms quick to follow. Strawson's way with his danger is not to struggle to get out of it, but simply to avoid it, while continuing his pursuit of justifying the claim that logic, epistemology and ontology are just three interdependent aspects of one unified enquiry.

Among those three, start with logic. To make a judgement is to apply some general concept to some particular case. To use concepts at all, we must be able to distinguish among *different* particular cases while at the same time recognizing them as being *alike* in being apt for the application of the same concept. The evident foundation for the distinctions that we do make among the particular things that we refer to is their location in a common spatiotemporal grid. We see two sheep, spatially different but gathered under the same concept; we hear two strikings of a bell, temporally different but gathered under the same concept.

At this point, it is critical to remember that Strawson makes a pivotal distinction between the uses of "particular" and "individual". The distinction is made and fully explicated in *Individuals*, especially in Part II, an account of which is found in Chapter 3 above. Anything whatsoever can be identifyingly referred to, and these objects of reference are all of them individuals. Particulars are the items having a location on the spatiotemporal grid, primarily material bodies. In our discourse, a concept may be referred to and therefore may serve either as a subject or as a predicate. In contrast, particulars in standard use are subjects but not predicates.

We distinguish in logic between subject and predicate, and in ontology between particular instances and general concepts. The bridge between those two distinctions is based on the empirical principle that all of our concepts have meaningful employment only in their application to the objects of our sensuous intuitions, and that the forms of those intuitions are exclusively those of space and time. Concepts may indeed serve as individuals referred to, but their ultimate significance is rooted in our empirical experience of particulars. Here Strawson concludes that his pursuit of relational connections among logic, epistemology and ontology is now at least in part successful. His ties to Kant are nowhere more evident.

Chapter 5: Sensible Experience and Material Objects

For Strawson, our experience of the world is thus always in the spatiotemporal context of "here" and "now". Sense perception is therefore the root of our making *true* judgements about the objective spatiotemporal world. This notion of sense perception making possible true judgements about the world is in turn rooted in the notion that there should be some reasonably regular relation of *causal dependence* of our experience in sense perception on the way things are in the world apart from our perception of them.

Plants and instruments of utility are themselves part of the objective world they respond to. Human conscious awareness differs in that we employ *concepts* in making judgements about that world. This could lead us to the view that the way we acquire knowledge about the world involves two radically distinct steps: first there is sense experience of the world, and then there is conceptual judgement, which issues from that experience. For Strawson, that account can be misleading, since it suggests the view that there are two distinct causal relationships, that our sense experience is causally dependent on the external world, and that in turn our concepts are causally dependent on that experience. Concept formation and sense experience actually interpenetrate far more closely than the dual causation image may suggest:

> For example, the best way, indeed normally the only way, of giving a veridical description of your current visual experience ... is to describe what you take yourself to be *seeing* out there is the world in front of you .... The point is that the concepts that are necessary for the *experience* description are precisely those that are necessary for the *world* description.
>
> (AM: 63, emphasis added)

If the conceptual judgements we make are to be true in their reference to an objective spatiotemporal world, then evidently they must use concepts of just those kinds of things that actually are in the world and of the properties they actually have. But now a problem may seem to arise. Our experience of the world is one of objects having both spatial location and spatial properties such as size and shape. We become aware of those properties and positions by all sorts of properties that are visual and tactile rather than spatial. We discriminate among particulars as quickly by their colour as by their spatial characteristics. When we learn about the actual causal mechanism of sight perception, we may then come to regard spatial location and properties as uniquely "objective", reducing all else to the merely "subjective". We may think that things in the objective world actually do have size and shape and location, while the property of "red" is simply a function of the kind of sensory apparatus we human beings happen to have. We may come to the conclusion that we do not perceive things as they "really" are, but only as they appear to us.

Strawson thinks that this conclusion, rightly understood, is perfectly acceptable. We need only to distinguish between two senses of "things as they really are". In the first sense, colour is excluded, since here the standard of reality lies within the domain of physical theory. In the second sense, colour is included, since here we are referring to the normal conditions of observation. Under those "intersubjective" conditions, the conditions common to all of us, things with spatial properties have characteristics other than the spatial ones. Both the theoretical and the normal models have their own validity. To be obsessed with the theoretical model alone is to lose the distinction between "subjective" and "intersubjective", and to forget the role of the objective in our normal and ordinary lives as social and intercommunicating persons. In those lives, objects must be perceived also to have visual and tactile qualities if they are to be perceived as occupying space. Things that have shape have colour as well.

The objective world of our experience is always both *from* a particular spatial point of view and *at* a particular time, a "here" and a "now". The very notion "now" requires the notions of a past remembered and a future that may be anticipated, and that in turn requires the notion of a relative persistence across time for at least some of the objects within our changing perceptions. Change as compared to mere succession requires something that in some sense does not change. Those identity-retaining and space-occupying individuals are the material bodies that make up the unified spatiotemporal framework of our world. Those bodies are the primary referents of our nouns and noun phrases, and in this fact Strawson finds the tie between our ordinary language and the objective world it reflects.

Chapter 6: Classical Empiricism and The Inner and The Outer

Strawson has declared, and shown his commitment to, the empiricist principle. There is more than one version of that principle. For Kant, all of our experience arises with sensation. Our intuitions or immediate experiences of the world are without exception sensuous. The forms of those intuitions, space and time, are blind without their use in concepts, but the concepts can in turn mean nothing apart from their direct or indirect relation to a possible experience of the real.

For Strawson, this Kantian empiricism differs markedly and saves us from the confusions inherent in classical British empiricism. There the entire general structure of our ideas is derived from a certain small basic part of itself, the *given*, namely, the time-ordered sequence in the subject's mind of his subjective mental states, especially his own sensory experiences. Those states are images of simple sensory qualities. This classical empiricism has in turn three varieties. In the first, our ordinary beliefs are a *theory* that stands in need of an explanation along the lines of the sort of rational justification we give for our complex scientific theories. In the second variety, our ordinary beliefs are simply those we are stuck with in our human condition. This is Hume's stance, the view that these beliefs neither need nor admit a further proof. The third type of classical empiricism holds that there are basic elements in the general structure of our thoughts, and that all other notions are "logical constructs" out of those elements.

Strawson opposes all three varieties of that empiricism. Against the first, the general structure of our thought is not derived from sensory experience. That general structure is instead presupposed by enquiry we may make into the foundation of our ordinary beliefs. Against the second, while Hume accepted our natural beliefs as beyond justification, he then searched for a causal account of why those are our beliefs, a search the terms of which once again presupposes the framework the search would question. The "logical atomism" of the third version is simply a particular instance of that reductionist model of philosophical analysis that Strawson has already found implausible, since there is here once again the recurring difficulty that what is presented in reduction as a simple element may tacitly contain precisely the complex idea that is being analysed.

Classical empiricism in all of its varieties may be seen as an "internalism" in the sense that it seeks its basis in a series of subjective mental states, with the existence of an objective physical world made problematic. Strawson finds the errors of this internalism turned upside down in the complementary error he terms "externalism". Here the existence of an objective physical world of objects interacting in space is what is taken for granted, and it is the reality of the subjective world that is challenged. The reductionism of the third variety of internalist classical empiricism is paralleled by the externalist reductionism of an ostensibly hard-headed or scientific approach.

One thing that might seem to support that externalist view is the claim that the characteristics of physical bodies interacting in space are definite and observable, while the characteristics of mental states are elusive and not observable. Strawson finds that claim absurd:

> Let us concentrate our attention on ... *observability in perception.* Suppose we are ... observing some rich and complex physical scene .... Then note that the perceptual experience of observing ... the scene is no less rich and complex than the physical scene itself *as we see it.* To try to effect an externalist reduction of the perceptual experience is not only intrinsically absurd; it is self-defeating; for it strikes at the very ground of the attraction of externalism itself: that is, the satisfactorily and definitely observable nature of the public, physical scene .... The full and rich description of the physical world *as perceived* yields incidentally and at the same time a full and rich description of the subjective experience of the observer. (AM: 75–6)

There is a further difficulty with externalism. Leibniz made the distinction between truths of reason and truths of fact, and other philosophers have spoken of the distinction between necessary and contingent truths, or between analytic and synthetic truths. Accounts of these distinctions make use of the notion of *meaning*, of the identity or inclusion or incompatibility of the *senses* of the *propositions* we use in sentences. Those meanings or senses are what Quine and others call "intensions". For the defenders of externalism, those intensions are internal subject states, and as such they are infected with "mentalism". They stand in invidious comparison to what is external and observable. Instead of speaking in terms of intensions, the externalist would have us turn our attention to such publicly observable features of language as spoken or written tokens of sentences and the outward patterns of behaviour in response to their use. It comes as no surprise that in his rejection of intensions the externalist has no use for a distinction between necessary and contingent truths, since all truth claims are subject to continuing empirical revision.

Strawson disagrees with the externalist position. As language users, our recognition of such features as incompatibility and necessity is possible only through the meanings or senses of the words we use. If this be mentalism, then so be it, and so much the worse for externalism. Some sort of "mentalism" is as necessary in our account of language as it is in our account of perception.

Thus the unbridled mentalism of classical empiricism and the unbridled physicalism of externalism are equally unacceptable to Strawson as comprehensive accounts of our system of ideas. We may wonder what Strawson might offer as an alternative. He asks us to attend to two other features of our experience, for neither of which he claims necessity, but both of which he finds pervasive. Those features are *agency* and *society*. We are beings capable of action, and we are social beings. Not only do I experience a spatiotemporal world of which I am myself a member, a world about which I make judgements, but I also *act* in that world. We are cognitive beings, *and* we are also agents. Those two roles are tied to each other because we favour or disfavour states of affairs that either are or may be, and we act to obtain what we believe desirable and to avoid its opposite. Our actions are based on our beliefs about the nature of things, and we consequently have a concern that those beliefs be true. In learning the nature of things, we learn at the same time our possibilities of action. When we act, we also then learn that by the nature of things there are limitations to those possibilities. Our roles as cognitive beings and as agents of change go hand in hand.

Some seeing is believing, and to believe is to be prepared to act in a certain way. It is not true that we first build up a cognitive picture of the world, develop habits of action, and then enter into social relations with other persons, confronting new situations and new questions. It is instead the case that all of our cognitive and volitional activity occurs from the outset in a social context of interpersonal contact and communication. This is especially true in the case of our language acquisition.

Our actions are tied to our beliefs, and we are therefore concerned that those beliefs be true. This leads Strawson directly to a closer consideration of the nature of truth and knowledge.

Chapter 7: Truth and Knowledge

There are two traditional theories about the meaning of "truth". The correspondence theory holds that a belief is true if and only if it corresponds to what is the case. "It is raining in Paris" is true if and only if it is raining in Paris. The coherence theory holds that a statement is true if and only if it is "a member of a coherent, consistent and comprehensive system of held beliefs" (AM: 83). Any apparent conflict may be more seeming than real, and Strawson finds it worthwhile to start with some commonly held platitudes about the general nature of the concept of truth:

- Beliefs are partly based on *personal experience.*
- But most beliefs are not first-hand. They are instead rooted in instruction and communication and are thus second-hand.
- Our beliefs include not only particular observations and expectations, but also general beliefs about the identity of objects across time and about the conditions under which our expectations may be realized.
- Candidates for belief may conflict directly with each other or indirectly in the context of a more general belief.
- There is a need for consistency in belief, since it is a necessary condition for an unstressed and successful accomplishment of our goals.
- In the context of a general body of beliefs, there will arise the question of the admission of a new candidate, possibly at the cost of expelling a present member.

Those six seem uncontroversial to Strawson and serve as a background to the question of the relationship between correspondence and coherence. Correspondence means that there is a reality independent of our experience and our judgement. Coherence emphasizes interrelatedness among our beliefs. Put in those terms, and in the context of the six uncontroversial platitudes, both theories have merit and are indeed complementary. Both are theories about truth, and that notion itself calls for some analysis.

The logical formula that it is true that p if and only if p seems to apply to all possible propositions. To say that all exemplifications of that apparently simple formula are true would not count as a theory of truth; something more would be needed. That usually takes the particular form of either a theory of *knowledge* or a theory of *meaning*, and this is not surprising, since the notion of truth is central to each. For a belief to count as knowledge, it must be true. Suppose that someone says that John is bald. That statement is true if and only if John is bald. It is apparent that in this case there is a certain correspondence between two things, between word and world. In Austin's perceptive words, it takes two to make a truth (AM: 88). There is a tie between word and world, and this is the basis of any theory of either meaning or knowledge. They are just two aspects of a single theory of truth.

Strawson finds that this closer analysis of the apparently simple "*p* if and only if *p*" has offered clarifying insight. He also thinks that this awareness of the correspondence in truth between word and world may also lead us to a too narrow notion of truth. Consider the claim that the statement "$7 + 5 = 12$" is true. Where is the correspondence of word and world in this case? Or consider the claim that the statement "John ought to care for his brother" is true. Where is correspondence here? Statements about mathematics or about morals seem not amenable to any word-to-world correspondence.

Strawson considers two frequently offered replies to these challenges. The first would simply deny that such statements are propositions at all in a proper sense. They are neither true nor false in the correspondence sense. They are instead rules or imperatives that serve as guidelines for acting in or reasoning about the world. The second reply would include Platonism in mathematics and something like Moore's ethical intuitionism in morals. Both are attempts to expand the notion of the real. For Platonism, the world of the Ideas has its own existential reality. For Moore, supervening the qualities and relations found in nature there are our non-natural ethical intuitions. It is as immediately evident that the wanton destruction of beautiful things is bad as it is that this leaf is yellow.

Neither Platonism in mathematics and logic nor intuitionism in ethics is in wide favour today, and Strawson looks for an alternative that would preserve a form of correspondence for word and world. He thinks the best approach is to begin with the relatively simple cases where the correspondence model does fit, and then proceed cautiously to go beyond that start to the more complex issues, being careful not to feed on either myth or illusion as we go along.

Having considered the relationship of a word–world correspondence to the notion of truth, Strawson turns to a parallel consideration of the notion of knowledge. He has argued that our capacity to recognize particulars as being of a certain kind is fundamental to both language and knowledge in general. That sound conviction carries with it an insidious temptation. Consider the case where we have a new and correct *observation* about how things are in the world. There is the question of how this observation is to fit into our presently established general picture of that world. This may lead us to seek the ultimate foundations for all of our beliefs. Any structure has foundations on which it is built, and to remove any part of that foundation is a threat to the structure as a whole. We come then to think that *correct observation* is the foundation of our entire thought structure. Err here and the whole structure falls.

While perhaps initially plausible, Strawson finds this foundation metaphor preposterous. The reason I have for a present belief is not always an observation, present or past, that I can immediately bring to mind. Moreover, the observations I do appeal to have themselves presuppositions, which are in turn not supported by immediate observation. The foundation metaphor rests on the thought that all of my beliefs are a pyramid structure, with observation at the base. For Strawson, my thought structure is not reductionist in that way. It is instead a series of connections among all of my various thoughts.

We might suppose more modestly that while observation is not always the immediate checkpoint, it is nonetheless the ultimate one. Even that cannot be the whole story. Many "observations" are based on prior beliefs. "Observation" often leads back to some authority figure or canonical text. Any serious doubt that I may have does itself *presuppose* a vast background of connections. Once again, a patient consideration of those connections found within my thought structure is a far more fruitful approach to philosophical analysis than the reductionism of the foundational metaphor.

We do indeed have the power of critical reflection on the whole world picture, which is being continuously shaped by my interaction with the world, but that power of reflection arises only after there is a prior body of belief. Strawson cites Wittgenstein (1969) in support of the view that when we first begin to believe anything, we believe not a single proposition but instead a whole interacting complex of propositions.

Strawson offers in conclusion not a theory, but a practical precept:

> Not every accepted belief or purported piece of information can be checked or tested against the evidence of our eyes and ears; but some can and should be. A radical and all-pervasive (i.e., a philosophical) scepticism is at worst senseless, at best idle; but one of the things we learn from experience is that a practical and selective scepticism is wise, particularly when what is in question are the assertions of interested parties or of people with strong partisan or ideological views, however personally disinterested they may be. (AM: 96)

Chapter 8: Meaning and Understanding

The "linguistic turn" in contemporary analytic philosophy has brought a new focus to the question of the relationship between the structure of our language and the structure of our thinking. Language serves to express thought. Language is the outward visible and audible *sign* of the inner thing. The structure of language is its grammar, and a major portion of Strawson's career in philosophy has been given over to a complementary and detailed account of the necessary structure of all of our thinking, the sort of structure Kant attempted to discern in the *Critique of Pure Reason*. For Strawson, the relation between these two structures is a two-way street. While language, as an outward sign of an inner thing, must depend on thought, it is no less true that thought depends on language, since we can think only what we are able to say and understand. Clear-thinking about how it is between language and thought will thus depend on what it means to say that we understand a sentence.

The number of sentences we can understand is without limit, but that understanding has just two necessary and sufficient conditions. We need a *grammar*, a finite set of the general types of the significant combinations of linguistic elements, and we need a finite *vocabulary* of those elements, the references of names and predicates. Among our various ordinary languages there are various grammars, but the intertranslatability of those languages suggests their fundamental underlying common structure. For Quine, all of the semantic structures of ordinary language can be reduced to the structures of formal logic, and the tie between thought and language is thereby established, but Strawson thinks that such a reductionist program has its own assumptions. It assumes that to understand a sentence is to grasp its truth conditions, to understand is to know what it means to believe that a sentence is true. If we also suppose that true predication means correctly applying a concept to an individual referred to, then logic offers us a few simple recursive rules relating to quantification and sentence composition that will enable us to generate an infinite number of sentences whose truth conditions are thereby known. On this programme and with its assumptions, logic gives us not only the model for what we seek, but also the necessary structural key to any adequate semantic theory for any ordinary language.

Not surprisingly, Strawson finds all sorts of difficulties in this reductionist model. To make it initially plausible, its supporters will have to resort to an ingenious paraphrasing of the sentences of ordinary language in order to arrive at their "true logical form". That exercise of ingenuity is for Strawson unrealistic, indeed slightly comic. It assumes that the point of the paraphrasing is to make clear how it is that the language user is able to understand the meaning of an unlimited number of sentences, but those meanings are obviously already mastered by the ordinary person who has no parallel implicit grasp of the nuances of formal logic. The urge to paraphrase becomes particularly acute in the case of sentences that report actions or events. Strawson finds Davidson's attempt, through paraphrasing, to reduce such sentences to the structures of formal logic particularly ingenious, but this exercise is as unnecessary as it is unrealistic. What we need first and above all to keep in mind is that our objective world is a spatiotemporal world:

> For, as I have emphasized earlier, it is a quite fundamental feature of our conceptual scheme that we conceive of the world as spatio-temporal and hence that we have the idea of places and times at which things happen or at which people act in various ways. What could be more simple and straightforward than the idea of a construction whereby we may tack on to the verbs of happening or action ... a phrase which answers ... when? and where? questions. The capacity to recognize such phrases *as having such a function* is all we need .... The thought that we need more ... begins to look like a symptom of an unreasoned determination to force ... as many as possible ... of the structural semantic principles of combination which we understand into the framework of standard logic. (AM: 103–4)

Strawson has been concerned throughout to show the interconnectedness of logic, metaphysics and epistemology. That connection is again made apparent when we recognize that our objective world is a spatiotemporal world, a metaphysical principle that must be invoked if we are to make progress in the philosophy of language, just as we need to invoke epistemology to make progress in metaphysics.

We attempt here to explain our mastery of an unlimited number of sentences in our ordinary discourse. Quine's reductionist method will not do, and we may well wonder what Strawson may offer as an alternative. He says that he is not prepared to provide a detailed and comprehensive project that will explain all; at most he can offer us a programme that will take us a little way. He says that a start has been made in his *Subject and Predicate in Logic and Grammar* (1974b), but that the successful execution of such a programme would call for "an unexampled combination of linguistic knowledge, philosophical insight, logical expertise, industry, and perseverance" (AM: 108). He is perhaps overly modest in his disclaimer. Those interested in the relationship between word and world, and the interconnectedness among logic, metaphysics and epistemology, will also find much that is worth considering in his *Individuals*, especially in Part II.

Chapter 9: Causation and Explanation

Strawson is concerned with the conceptual framework of all of our thinking. Two elements within that framework are the notions of causation and explanation. We sometimes presume causality as a natural relation, and we rightly associate it with explanation, but explanation is an intellectual or rational or intensional relation that holds among *facts* or *truths*, while causation holds among *things* in the natural world.

We have expressions that are used to cover both causation and explanation, for example, "due to". Often we do not distinguish between the two, and often we do not need to. We may say that particular happening A is the cause of particular happening B. That relationship in *nature* holds for whatever *descriptions* our language may provide for A and B, so that some A-involving fact *explains* some B-involving fact. We then rightly believe that the power of one fact to explain another fact must have some kind of root in the natural world. If we do not believe that, we would apparently be left with the "received view" of Hume, namely, his contention that "causality" has no existence outside our minds, that it is instead merely a subjective impression that we impose on the world.

For Strawson, that received view is partly right and partly wrong. It is true that there is neither a single relation nor a gathering of natural detectable relations that we can identify in our observation vocabulary as *the* causal relation. That negative starting-point can lead us by way of a premature generality to the wrong conclusion that causality has no foundation at all in our observation vocabulary, whereas in fact there are all sorts of actions that are directly observable and that are rightly called causal in so far as they bring something about. When we report such actions, we use a two-place predicate, and at least one of those two places is filled by designating some particular substance, typically the action of some agent on some patient:

> Thus one thing ... acts to bring about an effect, a new state of affairs ... by a characteristic exercise of causal power; and in observing such a transaction one already possesses the explanation (or at

least the immediate explanation) of the new state of affairs. There is no question of dissolving the transaction into a sequence of states of affairs – a sequence of "distinct existences" – and wondering whether ... the sequence constitutes a causal sequence. One has *observed* the change being *brought about* in some characteristic mode. (AM: 116)

Thus we simply observe the stone *break* the glass, the rolling boulder *flatten* the Alpine hut, the boy *close* the door. That *is* the cause, and that *is* the explanation. Hume sought the *impression* from which the *idea* of causality is derived. He ignored the common impression of force being exerted or suffered. He sought falsely to atomize the whole experience and then to find the impression that would serve as the connecting link for the elements. For Strawson, that misstep characterizes Hume's entire phenomenology of perception.

Our immediate explanations of causation in terms of gross observation may be succeeded by a search for more sophisticated explanations. At the further limits of that search, the utility of the gross models may diminish to the vanishing point, but that is a point no one occupies for very long and many of us do not occupy at all. The basic model for causality is the notion of attraction and repulsion, the foundation of all physical theory. This model of mechanical interaction as paradigmatically explanatory may be gross, but it is nonetheless both fundamental and the source of analogical application. Thus it is by analogy to physical push and pull that we speak of our emotions in terms of being drawn to or repelled by their objects.

The objection might be made that Strawson moves too quickly from the observable production of a particular effect, the stone breaking the glass, to a very general theory of the concept of causality. Strawson meets that objection and fortifies his own position by considering once again the concepts that we have of the types or kinds of things or substances we encounter in our experience. Those concepts are dispositional, that is, types of things have characteristic dispositions to act and react in certain ways under certain circumstances. We may indeed observe some particular action without knowing which circumstances are operative in this case, and we may indeed demand some further explanation, but we know in advance the range of possibilities that will fill the gap in explanation. The *general* notion of causality is already lodged within us, and it is implicit in our dispositional notion of kinds of things.

Hume notwithstanding, the notion of causality is not derived from bare regularities of succession among the events in our experience.

It is not true that our concepts of things are built up out of non-dispositional elements. Those concepts are dispositional from the outset, and Hume and the other reductionists have put the cart before the horse. Strawson finds that Kant is fundamentally right against Hume. The concept of causality is not derived *from* experience, it arises *with* experience. It is a presupposition of experience.

Strawson sees the attraction and repulsion of bodies as the fundamental model for the notions of causality and explanation. There are other models, notably that of human agency. It is not by way of Hume's "constant junction of impressions" that we human beings talk about why we act as we do. We know full well what we are doing and what we are trying to do. We have an immediate and not indirect knowledge of causal activity. Each of us can cause events, we see that there are other human beings with a like capacity, and we seek to influence their behaviour by providing them with appropriate motivations. We also see events in nature that are so vast that they are beyond human control or influence, and we have then attributed these effects to supernatural beings whose favour we have sought to gain by acts of worship and sacrifice, although with a poor yield in terms of practical success. Strawson's point here is that agency as a model for causality and explanation is no more supportive of Hume's account than is the model of physical attraction and repulsion.

In the march of science, theories of superhuman agency have given way to more successful theories that make no reference to motives. This greater success was the result of a greater understanding of causal power, which led to increased certainty in prediction and control. The notion of causal power is in turn inseparable from the notion of natural kinds and their propensities. When an expected response in terms of a current understanding of those powers and propensities has not been forthcoming, the result has been a search for a deeper level of explanation, one to be given in the terms of the strict laws of a physical theory that go beyond the level of ordinary observed regularity. For Strawson, the establishing of those laws has characteristically come about in a two-step process. There is the initial framing of a hypothesis, and this is followed by its testing in "carefully contrived observational situations" (AM: 127).

Strawson characteristically concludes that this continuing march towards an ever more general and ever more powerful physical theory should not lead us to think that our ordinary explanations of events in causal terms is rooted in a belief in some prior general and exceptionless discoverable law. It is instead true that our ordinary explanations in causal terms are not deficient, needing some further justification. The notion of causal efficacy is rooted in our very ordinary and common concepts.

Besides this unneeded "need" of a prior physical theory, Strawson finds another misleading account of the notion of the way causality is actually embedded in our ordinary ideas of things. This is the received doctrine that if circumstances X obtain, then the occurrence of event type a is a necessary and sufficient condition of event type b. The odd philosophical consequence of this doctrine is that we have no justification for calling the two events either "cause" or "effect"; indeed, we have no justification for distinguishing them at all. We may say only that they have a symmetrical mutual dependence. In opposition to that misleading doctrine, our common experience of causality maintains a natural asymmetry between type a and type b, since our embedded belief is that effects never precede their causes.

Chapter 10: Freedom and Necessity

Kant thought that there are three questions that are perennial in human thought in their *sic et non* forms: freedom of the will, the immortality of the human soul and the existence of God. Following his account of the concept of causality, Strawson turns naturally enough to a consideration of the freedom, or its absence, in acts of human willing. To give focus to this consideration, he begins with two theses of Spinoza:

(1) Freedom is an illusion, natural causality reigns.
(2) This illusion rests on a combination of (a) consciousness of our actions, and (b) ignorance of their causes.

Strawson will argue against both theses.

In accordance with Kant, it is commonly believed that we act under the idea of freedom. Kant held that this belief is incompatible with a belief in universal causality for reasons that Strawson finds doubtful. A more pedestrian view holds that freedom is incompatible with causality in the limited sense that someone being restrained by some physical force or psychological compulsion is not free to have acted otherwise. On that view, at least some of our actions are not free in the sense that they are limited by external or internal forces, but there would still remain questions on what further limitations there may be on the notion of a free will.

We are not totally ignorant of at least some of our actions having causes. If that is true in some cases, why not in all? Why not say with Spinoza that our present illusion of a will free of constraint is rooted in our present ignorance of the actual and necessary causes of our action? Why should there be any notion of free will at all? Strawson sketches three ways in which this notion arises as our natural belief.

A phenomenology of our sense of freedom starts with the fact that our desires and our preferences are not experienced as some kind of an alien presence, rather they are *ours*; indeed, there is a sense in which we *are* our desires. In contrast to them, there are indeed intrusive compulsions, where there is no sense of freedom. The absence of the sense of freedom in such cases is *not* simply due to my knowing the cause of the compulsion, since I may be ignorant of the cause and still regard the actions as alien intrusions.

A second aspect of our sense of freedom comes with a consideration of the way in which deliberation relates to our desires and preferences. We do not think of ourselves as mere spectators passively observing the contending struggles among our desires. We have instead a sense of deliberation resulting in that higher-order desire we call choice. This experience also strengthens our sense of self.

A third and related source of our sense of freedom comes from our repeated and ordinary experience of agency. We experience our actions issuing from our intentions, with those intentions issuing in turn from a combination of our beliefs and our desires. We have an immediate knowledge of our actions performed intentionally; we do not view them as a sequence of events we passively observe.

The sense of freedom we have for ourselves we attribute to others, and this natural fact is closely linked with the notions we have of moral judgement and moral desert, and consequently with the idea that the agent *could have acted differently*. But if universal determinism is so, then apparently all such attitudes are not appropriate. It is supposed by some that "He could have acted otherwise" is equivalent to "There was no sufficient natural impediment or bar, *of any kind whatsoever, however complex*, to his acting otherwise". Those accepting that equivalence find a consequent unresolvable conflict between the notions of moral desert and a universal determinism. It is an equivalence Strawson does not accept:

> I find it difficult, as others have found it difficult, to accept this equivalence. The common judgement of this form amounts rather to the denial of any sufficient natural impediment *of certain specific kinds or ranges of kinds*. For example, "He could (easily)

have helped them (instead of withholding help)" may amount to the denial of any lack on his part of adequate muscular power or financial means. Will the response, "It simply wasn't in his nature to do so" lead to a withdrawal of moral judgement in such a case? I hardly think so; rather to its reinforcement.   (AM: 136–7)

Our proclivity to moral attitude together with its link to our sense of freedom is a natural fact of the human condition. Our sense of freedom is in turn closely linked with our sense of self, since our awareness of our choices is at the same moment our awareness of ourselves. We see other persons as being linked as we ourselves are linked, and this is not a conclusion reached by analogical reasoning, it is instead the immediate feeling that we have towards each other as *other selves* in our common experience of human involvement and human interaction.

Strawson agrees that Spinoza has dealt with these attitudes and emotions as simply natural facts with analyses of admirable and unparalleled psychological insight. What Strawson disputes is the claim that the sense of freedom and self is incompatible with universal natural causality, the claim that our sense of freedom rests either on false belief or on ignorance. I can be knowledgeable about causal sources of my dispositions and nonetheless know them as *mine.* I can talk at great length about nature and nurture as the two sources of my dispositions, but all such talk is a relatively vague and inexact knowledge, and Strawson thinks that it is likely to remain so.

It may be argued that this vague and inexact knowledge of the present is progressively being replaced by an *exact* knowledge made possible by the advance of the physical and biological sciences. Suppose that we are able increasingly to identify every thought, feeling and impulse to action with some complex physical state. With such a programme, we would come to realize that the basis for our past belief in freedom was a product of ignorance. This would be altogether in the spirit of Spinoza. Strawson argues that such a programme cannot possibly be fulfilled:

> *X*, let us say, notices that *Y*'s last remark has caused embarrassment to *Z*, and, wishing to spare *Z*'s feelings, *X* himself makes a remark intended to change the direction of the conversation. Can we seriously contemplate the possibility of being able to give, in terms belonging exclusively to the exact physical sciences, a complete causal account of the origin of precisely this complex of thought, feeling, and action on *X*'s part? The idea is absurd; and not because there would not be world enough and time to work

out the solutions to such problems .... It is more fundamentally absurd because there is no practical possibility of establishing the general principles on which any such calculation would have to be based.   (AM: 140)

A full account of *X*'s behaviour would have to include all sorts of inexactitudes such as the sort of society in which he was raised and his feelings about *Z*. We could of course eliminate from our descriptions of human behaviour all use of the human terms of intention and motive, substituting for them terms of bodily movement. Under that programme, an explanation of the human scene in purely physical terms would indeed be within our possible grasp, but such a programme would by its very nature exclude on principle precisely the attitudes and feelings that are in question.

The interconnectedness among semantics, epistemology and metaphysics that Strawson affirms in *Analysis and Metaphysics* is also manifest throughout his entire career in philosophy. Regarding all three of these fundamental concerns in philosophy, there is an ongoing debate between realists and anti-realists. Tadeusz Szubka (1998) thinks that while Strawson is generally regarded as a realist, he is more properly seen as straddling the issue. Strawson declares himself to be firmly on the realist side.[5]

The debate between the realist and the anti-realist on semantics turns on the question of the relation between the meaning of any declarative statement and its truth conditions. For the realist, there is an identity of the two, a position that the anti-realist accepts only in a very qualified way. In practice, the discussion centres on what *understanding* a sentence means. Strawson maintains that understanding a sentence generally involves having an identifying knowledge of an individual referred to in the subject and an ability to recognize instances of the general characteristics found in the predicate. That twofold condition is one shared by the realist and the anti-realist. Strawson thinks that the division comes when Szubka makes a further inference:

> [Szubka] is tempted to infer that these two constraints ensure that the way in which an individual referred to exemplifies such a general characterization cannot be recognitionally transcendent. Hence he concludes ... that "there cannot be a radical gap between assertibility conditions and truth conditions and there is no obstacle to constructing the latter out of the former"; thus meeting the crucial condition of a modest antirealism.
>
> (Strawson 1998c: 193)

Strawson's reply is that where Szubka thinks that identificatory knowledge of an individual is the ability to recognize the individual under publicly assertible conditions, we can surely know the meaning of a sentence even if such conditions are not in fact available. We can certainly envisage what such conditions would be. We know full well the meaning of a sentence because we know *simpliciter* what it would mean for it to be true. In this way, Strawson maintains the realist thesis of the identity of the meaning of any sentence and its truth conditions.

The debate between the realist and the anti-realist is also manifest on the issues of epistemology and metaphysics. The link between those two issues is evident enough, since the claim of the epistemological realist that we can know a reality independent of ourselves is plainly dependent on the existence of such a reality. Szubka observes that the real question is whether our knowledge conforms to the objects of an independent reality or whether those presumed objects have to conform to the structure of our knowledge. If we accept the second alternative, then we may seem to have a Kantian view on the question, and a commitment to the anti-realist's position may seem to follow. Strawson's affirmation of his restructuring of Kant's Analytic would then place him in the anti-realist camp.

Strawson's reply is that we should proceed along that line with caution, since Kant explicitly refers to himself as an empirical realist about the spatiotemporal world of the natural scientist. Nonetheless, while Kant did affirm that empirical realism, he also maintained that reality *as it is in itself* is beyond the reach of human knowledge, and those two Kantian perspectives cannot be combined. This brings Strawson back to Szubka's question of whether our knowledge conforms to the objects of an external world or whether those objects conform to the structure of our knowledge. For Strawson, Szubka's question poses a false dilemma:

> Granted that the spatio-temporal objects of natural science and common experience are indeed "objects in reality" (as only an out-and-out idealist, certainly not Kant, would deny), then it follows … that our awareness of objects as spatio-temporal is a necessary condition of our making empirical judgments and hence of possessing any empirical knowledge of the natural world. Kant indeed expressed this point misleadingly enough by saying that space and time were, merely, *our* forms of sensible intuition. But unless we are prepared to embrace the out-and-out (Berkeleyan) idealism which Kant himself emphatically repudiates, there is no occasion for us to be misled. (*Ibid.*)

Strawson thinks that what the anti-realist is ultimately demanding from the realist is "grounds for saying that we may get to know what the world is like independently of any cognitive procedures, indeed in abstraction from any knowledge of it" (*ibid.*: 196, quoting Szubka). For Strawson, that demand is absurd. Sensibility and understanding are the mutually complementary sources of all of our knowledge. "Realism, reasonably understood, is the unarticulated metaphysics of the common man, as it is of the common natural scientist as well; and, in a suitably refined form, it is also the metaphysics of the reasonable metaphysician" (*ibid.*: 196–7).

One of the great merits of Strawson's career in philosophy is that he has brought contemporary analysis into a lively dialogue with philosophy's past. That past is largely one that for Strawson begins with Descartes and with Kant's concerns with his rationalist and empiricist forerunners. At the same time, Strawson acknowledges both Kant and Aristotle as the greatest of our predecessors, and he sees both as engaged in that descriptive metaphysics that separates them from the illusions and errors of the revisionists.

On questions of logic and semantics, Strawson finds some elements of the Aristotelian tradition helpfully corrective of some of the more extreme and absolute claims found in some contemporary logic. Strawson consistently maintains the interconnectedness of logic, epistemology and metaphysics. While he devotes time and detail to the continuing relevance of the Aristotelian tradition to logic, there is remarkably less attention given to the connected issues in epistemology and metaphysics. In so far as Aristotle is indeed also a "descriptive metaphysician", it is conceivable that the realism commonly perceived to be present in his *Metaphysics* and *Concerning the Soul* might stand in an interesting relation to the empirical realism of Strawson's restructured Kant.

This is not to suggest that such a comparison is one that Strawson himself should have undertaken. His ability to relate an insider's view of contemporary analysis and logic to the broad sweep of modern philosophy and to do that in continuing dialogue with his peers is his signal accomplishment. His writings are marked by an uncommon lucidity and grace. He has done more than his share to "keep the conversation going", and the views that so sharply divide him from many of his peers have consistently shed new light on the major issues raised by contemporary philosophers. Peter Strawson is surely one of the great philosophers of our time.

Notes

Introduction

1. L. E. Hahn (ed.), *The Philosophy of P. F. Strawson* (Chicago, IL: Open Court, 1998) is a particularly valuable "intellectual autobiography" in which Strawson, with wit and with insight, traces the course of his career in philosophy. The Hahn collection also contains a series of articles written by both exponents and critics of Strawson's writings together with his replies and an excellent bibliography.

Chapter 1: "On Referring" and *Introduction to Logical Theory*: The basic questions

1. "On Referring" was originally published in *Mind* **59** (1950), 21–52, but was reprinted with some new footnotes in Anthony Flew (ed.), *Essays in Conceptual Analysis*, 21–52 (London: Macmillan, 1956), and in Strawson's *Logico-Linguistic Papers*, 1–27 (London: Methuen, 1971). My page references to this article are drawn from *Logico-Linguistic Papers*.
2. They are: simple conversion, conversion *per accidens*, obversion (or permutation), and contraposition and inversion; P. F. Strawson, *Introduction to Logical Theory* (London: Methuen, 1952), 156–7.

Chapter 2: *Individuals: An Essay in Descriptive Metaphysics*: Towards a basic ontology

1. Strawson allows the possibility that there may be particulars that are not in both time and place, but he thinks that "it is at least plausible to assume that every particular which is not, is uniquely related in some way to one which is" (IE: 23).
2. Strawson uses a "weak version" of "material bodies" in which any supposedly purely visual three-dimensional bodies are allowed to qualify for membership. Thus such candidates as shafts of light and volumes of coloured gas are admitted to membership.

3. This passage is contained in Hume's article "Abstract of a Treatise of Human Nature".

4. Chisholm cites Jean-Paul Sartre, *L'Être et le Néant* (Paris : Librairie Gallimard, 1942), 134, 145, 652–3.

5. I have attempted to do this in *Leibniz and Strawson: A New Essay in Descriptive Metaphysics* (Munich: Philosophia, 1990).

6. From a letter to De Volder (1703).

7. From a letter to Bourguet (1714).

8. From a letter to Christian Philipp (1680).

9. From *The Monadology* (1714).

10. Strawson cites F. P. Ramsey, "Universals" in *Foundations of Mathematics and Other Logical Essays*, 116–17 (New York: Harcourt Brace, 1931).

11. Strawson cites Frege's "On Concept and Object" in *Translations from the Philosophical Writings of Gottlob Frege*, P. Geach & M. Black (eds and trans.), 3rd edn, 42–78 (Oxford: Blackwell, 1980), 54.

12. On the traditional question of the being of non-existents and its relation to present consideration of the issue of transworld identity, see Nicholas Rescher, "Nonexistents Then and Now", *Review of Metaphysics* **57**(2) (December 2003), 359–81.

13. For Strawson's reply, see *Philosophical Subjects: Essays Presented to P. F. Strawson,* Z. Van Straaten (ed.) (Oxford: Clarendon Press, 1980), 271–3.

14. In "Reflections on Knowledge, Truth, and Ideas".

Chapter 3: *The Bounds of Sense*: Kant's first *Critique* under analysis

1. Strawson notes that all of his quotations from the *Critique*, with very few modifications, are drawn from Kemp Smith's translation, and that references are given with the usual "A" and "B" numbering, both numbers being given for passages common to the first and second editions.

2. Hans-Johann Glock (ed.), *Strawson and Kant* (Oxford: Oxford University Press, 2003) is a most helpful collection of essays on the two philosophers and the relationship of their views.

3. For the arguments on connectedness, unity and objectivity, see pp. 103–7 above.

4. Strawson's reply is in Hahn (ed.), *The Philosophy of P. F. Strawson*, 146–50.

5. McDowell's reference is to Anscombe's "The First Person", in *Mind and Language*, S. Gutteridge (ed.), 45–65 (Oxford: Clarendon Press, 1975).

Chapter 4: *Skepticism and Naturalism*: Hume revisited

1. From Edward Gibbon's *Memoirs of my Life and Writings* (1796).

2. The terms "catholic" and "liberal" here have neither religious nor political significance in Strawson's usage.

3. In the quotations from this work that follow, the italics are generally Strawson's.

4. Cf. Strawson's earlier *Freedom and Resentment and Other Essays* (London: Methuen, 1974).

5. Strawson cites the end of section VII of Reid's *Inquiry into the Human Mind*, published in 1764.
6. Mackie, *Ethics: Inventing Right and Wrong* (London: Penguin, 1977).
7. Strawson does not here explicitly refer to the events recorded in the *Crito*, but the instance may perhaps serve as an example of our common practice.
8. Strawson's reply is in Hahn (ed.), *The Philosophy of P. F. Strawson*, 288–92.
9. Putnam cites Strawson's *Introduction to Logical Theory* (ILT: ch. 9).
10. Strawson's reply is found in *Philosophical Studies* **9**(1–2) (Jan.–Feb. 1958), 33–48.

Chapter 5: *Analysis and Metaphysics*: Summing up

1. John Milton, *Mask of Comus* (l. 476).
2. Here there is a certain limited similarity to the way in which learning to play a musical instrument is done in what is sometimes called the Suzuki method. The beginner is not initially taught the rules for reading a musical score; instead the instructor plays, the student copies, and timely corrections are made. Only later may "reading music" come into use.
3. Readers of Plato's *Republic* will recall successive attempts by Socrates and his friends to be clear about a common concept of justice.
4. Strawson cites Wittgenstein, *Philosophical Investigations*, G. E. M. Anscombe (trans.) (Oxford: Blackwell, 1973), §118.
5. Strawson's reply is also found in Hahn (ed.), *The Philosophy of P. F. Strawson*, 192–7.

Bibliography

Works by Peter Strawson

1948. "Necessary Propositions and Entailment Statements". *Mind* **57**: 184–200.

1949a. "Ethical Intuitionism". *Philosophy* **24**(88): 23–33.

1949b. "Truth". *Analysis* **9**: 83–97.

1950. "On Referring". *Mind* **59**: 21–52.

1952. *Introduction to Logical Theory*. London: Methuen.

1953. "Particular and General". *Proceedings of the Aristotelian Society* (1953–54): 233–60.

1954a. "A Reply to Mr. Sellars". *Philosophical Review* **63**: 216–31.

1954b. "Wittgenstein's *Philosophical Investigations*". *Mind* **58**: 70–99.

1955. "A Logician's Landscape". *Philosophy* **30**: 229–37.

1956. "Singular Terms, Ontology and Identity". *Mind* **65**: 433–54.

1957a. "Logical Subjects and Physical Objects". *Philosophy and Phenomenological Research* **17**: 441–57.

1957b. "Propositions, Concepts and Logical Truths". *Philosophical Quarterly* **7**: 15–25.

1958. "On Justifying Induction". *Philosophical Studies* (1958): 20–21.

1959. *Individuals: An Essay in Descriptive Metaphysics*. London: Methuen.

1961a. "Perception and Identification". *Proceedings of the Aristotelian Society* supp. vol. **35**: 97–120.

1961b. "Singular Terms and Predication". *Journal of Philosophy* **58**: 393–412.

1964. "Identifying Reference and Truth Values". *Theoria* **30**: 96–118.

1966a. *The Bounds of Sense*. London: Methuen.

1966b. "Paradoxes, Posits and Propositions". *Philosophical Review* **76**(2) (April 1967): 214–19.

1968. "Bennett on Kant's Analytic". *Philosophical Review* **77**: 332–9.

1971. *Logico-Linguistic Papers*. London: Methuen.

1974a. *Freedom and Resentment and Other Essays*. London: Methuen.

1974b. *Subject and Predicate in Logic and Grammar*. London: Methuen.

1976. "Scruton and Wright on Anti-Realism etc". *Proceedings of the Aristotelian Society* (new series) **77** (1976–77): 15–27.

1979. "Perception and its Objects". In *Perception and Identity: Essays Presented to A. J. Ayer*, G. F. MacDonald (ed.), 41–60. Ithaca, NY: Cornell University Press.

1980. "Belief, Reference and Quantification". *Monist* (1980): 143–60.

1985. *Skepticism and Naturalism: Some Varieties*. New York: Columbia University Press.

1987. "Concepts and Properties, or Predication and Copulation". *Philosophical Quarterly* **37**, 402–6.

1992a. *Analysis and Metaphysics: An Introduction to Philosophy*. Oxford: Oxford University Press.

1992b. "The Incoherence of Empiricism". *Proceedings of the Aristotelian Society* supp. vol. **66**: 99–138.

1997. *Entity and Identity*. Oxford: Oxford University Press.

1998a. "Intellectual Autobiography". In *The Philosophy of Peter Strawson*, L. E. Hahn (ed.), 3–21. La Salle, IL: Open Court.

1998b. "Reply to John McDowell". In *The Philosophy of Peter Strawson*, L. E. Hahn (ed.), 146–50. La Salle, IL: Open Court.

1998c. "Reply to Szubka". In *The Philosophy of Peter Strawson*, L. E. Hahn (ed.), 192–7. La Salle, IL: Open Court.

2003a. "A Bit of Intellectual Biography". In *Strawson and Kant*, H.-J. Glock (ed.), 7–14. Oxford: Clarendon Press.

2003b. "Reply to Hilary Putnam". In *The Philosophy of Peter Strawson*, L. E. Hahn (ed.), 288–92. La Salle, IL: Open Court.

Collections

There are four particularly valuable collections of essays on Strawson:

Glock, H.-J. (ed.) 2003. *Strawson and Kant*. Oxford: Clarendon Press. [Includes Strawson's "A Bit of Intellectual Autobiography".]

Hahn, L. E. (ed.) 1998. *The Philosophy of P. F. Strawson*. La Salle, IL: Open Court. [Includes Strawson's replies to his critics, and an "Intellectual Autobiography of P. F. Strawson".]

Sen, P. K. & R. R. Verma (eds) 1995. *The Philosophy of P. F. Strawson*. New Delhi: Indian Council of Philosophical Research.

Van Straaten, Z. (ed.) 1980. *Philosophical Subjects: Essays Presented to P. F. Strawson*. Oxford: Clarendon Press. [Includes Strawson's replies to his critics.]

References

Anscombe, G. E. M. 1975. "The First Person". In *Mind and Language*, S. Gutteridge (ed.), 45–65. Oxford: Clarendon Press.

Behling, R. W. 1998. "Two Kinds of Logic?". See Hahn (1998), 111–26.

Brentano, F. 1925. *Versuch über die Erkenntnis*. Leipzig: Felix Meiner.

Brown, C. 1990. *Leibniz and Strawson: A New Essay in Descriptive Metaphysics*. Munich: Philosophia.

Carnap, R. [1928] 2003. *The Logical Construction of the World and Pseudoproblems in Philosophy*, R. A. George (trans.). Peru, IL: Open Court.

Carnap, R. 1950. "Empiricism, Semantics and Ontology". *Revue Internationale de Philosophie* **11**: 20–40. Reprinted in *Semantics and the Philosophy of Language*, L. Linsky (ed.), 208–30 (Champaign, IL: University of Illinois Press, 1952).

Chisholm, R. 1969. "On the Observability of the Self". *Philosophy and Phenomenological Research* **30**(1) (September): 7–21.

Chung M. Tse 1998. "Strawson's Theory of Subject and Predicate". See Hahn (1998), 373–82.

Davidson, D. 1980. *Actions and Events*. Oxford: Oxford University Press.

Evans, G. 1980. "Things Without the Mind – A Commentary upon Chapter Two of Strawson's *Individuals*". See Van Straaten (1980), 76–116.

Flew, A. (ed.) 1956. *Essays in Conceptual Analysis*. London: Macmillan.

Frege, G. 1980. "On Concept and Object". In *Translations from the Philosophical Writings of Gottlob Frege*, P. Geach & M. Black (eds and trans.), 3rd edn, 42–78. Oxford: Blackwell.

Glock, H.-J. (ed.) 2003. *Strawson and Kant*. Oxford: Oxford University Press.

Hacker, P. M. S. 2003. "On Strawson's Rehabilitation of Metaphysics". See Glock (2003), 43–66.

Hahn, L. E. (ed.) 1998. *The Philosophy of P. F. Strawson*. Chicago, IL: Open Court.

Heidegger, M. 1962. *Being and Time*, J. Macquarrie & E. Robinson (trans.). London: SCM Press.

Hintikka, J. 1972. "Leibniz on Plenitude, Relations, and the 'Reign of Law'". In *Leibniz: A Collection of Critical Essays*, H. G. Frankfurt (ed.), 155–90. Garden City, NY: Anchor Books.

Hume, D. 1955. *An Enquiry concerning Human Understanding*, C. W. Hendel (ed.). New York: The Liberal Arts Press.

Hume, D. 1955b. *A Treatise of Human Nature*. In *Hume Selections*, C. W. Hendel (ed.). New York: Scribners.

Ishiguro, H. 1980. "The Primitiveness of the Concept of a Person". See Van Straaten (1980), 63–75.

Kant, I. 1929. *Critique of Pure Reason*, N. Kemp Smith (trans.). Basingstoke: Macmillan.

Langton, R. 1997. *Kantian Humility*. Oxford: Oxford University Press.

Leibniz, G. W. 1970. *Philosophical Papers and Letters*, L. E. Loemker (ed.). Dordrecht: Reidel.

Leibniz, G. W. 1981. *New Essays on Human Understanding*, P. Remnant & J. Bennett (eds and trans.). Cambridge: Cambridge University Press.

Mackie, J. L. 1976. *Problems from Locke*. Oxford: Oxford University Press.

Mackie, J. L. 1977. *Ethics: Inventing Right and Wrong*. Harmondsworth: Penguin.

McDowell, J. 1998. "On Referring to Oneself". See Hahn (1998), 129–45.

Moore, G. E. 1903. *Principia Ethica*. Cambridge: Cambridge University Press.

Moore, G. E. 1925. "A Defense of Common Sense". In *Contemporary British Philosophy*, J. H. Muirhead (ed.). London: Allen & Unwin. Reprinted in G. E. Moore, *Philosophical Papers* (London: Collier, 1950), 32–59.

Moore, G. E. 1939. "Proof of an External World". *Proceedings of the British Academy* **25**: 273–300.

Moore, G. E. 1953. *Some Main Problems in Philosophy*. London: Allen & Unwin.

Nagel, T. 1979. "Moral Luck". In *Mortal Questions*, 24–38. Cambridge: Cambridge University Press.

Putnam, H. 1998. "Strawson and Skepticism". See Hahn (1998), 273–87.

Quine, W. V. 1953. "Two Dogmas of Empiricism". In *From a Logical Point of View*, 20–46. Cambridge, MA: Harvard University Press.

Quine, W. V. 1960. *Word and Object*. Cambridge, MA: MIT Press.

Quine, W. V. 1972. *Methods of Logic*, 3rd edn. New York: Holt, Rinehart and

Winston.

Ramsey, F. P. 1931. *Foundations of Mathematics and Other Logical Essays*. New York: Harcourt Brace.

Rescher, N. 2003. "Nonexistents Then and Now". *Review of Metaphysics* **57**(2) (December): 359–81.

Rotenstreich, N. & N. Schneider (eds) 1983. *Spinoza: His Thought and Work*. Jerusalem: Israel Academy of Sciences and Humanities.

Russell, B. 1905. "On Denoting". *Mind* **14**(4) (October): 479–93.

Russell, B. 1956. *Logic and Knowledge*. London: Allen & Unwin.

Salmon, W. 1957. "Should We Attempt to Justify Induction?". *Philosophical Studies* **8**(3) (April): 33–48.

Sartre, J.-P. 1942. *L'Être et le Néant*. Paris: Gallimard.

Snowdon, P. F. 1998. "Strawson on the Concept of Perception". See Hahn (1998), 293–310.

Stroud, B. 1979. "The Significance of Skepticism". In *Transcendental Arguments and Science*, P. Bieri, R. P. Horstmann & L. Kruger (eds), 277–97. Dordrecht: Reidel.

Szubka, T. 2003. "Strawson and Antirealism". See Hahn (1998), 175–91.

Urmson, J. O. 1961. "Critical Notice / *Individuals: An Essay in Descriptive Metaphysics*, by P. F. Strawson". *Mind* **70**: 258–64.

Van Straaten, Z. (ed.) 1980. *Philosophical Subjects: Essays Presented to P. F. Strawson*. Oxford: Clarendon Press.

Vermazen, B. & M. Hintikka (eds) 1985. *Essays on Davidson: Actions and Events*. Oxford: Clarendon Press.

Wittgenstein, L. 1958. *Preliminary Studies for the "Philosophical Investigations", generally known as the* Blue *and* Brown Books. Oxford: Blackwell.

Wittgenstein, L. 1969. *On Certainty*, G. E. M. Anscombe & G. H. von Wright (eds and trans.). Oxford: Blackwell.

Wittgenstein, L. 1973. *Philosophical Investigations*, G. E. M. Anscombe (trans.). Oxford: Blackwell.

Index

Analysis and Metaphysics 12, 167–98
analytic philosophy
  and the grammarian 169–70, 173
  and therapy 168–70, 173
  as reduction or as connection 171–3, 177
Anscombe, G. E. M. 131–4
a priori knowledge 96, 100
Aristotle 2, 4–6, 15, 17, 23, 39–43, 47–8, 52, 96, 170, 198
Armstrong, D. M. 158
ascribing and referring uses distinguished 21–2, 75–6, 83
Austin, J. L. 2, 5, 7, 14, 151
Ayer, A. J. 6–7, 139, 141

basic particulars 56–9
Behling, R. W. 47–8
Bergson, H. 139
Berkeley 52, 95, 98, 101, 111–12, 121, 128, 138, 141, 144, 175, 197
blind persons 63
bodies as basic particulars 53–9, 75
Bounds of Sense, The 8, 56, 91, 93–141, 143, 162–6, 173, 178
Bradley, F. H. 139
Brentano, F. 67

Carnap, R. 67, 139, 144–5, 147
Catholic University of America 9
causality 12, 110–13, 146, 180–82
  and explanation 190–93
change and succession compared 181
Chisholm, R. 67–8
Chung, M. Tse 90–91
coherence and correspondence theories of truth 178, 180, 184–5
Collège de France 9
Collingwood, R. G. 149, 153

Columbia University 10, 143
common-sense realism 153, 198
complete individual concepts for Leibniz 71–2
completeness
  and particulars and universals 52–83
  as the source of illusion 114
concepts of the understanding and sensuous intuitions 95, 179
contextual requirement in ascriptive use 20–21
Critique of Pure Reason 8, 15, 91, 93–4, 149, 188
  structure 94
  Strawson's general review 94–9

Davidson, D. 12, 157, 167, 189
definite descriptions 17–23
demonstratives and the identification of particulars 6, 53, 80
Descartes and the Cartesians 7, 12, 52, 66, 68, 73, 89–90, 94–5, 108, 115–17, 130–33, 138, 141, 144–5, 155, 162, 166, 170, 198
deus deceptor 145, 171

empiricism 94–5, 98, 139, 178–82
  classical British and Kantian compared 178, 182
entailment 26 ff.
epistemology and logic and ontology 178–9, 189, 197–8
Euclidian geometry 96, 123
Evans, G. 10, 61–4
existential import 4, 39–43, 84–7, 176
external bodies 146, 149, 151, 164–6

feature-universals 82

freedom and necessity   12, 125, 150–54, 193–8
Freedom and Resentment   89
Frege, G.   5–7, 75, 175
formal logic and ordinary language   23, 25, 29–30, 42–3

Geach, P. T   2, 6
Gibbon, E.   12, 143, 162
God   15, 71, 115, 124–8, 194
Grice, H. P.   2
group mind   69–70

Hacker, P. M. S.   139–41
Heidegger, M.   139, 149, 168
Hero and Seer   61–4
heuristic *as if*   98, 114, 126
Hintikka, J.   73
Hobbes   73
human nature   69
Hume   10, 12, 15, 67–9, 82, 95, 139, 141, 167, 182, 190–92
   and causality   12, 146
   and external bodies   146, 149, 151
   and induction   146, 149, 151
   and nature   146–7, 149
   and passions and reason   145–6

identification of particulars   53–4
identity (numerical and qualitative)   54–5
identity of indiscernibles   71
identity theory of mental and physical   155–8
immortality of the soul   193
India   10
Individuals: An Essay in Descriptive Metaphysics   7–9, 21, 38, 49, 51–91, 93, 100, 105, 116–17, 132–4, 139, 141, 149, 155, 163, 175, 190
individuals and particulars distinguished   1, 51
inductive reasoning and probability   45–7, 146, 149, 151, 166
inner and outer and classical empiricism   181–4
intensions and meaning   159
Introduction to Logical Theory   4–6, 12, 23–48, 93, 163
Ishiguro, H.   10, 89

James, H.   156
Jerusalem   10
justification for deductive and inductive statements   45–7

Kant   7, 10–12, 14–15, 56, 71, 91, 139, 165–7, 170, 178, 192–3, 197–8
   and *The Analogies of Experience*   108–10
   and *The Antinomy of Pure Reason*   8, 98, 118
   and *a priori* knowledge   96, 100
   and body   116
   and causality   110–13
   and completeness as the source of illusion   114
   and concepts of the understanding   94–7, 99–100, 103–11
   and cosmos   115, 118–24
   and the *Critique of Practical Reason*   127
   and freedom   125, 152
   and God   115, 124–8
      and the cosmological argument 125–6
      and the ontological argument 126
      and the teleological argument   126–7
   and the heuristic use of as if   98, 114, 126
   and moral philosophy   3, 8, 114, 125, 127, 137
   and noumenon and phenomenon   95–6, 99, 105, 111–12, 118, 124–5, 129, 136–7
   and objectivity and unity   103–7
   and permanence   107–10
   and person   116
   and rational psychology   115
   and *The Refutation of Idealism*   100, 108
   and religion   8, 95, 137
   and sensuous intuitions   6, 8, 95, 97, 99–103, 115
   and self-consciousness   8, 97, 101, 105–6, 108–9, 115–16
   and simples   114, 123
   and solipsism   122
   and soul   115
   and the spatiotemporal world   6, 8, 12, 99–103, 111, 118
   and Spinoza   128
   and syllogistic forms of traditional logic   114
   and theology   115
   and thesis and antithesis   114–28
   and things-in-themselves   8
   and *The Transcendental Aesthetic*   94, 99–103
   and *The Transcendental Analytic*   8–9, 94, 96, 99–113
   and *The Transcendental Deduction of the Categories*   97, 105
   and *The Transcendental Dialectic*   8–9, 94, 98, 113–28
   and transcendental idealism   100, 102
   and *The Transcendental Logic*   94, 103
   and the transcendental unity of apperception   116–17
Keats   168

knowledge 196–8
  its kinds according to Leibniz 89

Langton, R. 112–13
Leibniz 7, 21, 52, 55–6, 67, 70–74, 89, 117, 138, 141, 183
linguistic rules and particular languages 25
linguistic turn 188
Locke 22, 55, 67, 82, 87, 166, 170
logic
  and appraisal 24–6
  Aristotelian 39–43
  and epistemology and ontology 178–9, 189, 198
  and first-order statements 26
  formal logic 26–32
    and ordinary language 4–5, 23–32, 35–7
  and the lexicographer 28
  two kinds 44–5
  variables 27ff.
logical atomism 182

Mackie, J. 151, 158
McDowell, J. 10, 130–35
meaning
  and mentioning confused by Russell 19
  and understanding 188–90
  of universal and particular terms in our discourse 158–66
mental and physical 154–8
metaphysics
  descriptive and revisionary 52, 138–40, 148, 198
  and epistemology and logic 174–6, 197–8
Milton 168
mind–body relationship 7
monads 70–74, 117
Moore, G. E. 2, 5, 12, 144, 174–6, 186
moral philosophy 3, 8, 11, 24, 125, 137, 150–58

Nagel, T. 150
naturalism 148
  hard and soft 143–4, 152 155, 162
nature 146–7, 149
Newtonian physics 96, 102, 107–8
Nietzsche, F. 168
nominalists and realists 11, 84–7, 160–62
no-ownership view of perceptions 66–8, 89
no-space world 60–65, 100, 109

object and concept contrasted 76
Ockham 67
"On Referring" 3, 5, 6, 12, 17–23, 25, 29, 38, 45, 48, 51, 93
ordinary language and formal logic 4–5,

23–32, 35–7, 42–43, 87, 170–72, 177, 181, 189
ontology and logic and epistemology 178–9, 189
other minds 150
Oxford 1–3, 9, 12–13, 139, 167

particulars 6
  bare 83
  and individuals distinguished 7, 51
  introduced into discourse 81–3
  and universals contrasted 77, 91
passion and reason 145–6
past, its reality and its determineateness 150
Pears, D. F. 2
Perception and its Objects 63
permanence 107–10
persons 72, 88–90, 105, 116
  as basic particulars 56, 64–70, 75
Philosophia (Israel) 10
Plantinga, A. 128
Platonism 85–7, 161, 186
Popper, K. 169
possible and compossible 73
predicates
  M- and P-, 7, 69–70, 72, 88–9, 106, 133
  and subjects 7, 51, 74–83
predicative formulae and quantifiers 38–9
presupposition 4, 42–3, 93, 95, 100, 187
process-things 58
proper names 59
Proust, M 156
Putnam, H. 2, 15, 162–6

quantification 23, 38–9, 104, 176–7
Quine, W. V. 2, 5–6, 12, 34, 48, 52, 80, 159, 161, 176–7, 183, 188–9

rationalists 94–5, 98, 139
reidentification of particulars 54–6
Ramsey, F. 75, 77
realists 12, 196–7
  common-sense and scientific 143–4, 153
  and nominalists 11, 84–7, 160–62
reductionism 155, 159–61, 177, 182–3, 187–9
referring and ascribing uses distinguished 21–2, 75–6, 83
referring to oneself 66–9, 106, 116
Reid, T. 150
re-identification of particulars 54–6
relational statements 43–4
religion 8, 15, 95, 137
resurrection 70
rhetorical appraisal 23
Russell, B. 5, 23, 48, 67, 86, 131, 139, 169, 172, 175

and *Enquiry into Meaning and Truth*
20
and *Human Knowledge* 20
and the theory of definite descriptions
3, 5, 17–23
Ryle, G. 2–5, 9

Salmon, W. 163
Sartre, J-P. 67, 168
scepticism 55, 77, 95, 141, 143–4,
148–9, 155
Schlick, M. 7, 66
Searle, J. 2
self and self-awareness 8, 65–9, 97,
101, 105–6, 108–9, 115–16, 145
sensible experience and material objects
180–81
sensuous intuitions 178
and concepts of the understanding
95, 179
sentences
and the uses of sentences 19
and utterances distinguished 4,
19–20
and statements distinguished 4, 25,
27, 29–30, 51
Shakespeare 156
singular terms
and reference 48
and predication 51
Sino-British Summer School in
Philosophy (Beijing) 9
Skepticism and Naturalism 10, 143–66
Smart, J. J. C. 158
Snowdon, P. 15
solipsism 61–5, 88, 122
sounds 59–64, 100, 173
Spain 10
spatiotemporal framework 6, 8, 12, 53,
88–103, 111, 118, 180–81, 184
Spinoza 10, 12–14, 73, 128, 151, 162,
167, 193–6
Stroud, B. 144–5, 148
subjects
and existential import 84–7

grammatical and logical distinguished
7, 18
and predicates and their criteria 7,
51, 74–83
grammatical and category criteria
distinguished 74–81
and particulars and universals 7, 75
*Subject and Predicate in Logic and
Grammar* 9, 189
subjective and intersubjective 181
substance 22
syllogisms 39–43
systems and their limitations 31–2
Szubka, T. 196–8

Tolstoy 156
token-reflexive force 6
truth
analytic and synthetic 183
contingent and necessary 159, 183
as coherence or correspondence 178,
180, 184–6
and knowledge 184–7
truth-functions 26, 32–7, 104
truth tables 4, 32–4
tutors 3

undergraduate and graduate teaching 13
universals
and assertive tying 78–9
and particulars contrasted 77
Universities of Colorado, Wisconsin, and
Wyoming 13
Urmson, J. O. 2, 88–9

verificationism 144–5
Vienna Circle 139
Voltaire 73

Wittgenstein, L. 5–7, 11, 15, 66, 130–31,
133, 139–40, 145–7, 149, 160–61, 165,
168, 171, 187

Yale University 13
Yugoslavia 10